Psychology in Human and Social Development

Social Development

Lessons from Diverse Cultures

A Festschrift for Durganand Sinha

Edited by
John W. Berry
R.C. Mishra
R.C. Tripathi

Sage Publications
New Delhi/Thousand Oaks/London

234035   150·9 BEL   OH

First published in 2003 by

Sage Publications India Pvt Ltd
B-42, Panchsheel Enclave
New Delhi 110 017

Sage Publications Inc
2455 Teller Road
Thousand Oaks, California 91320

Sage Publications Ltd
6 Bonhill Street
London EC2A 4PU

Published by Tejeshwar Singh for Sage Publications India Pvt Ltd, typeset in 10/12 Book Antiqua by S.R. Enterprises, New Delhi, and printed at Chaman Enterprises, Delhi.

Library of Congress Cataloging-in-Publication Data

Psychology in human and social development: lessons from diverse cultures: a festschrift for Durganand Sinha / edited by J.W. Berry, R.C. Mishra, R.C. Tripathi.
    p. cm.
    Includes bibliographical references and index.
    1. Psychology — Developing countries — Congresses. I. Sinha, Durganand. II. Berry, John W. III. Mishra, R.C., 1952–IV. Tripathi, Rama Charan.
BF121.P8265   2002   150'.9 — dc21   2001048775

ISBN: 0-7619-9534-X (US-Hb)   81-7829-013-8 (India-Hb)
      0-7619-9535-8 (US-Pb)   81-7829-014-6 (India-Pb)

Sage Production Team: Payal Mehta, N.K. Negi and Santosh Rawat

Contents

6 ✻ Psychology in Human and Social Development

List of Figures and Tables

Acknowledgements

T he idea to bring out a volume in honour of Durganand Sinha, one of the leading Third World psychologists, was mooted by several psychologists attending the International Congress of Psychology at Kyoto in 1992, prominent among them were J.W. Berry, J.B.P. Sinha, and Janak Pandey. They were of the view that the efforts of Durganand Sinha to bring the issues of development centre stage in psychology should be recognised in the form of a *festschrift* for him. Accordingly, they prepared a proposal and letters were sent to several scholars, some of whom were old friends and others were associates and students of Durganand Sinha who had worked on approaches and problems related to sociocultural development. Janak Pandey, Director, G.B. Pant Institute of Social Sciences, Allahabad, successfully convinced John Adair, Chairman of the Scientific Programme Committee of the International Congress of Psychology at Montreal in 1996, to organise a symposium in honour of Professor Durganand Sinha. The symposium, organised by R.C. Tripathi, was attended by eminent psychologists including Wayne Holtzman, R. Diaz Guerrero, R.N. Kanungo, H.S.R. Kao, and R.C. Tripathi who presented their papers which are included in this volume. At Montreal, J.B.P. Sinha and Janak Pandey expressed their inability to work on this project because of other preoccupations and subsequently R.C. Mishra and R.C. Tripathi were requested to give final shape to the project. The support of the Centre for Advance Study in Psychology, University of Allahabad, Banaras Hindu University, and Queen's University was largely instrumental in the successful completion of this project.

Tejeshwar Singh of Sage Publications readily agreed to consider this volume for publication.

Many friends and colleagues of Professor Durganand Sinha have been gracious in their support for this volume. They have worked silently but do not wish to be named. We express our grateful thanks to them and to all the others.

❧ ONE ❧

Introduction

The Journey

For a long time psychology has been obsessed with the idea of becoming a science like physiology, chemistry and other natural sciences. This idea has acted as a strong motivational force in shaping its development in modern times. It has unhesitatingly borrowed concepts, ideas and methods from the natural sciences. It has evolved its theoretical structures based on models used in the Western world of science. This largely gave psychology the identity of an academic discipline with its primary goals as understanding, explanation and prediction of behaviour. The laboratory was regarded as the best site for the study of a variety of micro level phenomena with little concern for the problems requiring global or macro level treatment. Observation of behaviour under controlled and artificially created experimental conditions became the most dominant orientation of psychological studies. The knowledge thus generated has played a significant role in giving psychology the texture of both a basic and applied science and also in creating a belief about the universality of human behaviour.

The science-oriented concern of psychologists led to the development of the discipline as a "culturally decontextualised" science of behaviour (G. Misra & Gergen, 1993). In the pursuit of establishing its scientific credentials the study of the role of social, cultural, economic, and other macro level variables was marginalised. They were often considered as potential sources of error in data and efforts were made by psychologists to control them in the best possible way. Such a psychology, called "mainstream psychology", developed and flourished across the world for nearly a century.

A radical departure from the dominant experimental tradition became evident with the emergence of cross-cultural psychology during the late 1960s. One of the forebearers of this emerging discipline in psychology was Durganand Sinha along with Gustav Jahoda, Jan Deregowski, and John Dawson. As this discipline further developed, culture came to be regarded as the context or system, and human behaviour as adaptive to this context (Berry, 1983). Thus, understanding behaviour necessitated an analysis of the cultural context in order to delineate the numerous variables that may be associated in significant ways with variations in human behaviour. Sinha's work on behaviour in a catastrophic situation in the early 1950s and later on the role of caste in anxiety clearly highlighted the role of culture.

Outgrowing the Western Approach

The movements of cross-cultural, cultural, and indigenous psychology led to a concern for outgrowing the alien framework in the study of human behaviour (Sinha, 1980). The concern for developing psychology rooted in the indigenous cultural soil or tradition is explicit in the writings of Sinha and other scholars in recent years. Three decades ago, Sinha (1965) pointed out that the development of science in any country should be in tune with the sociocultural realities of life of its people if it has to serve any good. As these realities tend to differ sharply in Eastern and Western societies, Sinha (1965) argued that by closely adhering to the Western model of behaviour in their work Indian psychologists had failed to present a vigorous scientific psychology; instead they "... have at best been able to develop a pale and insipid edition of American or British psychology" (p. 6). In subsequent work, Sinha (1977a; 1980; 1981a; 1993) urged Indian and Third World psychologists to outgrow the alien framework in their research by evolving perspectives that were in tune with their own sociocultural realities. This finally culminated in the plea for indigenisation of psychology (Sinha, 1997).

Similar voices of concern were raised in many other parts of the world including Europe (Faucheux, 1976; Moscovici, 1972), Canada (Berry, 1974; Berry & Wilde, 1972), and the US (Kennedy, Schierer, & Rogers, 1984; Much, 1995; Russell, 1984; Sexton & Misiak, 1984), besides Asia, Africa, and Latin America. The development of local and culturally appropriate psychologies is considered essential for obtaining a more comprehensive understanding of human behaviour, and for making psychology relevant to the needs of people. It is hoped that some positive differences can be made in people's lives by the inclusion of issues and problems of concern to them. An attempt is made to test the generalisability of the existing principles, theories and models of human behaviour, and to eschew ethnocentrism that persists in psychology.

Sinha was among the first to recognise the differences between Eastern and Western psychological orientations (Sinha, 1965; 1993). At the same time, however, he felt that the differences between the two traditions not only led to the pursuit of different goals, but also deprived psychologists of the benefits of mutual communication and exchange, therefore, a synthesis between the two approaches was needed. His work on individualism and collectivism which seeks to dissolve this dichotomy is illustrative of this effort. The situation has considerably changed during the last one decade or so as the dominant Western approach has been severely criticised by scholars even in the Western hemisphere. This new found awareness has encouraged new lines of thinking about cognitions, emotions, personality, and mental health (see the contributions by Misra and Diaz-Guerrero in this volume). Phenomena like self-actualisation, peak experiences, and transcendental meditation, which were earlier perceived as highly subjective experiences and excluded from the mainstream of psychological inquiry, are now duly recognised even in professional circles. Several concepts are being rendered in terms which were earlier labelled as "mentalistic" (Langner, 1983). The change in the language and content of Western psychology indicates that psychology is regaining its mind. A need has been expressed for not only translating psychological knowledge into the language of everyday experience, but also for treating commonsense as an important source of knowledge (Fletcher, 1984; Smedslund, 1995). Against the backdrop of these changes in the orientation of Western psychologists, concepts of self, personality, motivation, states of consciousness, processes of mind, and yogic as well as other methods of improving individuals' health and wellbeing in the present stressful era have great potential for extending Western knowledge. Concepts of *samskara* (see Saraswathi in this volume) and the practice of *maitri bhavana* (K. Mishra, 1997) have enormous potential to promote development of individuals and groups respectively.

In his paper, Paranjpe observes that in the modern era the ecological crisis coupled with the fear of nuclear war have led to a repudiation of technology, and there is a greater likelihood that the domination of natural sciences over humanities would diminish. With the gradual disappearance of the colonial mentality in both the "developing" and "developed" countries, an interpretive turn in the social sciences is evident. Hermeneutics, which encourage alternative interpretations instead of insisting on finding a universal, univocal perspective demanded by the natural sciences, are making inroads into psychology. Several other new perspectives are also in evidence (Smith, Harré, & Langenhove, 1995). Similarly, Misra, in his paper, argues for a model based on "the language and practice of real people in real/concrete interactional or transactional situations".

At the level of methodology too, the emphasis is gradually shifting from experimentation to the use of observational and ethnographic methods including qualitative description of behaviour. The relevance of the reductionistic approach and experimentation is being repeatedly questioned (see Misra's contribution in this volume). The *ecological validity* (Berry, 1980a) of experiments is also being questioned. Experimental psychologists are expected to transcend the reductionistic level to incorporate macro level analyses of behaviour by focusing on the learning, experiential, and ecological contexts of human behaviour (Berry, 1980a). Such efforts would inform them not only about several relevant variables, but also demand a change in their methodology with respect to sampling, selection and designing of tasks, framing instructions, etc. It is hoped that the focus of cross-cultural psychologists will shift from the holistic level to the analyses of experiential and learning contexts of individuals to identify relevant variables for their research, and test them in culturally appropriate experimental situations. Such efforts will not only provide experimental and cross-cultural psychologists with a meeting ground where they can share their experiences, but also complement each other's activities.

Applying Psychology for Development and Change

Encouraged by the idea of making psychology socially relevant, many scholars have turned their attention to the study of pressing problems of their respective societies (Sinha, 1969; Sinha, Tripathi, & Misra, 1982). It is largely due to this concern that Durganand Sinha successfully argued for a division on "Psychology and National

Development" in the International Association of Applied Psychology. Socioeconomic disadvantages, poverty, health, education, population, and environmental issues are being studied in the developed as well as developing countries (see the contributions by Carlson and Das, and Mohanty in this volume). These efforts signify a clear movement from the pursuit of "mainstream psychology" to the development of an "applied social psychology" (Misra, 1990; Tripathi, 1988a).

The study of sociocultural factors underlying the developmental processes of individuals and groups is the most commonly shared concern in applied social psychological research. It may be mentioned here that in many developing countries several well-designed programmes have been introduced at the national level with the aim of achieving integrated development. These programmes have largely focused on sustained economic growth through the processes of industrialisation, organisation building, and application of science and technology to various productive processes. The papers by Kao and Sek-Hong, and by Kanungo and Conger focus on leadership issues of organising which plays a central role in achieving organisational effectiveness. The efforts made in this direction have contributed to some extent to the economic development and material prosperity of the people at large.

A variety of negative consequences of development has been reported for the beneficiaries of development programmes. Such a state of affairs has necessitated a re-examination of the concept of development and its related processes. The technoeconomic parameters of development have been seriously questioned, and a number of noneconomic aspects of development have been identified. The role of cultural and social institutions (e.g., traditions, values, family, and social network) has been highlighted (Kao & Sinha, 1996; Sinha & Kao, 1988). The emphasis has now shifted from "development" to "endogenous development". The latter centres on man and corresponds to the internal characteristics of society. It takes into consideration the historical experiences, social institutions, and cultural traditions of the societies in question (Alechina, 1982; Schwindler, 1984).

A distinction has sometimes been made between individual and social development, although both are highly interrelated. Individual level development refers to progressive changes that take place among individuals in an orderly and predictable manner. Through these changes individuals become increasingly competent to carry out a wide variety of activities which did not form a part of their behavioural repertoire earlier. Social development requires an increase in the capacities of a society as a whole to organise for its own objectives and to carry out its programmes more effectively. It often requires changes in social institutions and the prevailing social structure of a community. Thus, while in the former case, the target is the "individual", in the latter case, the target of change is "society" as a whole. In both cases, however, development involves the notion of "empowerment". Pareek (1988) observed that development in psychological terms refers to the creation of a sense of power in individuals and collectives in a society, and their utilisation of this power to solve problems. It implies the stimulation of certain characteristics in individuals and collectives. Most of the intervention programmes designed in the context of development basically focus on the empowerment of individuals and groups through certain organised set of activities. An inherent assumption is that the behaviour of individuals or communities would exhibit change in the expected direction as a result of their empowerment. Tripathi (1988b) argued that not all changes taking place among individuals or groups necessarily reflect development. In order to qualify a change as development, it must satisfy the criteria of *openness* and *embeddedness*. The first criterion suggests that the change in a condition should make the system more open and receptive than what it was earlier. The second criterion emphasises that change should lead to greater involvement and integration of individuals in a given system. The degree to which the empowerment of individuals or groups encourages changes to fulfil these criteria, would define the level of development. Berry's paper discusses strategies for enhancing national unity through the ideology of multiculturalism in Canadian society.

More recent conceptualisation of development has included a deep concern for quality of life (QOL). The primary question being asked in this respect is whether development contributes to a high QOL (Orley, 1994); a number of indicators of QOL for individuals and groups have been developed. Strategies have been evolved for the assessment of QOL (The WHO QOL Group, 1996). These indicators cover six broad domains of life – physical, psychological, independence, social relationships, environment, and spiritual. Various facets of behaviour related to each domain have been pointed out. These may be collectively used as the criteria for evaluating QOL at the individual or group level. It is interesting to note that not even a single economic or technological factor finds a place among the indicators of QOL. The question of how empowerment of communities and individuals can be used to improve QOL has been examined by Holtzman in his paper.

The idea that in the course of development, individuals become increasingly more competent to cope with an array of problems that confront them has raised certain issues. An important issue is the search of meaning of competence in the local context, i.e., what sort of behaviours on the part of individuals are considered to provide evidence for competence in a given sociocultural setting. Analyses reveal that the notion of competence varies considerably across societies. The analyses of cultural norms of competence, cultural practices, beliefs that prevail in a given society as well as parenting and child rearing styles can provide useful information on the nature of child development in different societies. Thorough analyses of family, school and work contexts using ethnographic approaches can provide a wealth of information on different dimensions of development (e.g., intellectual, emotional, and social). However, none of these contexts attracted the attention of psychologists till a few years ago but today they have aroused their interest (see papers by Bharat and Saraswathi in this volume). With conceptualisation of the "developmental niche" (Super & Harkness, 1986; 1997), the analysis of physical and social settings, culturally regulated customs of child care and the psychology of caregivers has emerged as an important concern from the point of view of implementation of various educational programmes for adults belonging to many disadvantaged or underprivileged groups. Eldering and Leseman (1993) delineated several cultural problems in implementing intervention programmes. There is enough evidence to suggest that culture imposes several limitations on interventions which deal with vital aspects of social life and which are not in tune with the dominant norms and values of a society. On the other hand, it is fairly smooth in the case of superficial and less vital aspects of a community's life (e.g., experiential enrichment of children). An intervention strategy of development, which takes into account the prevailing ethos of a community, has greater chances of success than the one which fails to make use of cultural parameters (see Tripathi's paper in this volume). Thus, understanding human development from any point of view entails a thorough understanding of culture. A culturally appropriate psychology can be developed and practised only on the basis of a cultural understanding of individuals or groups.

❧ TWO ❧

Contemporary Psychology and the Mutual Understanding of India and Europe

❧ A.C. Paranjpe ❧

Today many psychologists in India have accepted the characterisation of India as a "developing" country that must emulate the "advanced" countries. This position implies that technological advance is the epitome of "progress". As noted by Bury (1932), the "idea of progress" is a product of the intellectual history of Europe. It is not only Eurocentric, but is also deeply coloured by Hegel's notions of the irreversible nature of history, and of the inevitable superiority of the European civilisation in the march of history. Hegel's understanding of India was dialectical opposite of Schopenhauer's rather naive idealisation of ancient Indian culture, and both need a corrective. Influenced by Comtean positivism, presentism, and scientism, most psychologists in India have developed an amnesia for the long history of the exchange of ideas between India and Europe. In contemporary Western thought, positivism has been declared dead; the idea of progress through technology is questioned due to the fear of nuclear holocaust and impending ecological disaster; philosophy has taken a hermeneutic turn, and Euro–American psychology is following suit. The rise of an interpretive social science and hermeneutical psychology signals the prospect of a holistic understanding of alien cultures. With its own rich tradition of textual interpretation and its practical use in personal edification, as in the techniques of Vedanta, India has much to offer to enrich hermeneutic and existential psychologies. With the gradual lessening of the colonial mentality in both the so-called "developing" and "developed" countries, the time is ripe for psychological insights of the hermeneutic traditions of India and Europe to converge.

Contemporary Psychology and the Postcolonial Mentality

The characterisation of countries of the world in terms of the "developed" Western nations as opposed to the "developing" countries of the Third World is as common in the international sphere of politics as in psychology. This is clear from Americanised curricula and textbooks, tests and techniques translated and adapted from the West, and the common lack of indigenous concepts in teaching as well as research. Overreliance on, or widespread imitation of, Western ways in psychology as well as many other fields implies the assumption that technological advancement of Western cultures is the epitome of "progress", which is worth emulating. In his writings in the mid-1960s Durganand Sinha (1965) noted that in their work most Indian psychologists used American models and had largely ignored the rich intellectual legacy of their own culture. During the quarter century that has passed since Sinha made these remarks, the situation has not significantly changed. More recently, Sinha (1986) attributed the Western character of psychology in India (and rightly so) to India's colonial past. Lord Macaulay, the chief architect of the educational policy of the British Raj, had aimed at creating "a class of persons, Indian in blood and colour, but English in taste, in opinions, in morals, and in intellect" (Macaulay, 1835/ 1972, p. 249). If Lord Macaulay were to wake up in present day India like Rip Van Winkle, he would be pleased to meet psychologists who know far more about the latest Anglo–American psychology, but little or nothing about the psychological insights of Yoga.

Some research findings have indicated that children from socially disadvantaged backgrounds tend to attribute their failures to internal factors such as own lack of ability, rather than to external factors such as discrimination or luck (Stephan, Passer, Kennedy, & Aronson, 1978). It should not therefore come as a surprise that colonised people often attribute their defeat to the inferiority of their ancestral culture, or to the native conceptions of knowledge. Collective self-hate and identification with the aggressor are among the common psychological consequences of defeat and colonisation. As noted by Ashis Nandy (1983), the colonial mentality has persisted in India decades after the attainment of independence.

In the postcolonial era, the colonised people have been categorised as "underdeveloped" societies in need of "development". Development is but another name for the idea of *progress*, which developed in Europe since the period of Enlightenment as Bury (1932) demonstrated in his well-known work. An important factor in the notion of progress is Francis Bacon's ideas of knowledge as power, and of the use of knowledge in controlling nature for "improving the estate of man". The development of scientific knowledge, and its technological application leading to large-scale prosperity, is clearly one of the greatest triumphs of the European civilisation. It is perfectly understandable that the formerly colonised people wish to emulate the European colonisers in attaining prosperity through science and technology. A psychology aimed at "prediction and control" is part and parcel of the "science and technology" package, and it has its own place in developing as well as developed countries. Thus, the need for the control of maladaptive or deviant behaviour is common to all societies, and the behaviourist technology of behaviour modification has carved its niche in educational and correctional institutions everywhere. However, a developing society as a whole is predominantly a society of the dispossessed; when compared with the developed societies, it lacks power that is needed to exercise control. What is particularly relevant for a developing society is not a psychology geared to the exercise of control, for this implies having power to do so, and power is a commodity in short supply, so to speak. For sections of humanity that are collectively dispossessed — ethnic minorities, women, colonised peoples, etc. — what is particularly needed is a psychology guided by emancipatory interests. Thus, for example, a child from a Black American ghetto has little use for an IQ test that shows him to be less capable than he may actually be due to his unfamiliarity with White middle class language and values, and thereby allows the "system" to deprive him of due respect or opportunities in training and employment. Black Americans would prefer a psychologist who develops an IQ test in the ghetto language which reverses the advantages of Black and White test makers, and helps through such demonstration the emancipation of Black children from the power psychologists who predict and control their behaviour. A similar, emancipatory intent of the feminist critique of contemporary psychology should be obvious, and underdeveloped societies deserve to follow suit.

A technologically "less developed" country like India is not a "have not" country so far as indigenous contributions to psychology are concerned. It has a rich intellectual tradition; its libraries are stocked with philosophical treatises of psychological significance; indeed, they are a virtual mine of psychological insights. Traditional systems of thought such as Yoga, and varieties of Buddhism contain psychological concepts, theories, methods of investigation, and techniques for self-control (Paranjpe, 1984; Paranjpe, Ho, & Rieber, 1988). It can be demonstrated that most of these have contemporary relevance, and not merely historical interest. A psychology based on indigenous roots has potential universal applicability even as a psychology of European origin does. However, psychologists in India have been slow in tapping this treasure in their own backyard, so to speak. The colonial mentality and the overpowering influence of the idea of "development" and "progress" is in no small measure responsible for this apathy. The Eurocentric character of the ideas of development and progress cannot be overemphasised. This is not to say that progress in this sense is morally unjustifiable, but simply that the imbalance of power and prestige between the developed and developing countries has overshadowed values traditionally cherished by the latter.

G.W.F. Hegel's idea of history as an irreversible march to progress from the past to the future has contributed significantly to the Eurocentric character of the ideas of progress. In sharp contrast to this Hegelian notion, classical systems of Indian thought assumed that history moves in cycles of four stages of successively declining moral standards (Deshpande, 1979). Turning back to Hegel, it is interesting to note that in his view, what is prior is always integrated into, cancelled, and superseded by what is posterior. If this is correct, there is no point in going back to ancient sources; any attempt to explore the ancient sources of ideas of contemporary relevance is ruled out as a false enterprise. This stands in sharp contrast to the Indian notion of cyclical nature of time. It also goes against the traditional Indian view that important philosophical and psychological insights contained in the Upanishads have eternal significance, and that they need to be reinterpreted in each age as language and social context undergo historical change. The indigenous psychology of India is therefore allied with India's own distinctive tradition of hermeneutics (Mimansa). This gives rise to a problem in psychology, since the European intellectual tradition has created a sharp division between the natural sciences (*Natruwissenschaften*) devoted to prediction and control, and the humanities (*Geisteswissenschaften*) (Dilthey, 1976) that are hermeneutical or interpretive, and modern psychology has chosen to be in the former camp. The indigenous Indian approach to psychology is at double odds with modern psychology because it not only belongs to an alien ancient Eastern culture, but is also classed in the culture of humanities that is sharply separated from the estranged culture of science and technology within the Western world (Snow, 1956/1963).

Returning once again to Hegel it is interesting to note that he was not unaware of ancient Indian thought; indeed, he was too close to the German Indological scholarship that flourished in German universities at that time to remain ignorant about it. As far as the ancient times are concerned, Hegel even granted the superiority of the pristine Indian culture over its Western counterpart. However, he believed that the "world spirit" (*Weltgeist*) had moved from the East to West over the centuries, and assumed an unquestioned superiority of European thought in modern times. Hegel declared that the "Europeanization of mankind" was inevitable in times to come. Husserl was an intellectual heir to Hegel on this issue, strongly reiterating the inevitability of the Europeanisation of mankind. Husserl provided a specific argument for the inherent inferiority of traditional Indian thought: in his view, India lacked a purely theoretical interest typical of the Greek–European view of knowledge, and was dominated by ethical and "religious" interests instead (Husserl, 1954/1970). At least one Indian philosopher, Ramakant Sinari (1965), adopted this Husserlian view in his assessment of Yoga. Another version of this view would be to denigrate the Yogic view of psychology in the name of a value-free science.

During the century and a half that has passed since Hegel forecasted the Europeanisation of mankind, there has been an unprecedented development in European countries of science and technology, as well as economic and military power. By the end of the twentieth century, the entire world had been completely Europeanised, and the combined influence of Europe and America has made Hegel's words sound prophetic. At least as far as psychology is concerned, Europeanisation around the world is very nearly complete; the whisper of indigenous psychologies is barely audible in psychological discourse.

Positivist Notions of
Psychological Knowledge

In my view, an important reason for the muting of the voices of indigenous psychologies is positivist notions of psychological knowlege that have dominated psychology over the latter half of the twentieth century. Inspired partly by Hegelian notion of progress, Auguste Comte (1798–1857) formulated his famous "law of three stages", which states that knowledge in any field passes through three successively superior stages: theological, metaphysical, and "positive" scientific (Comte, 1830/1970). Although Comte himself conceived of a scientific sociology as the highest of disciplines, and even founded a "religion" based on its principles, neo-positivists like Carnap became involved with a distinctly secular inquiry modelled after physics as the highest form of search for knowledge. Developing contemporaneously on parallel lines, behaviouristic psychology developed in the US as a natural science. Behaviourism, which dominated psychology all over the world for several decades, considered metaphysics or philosophy as a less advanced form of inquiry than science even as positivism did. Many behaviourists followed Comte in viewing theology as the most primitive form of inquiry, and strongly rejected concepts like the soul or self due to their theological background. Indeed, early behaviourists like Max Meyer (1922, p. 410) were openly and strongly anti-religious.

The anti-philosophical and strongly anti-religious stance of behaviourist and other varieties of modern psychology is a major impediment to the acceptability of psychological thought indigenous to Asian cultures. Some of the most significant psychological insights of the East are associated with the meditative practices of Yoga, Zen and other such systems of spiritual development, and these are often mistaken as inextricable aspects of religious practices of Hinduism and Buddhism. Therefore, despite the non-sectarian nature and ostensibly universal relevance of the fundamental psychological insights of Yoga and Zen, they tend to be considered irrelevant to secular scientific inquiry. Moreover, the Comtean view of the progress of knowledge, which implicitly assumed by many modern Western thinkers, considers the earlier developments in the history of ideas as obsolete and irrelevant. As such, contemporary psychologists reflect what T.H. Leahey (1987) called a "presentist" or "whiggish" attitude. Given that important psychological insights of the East are explained in medieval and ancient texts, most psychologists tend to treat them as basically irrelevant for the "cutting edge" of scientific inquiry presumably situated in the latest studies.

Ironically, Comte's thesis, which makes the study of the history of ideas appear redundant, was itself a product of historical analysis. As demonstrated by Scheler (1970), Comte's thesis of the development of thought is distinctly Eurocentric. Its three "stages" reflect the theological roots of modern science in Descartes' time, the development of "natural philosophy" in Newton's time, and the anti-metaphysical stance of Comte's own positivist view of knowledge. Had Comte been better acquainted with the history of ideas in India, argued Scheler, he would have concluded differently. As I have argued elsewhere (Paranjpe, 1984), the anti-religious character of contemporary psychology is clearly attributable to the long-drawn conflict between science and the Church, a conflict that appeared in the 1920s in the form of the infamous trial of John T. Scopes for teaching Darwin's theory, and more recently on American campuses in the form of heated debates between evolutionists and creationists. However, the history of Indian thought witnessed nothing of this sort; Indian thought is not inimical to the theory of evolution or any such doctrine; nor are Indian religions institutionally so organised as to set up an inquisition to guard the interests of the orthodoxy. Some of the most significant psychological insights of the Indian cultural tradition relate to spiritual self-development and self-realisation, an enterprise that has broad, potentially universal relevance far beyond the "religious" element associated with it. Nevertheless, the apparent alliance between the "spiritual" (*adhyatmic*) and the "religious" perceived widely in the West poses a serious block in the communication between psychologies indigenous to India and Europe.

When Comtean positivism led to the development of a variety of neo-positivist philosophies, Rudolph Carnap (1949; 1932–33/1959) proposed a distinctly univocalist approach to knowledge through a programme for the "unity of science". Under this programme, statements of all sciences were considered ultimately translatable into the language of physics, so that the language of physics would be the single and only language of the entire body of knowledge organised in the form of a "unified science". An implication of this programme for the unity of science is that a plurality of approaches to psychology are considered as unnecessary as the many tongues of Babel. A univocalist approach of the Carnapian vintage has been so entrenched that some 20 years ago when I began to speak at the meetings of psychologists about distinctive approaches to psychological issues found in India's indigenous intellectual tradition, such approaches were dubbed as belonging to an "Indian psychology" that was as ludicrous as "German physics" or "Russian genetics".

In the field of cross-cultural psychology, a different form of univocalist ideal is cherished. It is widely recognised in this field that all theories of psychology, including those of Euro–American origin that currently prevail, are "emic", i.e., influenced one way or another by their cultural origin, and hence of questionable universal applicability. The aim is to remove the cultural limitations of all emics so as to ultimately lead to a single, universal "etic" psychology (Berry, 1969). Although this singular "etic" is not commonly and explicitly fashioned after the Carnapian model of the unity of science based on the reduction of all sciences to physics, it nevertheless aims at the search for panhuman "laws" which are universal in the way that the laws of physics are. While cross-cultural psychology today recognises the importance of cultural diversity, the widely cherished ideal of an "etic" is unmistakably univocalist, and it repudiates theoretical pluralism no less than does Carnapian positivism. (This does not of course deny *cultural* pluralism; indeed, some of the proponents of an etic psychology are strong advocates and defenders of cultural pluralism.) Notwithstanding the fact that psychologists in this field even speak of indigenous psychologies with some degree of respect, their advocacy of an etic clearly undermines theoretical pluralism which indigenous psychologies treat as aberrations that must be overcome, and ultimately dissolved.

Most cross-cultural psychologists share the Whiggish attitudes prevalent in other fields; their publications reveal a distinct disdain for history. The typical cross-cultural psychologist tries to understand behaviour almost entirely on the basis of samples of contemporary behaviour, and pays little or no attention to the history of cultures he or she wishes to study. The neglect of the history of cultures seems to be justified in the eyes of the cross-cultural psychologist because behaviour is viewed as being governed by general, universal, and timeless laws; cultures are but specific conditions under which the operation of the general laws is to be studied. Granted that it is possible to conceive of such universal laws, the typical cross-cultural psychologist goes about his or her work as if there is nothing to be learned from the historical attempts to understand the cultures under study. Contemporary cross-cultural psychologists and ethnographers are certainly not the first to try to understand the different cultures of the world. In my view, there is much to learn from the long history of the mutual understanding of India and Europe.

Some Lessons from the History of Cross-cultural Understanding

Over the past millennia, countless travellers, traders, conquerors, administrators, scholars, missionaries, and others have travelled between distant places in the East and the West, and many of them have left behind detailed accounts of their experiences and ideas for posterity. The German–American Indologist Wilhelm Halbfass (1988) painstakingly sketched an account of the mutual understanding of India and Europe as reflected in a vast array of writings in many languages that date back to the earliest known times down to the present. While sifting through highly diverse writings of different types of authors — particularly administrators, scholars, and missionaries — Halbfass tried to analyse the variety of issues involved in the hermeneutic situations in their typical contexts. He noted some consistent East–West differences: the inexhaustible curiosity of Westerners in contrast with India's typical disdain for foreigners and their ways, for example. He also pointed out some persistent common problems in mutual understanding. There is much for the cross-cultural psychologist to learn from Halbfass's analysis. To illustrate the point, a few of Halbfass's observations may be noted.

Time and again, century after century, the historian obtains examples of persistent *biases* in intercultural communication that manifest ethnocentrism and xenophobia among travellers, administrators, missionaries, and scholars. Thus, there are instances of learned Christian missionaries who persistently despise the native religious beliefs and practices despite serious attempts to understand them. On the other hand, there are learned philosophers and grammarians from India who denigrate foreign ideas and linguistic practices. Although distrust and rejection of alien ideas and ways of life are most common, there are interesting cases of ambitious attempts at integrating Indian and foreign ideas. There was, for example, in the fifteenth century an attempt by Emperor Akbar to blend the elements of different religions into a single new mould; and in the early nineteenth century a similar attempt was made by Raja Rammohan Roy. However, both met with little or no success. Halbfass identified Hegel and Schopenhauer as prototypical examples of two mutually opposite types of reactions: the former insisting on the superiority of Europe over India, while the latter strongly idealising the ancient Indian culture. Are there any lessons to learn from such examples of the past? Yes, I believe.

In some ways, history is repeating itself. Today, as for centuries in the past, it is the West that is seeking out India, rather than the other way around. Although Indians have settled abroad in larger numbers than ever before, and despite the fact that many are studying other cultures, most of them are looking at the world from Western conceptual frameworks rather than their own. The contemporary psychologist may note the pervasive and subtle nature of ethnocentrism in cross-cultural understanding, the limits of syncretism, the danger of pseudo-logic in arguing the superiority of one culture over the other, or of the uncritical fascination of the exotic East. The uncritical acceptance of Western models in India may be as dangerous as the frequently naive fascination for Eastern techniques of meditation and the fabulous "altered states of consciousness" they promise. Although the methodological devices of the modern psychologist such as back translation of tests may overcome some sources of bias, the widely shared fascination of empirical methods scratch no more than the facade of a complex culture. As well, the uncritical acceptance of empirical methods in the name of science may conceal an underlying cultural imperialism, a legacy of the colonial past.

One of the most interesting issues in intercultural understanding is presented by Halbfass's account of Roberto Nobili (1577–1656), the well known Italian Jesuit missionary. Nobili was convinced that it was most important for him to understand the language and customs of the natives among whom he strived to spread the words of the Lord. He not only mastered the local language well enough to be now recognised as the father of Tamil prose, but also adopted the local customs in dress and manners. He recognised the enormous complexity of the associational context and the associational horizon of the Hindus. He attempted to isolate and ignore the relatively superficial cultural differences — such as wearing tusks and sacred

threads — and focused instead on the compatibility of the fundamental themes of the cultures, such as Vedantic monism and Christian monotheism. The essentially holistic nature of Nobili's approach
to cross-cultural understanding, and his effort to focus on the deeper
meanings of the central themes of culture, stand in sharp contrast to the
molecularistic approach of contemporary cross-cultural psychology
and its overemphasis on method rather than meaning. Leaving aside
the proselytising aspect of Nobili's work, and the obvious biases
following his deep commitments to his creed, the contemporary cross-
cultural psychologist may find something worthwhile to learn from
his approach to cross-cultural understanding.

On a different note, a memorable lesson of history is indicated by
the Indian philosopher K.C. Bhattacharyya who called for exercising
caution in accepting claims to "universal reason" — a veiled reference to Kantian philosophy, a field study in which he had acclaimed
expertise. Writing in the early 1930s when Mahatma Gandhi had
given a call for *swaraj* or self-rule by repealing the colonial rule,
Bhattacharyya (1931/1954) appealed to his compatriots to try to
attain "swaraj in *ideas*". This may appear to one's ears trained in the
universalism of science as a pernicious encroachment of territorial
chauvinism on the benign field of the search for knowledge. If one
looks at it another way, Bhattacharyya's appeal may be interpreted
as a reminder of the emancipatory role of knowledge that is often
forgotten. The reckless neglect of their own intellectual legacy that
continues to afflict a majority of psychologists in India indicates
that Bhattacharyya's words of caution would be of relevance even
today. Assuming for a moment that psychological insights of the
Indian tradition are indeed relevant today, and are also potentially
useful to many people around the world as some claim, then that
legacy will be wasted unless someone takes the time to interpret the
tradition and to introduce it to the international community of scholars. I interpret Bhattacharyya's call for a collective self-rule in ideas
to mean that self-deprecating attitudes are as pathological in the
search for knowledge as is servile acceptance of an exploitative foreign rule in the field of politics.

Against this background, it may be noted that at least a small
number of psychologists recognised the pernicious after-effects of
colonialism (Ho, 1988; Nandy, 1983; Sinha, 1986), and several scholars from different parts of the world have begun to seriously study
indigenous perspectives (Heelas & Lock, 1981; Paranjpe, 1984; 1988).

The multitude of perspectives that are thus coming to light for the first time in the history of psychology will not be widely heard unless the univocalist demands are not weakened and pluralism is encouraged. There are certain recent trends which indicate that such changes have begun to occur in the contemporary intellectual climate, and these are worth noting.

Some Recent Trends of Thought and Prospects for Indigenous Perspectives

As noted, one of the strongest forces that promoted univocalism and weakened pluralism was the neo-positivist conception of unified science. One-third of a decade has passed since the philosopher John Passmore (1967) declared the demise of positivism. Although there is some empirical evidence that elements of positivism are still solidly implanted in the perspectives of psychologists in North America (Powell et al., 1991), there is also widespread talk of a "post-positivist psychology". In the philosophy of science, typical foundationist conceptions of knowledge on which univocalism was based are being challenged (Rorty, 1979). T.S. Kuhn, who in his earlier work (Kuhn, 1970) had argued that the competition of multiple perspectives in psychology suggested its "pre-paradigmatic status", and alluded to the desirability of psychology being univocalist like physics, has in his later work discussed his "discovery of hermeneutics" (Kuhn, 1977, p. xiii). Indeed, for Kuhn, a hermeneutic or interpretive element is important not only in history or other disciplines of the humanities, but also in the natural sciences. As well, there is a strong interpretive turn in the social sciences (Rabinow & Sullivan, 1979). Hermeneutics are not only becoming increasingly popular, but are also making inroads into psychology (Packer, 1985). Given the open nature of hermeneutic inquiry, which encourages alternative interpretations rather than insist on finding universal, univocal perspectives demanded by the natural sciences, the current shift of psychology to hermeneutics is conducive to pluralism. The rise of critical theory has encouraged critical and emancipatory interests in the search of knowledge (Habermas, 1971). Unlike in the past several decades when advances in technology were led by, and contributed to, further development in the prestige and support of the natural sciences, the ecological crisis and the fear of nuclear war are leading to a repudiation of technology, and to a relative diminution in the dominance of natural sciences over the humanities. This implies that the practical interests of knowledge and its indiscriminate use in the name of "progress" may not occur at the expense of the advancement of knowledge in many fields is leading to an increased tolerance of alternative points of view in academia as never before. Ethnic minorities within nations are demanding that their distinctive perspectives cannot be simply ignored, and ethnomethodology is coming to their service. European perspectives may no longer dominate as in the past; the formerly colonised peoples are beginning to develop and publicise their distinctive, indigenous perspectives. These developments are contributing to an increasingly strong spirit of pluralism. With the growth of this spirit, one has only the relative narrowness of Eurocentric frameworks to lose. This is not to say that European contributions will no longer flourish; the rise of indigenous psychologies may only add to the richness and diversity of forms of knowledge available to members of humanity.

THREE

Implications of Culture for Psychological Knowledge

☀ Girishwar Misra ☀

ultures, in the form of shared organisations of human creations like symbols and ideas, are often revealed to us as
storied texts or narratives and while trying to understand
them, we construct them by reading those texts, interpreting them
and communicating about them using various tactics such as translation, representation, and elaboration. Both psychologists and anthropologists, if it is granted that the individual human entity is
part of the Whole, are in the same business, that is, culture. However, because of the *lila*, the sport of the Supreme Being depicted in
one of the Hindu narratives, the culture–psychology dialogue has
not been as harmonious as it should be. Due to *avidya* (in the form of
disciplinary bias and extradisciplinary considerations) human beings are engaged in several misconstruals. This realisation led to
reflection on the ways this construal has taken the present shape.
What follows is a narrative account of reflections — a modest effort
to prepare for a journey toward liberation, that is, seeking the much
wanted union of culture and psychology. In doing so, first the idea
of culture and its treatment in the discourse of psychology and some
of the fields of inquiry will be delineated. This is followed by a reformu-
lation of the position of culture vis-à-vis psychological discourse,
the implications of which are illustrated by exploring aspects of an
Indian with a Western conception of human action.

Culture: The Very Idea

Although the concept of culture has a very long tradition in the
human sciences, yet there is a lack of consensus on its characterisation. It appears to be a fuzzy, yet a relevant concept (Freilich, 1989).

Nevertheless, some understanding has been achieved and the available theoretical perspectives suggest that culture may be viewed as a collective product constituted by *values, beliefs, perceptions, symbols,* and other *humanly created artifacts* which are *transmitted* across generations through language and other mediums. In a way, culture reflects the value-seeking process of human beings and implicates a world-view or design for living. In the ultimate analysis, cultures emerge to be *meaning systems* which define, inform, and constitute the range of one's understanding and intelligibility. The effort after interpreting behaviours makes sense only by taking into account the constraints and enablements contained in a given culture.

Scholars usually differentiate between culture (i.e., human construction) and nature (i.e., structures and processes that exist and occur independent of human action) since the domains constituting culture are acquired and not genetically given. However, being traditions, cultures are also "given" in a concrete form as symbols and signs. Not only this, once the cultural process is set in motion, cultural evolution also begins and informs the development of human nature. A moment's reflection on the contents of culture suggests that it is inescapably psychological in its composition. Perhaps, the two are intertwined in such a manner that it is not possible to think of human nature independently of culture. The difference between the two is only of the level of analysis and abstraction; one focuses on individual level processes and their modifications, while the other goes further and attempts to uncover the pattern or structure at a global level. In this dialogue, biology and ecology also play an important role. Human beings are biological organisms too and have many genetically programmed dispositions which are expressed in behaviour in a specific ecological–environmental context. As Cole (1990) argued, "culture is the unique medium of human existence, a medium that acts both as constraint and tool of human action. This medium has co-evolved with the biological constitution of our species" (p. 282). In this way, culture becomes a co-determiner of behaviour with nature. Culture and behaviour, thus, are reciprocally related and the dichotomy is false (D'Andrade, 1990), created only for analytical convenience and disciplinary priorities. Against this background the cultural constitution of psychology will be examined. This would help understand why culture is conceived in psychological discourse in the way that it is.

Culture of Psychology:
A Story of Intimate Strangers

"Culture" as a domain of inquiry in its own right was recognised as early as 1888, when Wundt published *Volkerpsychologie*. Wundt (1900–1920) unambiguously thought that "all phenomena with which mental sciences deal are, indeed, creations of the social community" (p. 2). According to him, folk psychology "relates to those mental products which are created by a community of human life and are, therefore, inexplicable in terms merely of individual consciousness, since they presuppose the reciprocal actions of many. This will be for us the criterion of that which belongs to the consideration of folk psychology" (Wundt, 1900–1920, p. 3). A strong sociohistorical tradition existed in the eighteenth century (see Jahoda, 1990, for a detailed historical account), but in the subsequent growth of psychology it was marginalised and remained invisible for a fairly long time. Traditional psychology has been less sensitive to intra- as well as intercultural variations in its disciplinary voyage. Being primarily a Euro–American product, it has remained a monocultural academic enterprise. Nevertheless, it projects an universalistic image which was invoked by the value (culture) free idea of science and reinforced by economic imperialism and colonial rule in the majority of non-Western nations. This has led to a distorted, incomplete and biased representation of human functioning (Sampson, 1977). In the context of contemporary sociopolitical arrangements characterised by cultural pluralities and with new insights into the nature of science and its practice, which have demystified and recognised it as an essentially human activity (Woolgar, 1988), a rethinking about the forms and foundations of psychological knowledge has become imminent (G. Misra, 1991b). To this end, an understanding of the role of culture in psychological discourse merits special attention.

The interest of psychologists in culture has focused on its *instrumental* role in the emergence and development of behavioural competence, rather than on understanding the phenomenon of culture *per se*. In contrast, anthropologists have been preoccupied with studying culture as a *supra-individual level reality* and used individual level data toward the construction of structure and pattern. "What constitutes culture?" cannot be adequately answered without understanding

"What culture does?" and vice versa. The complimentarity of the perspectives of psychology and anthropology has yet to be realised (Jahoda, 1982). It is important to examine how psychology took the stance of the instrumental function of culture.

The project of experimental psychology which was institutionalised and constituted the practice of mainstream psychology found Wundt's initial concerns with culture quite uncomfortable and incommensurate with the pursuit of its scientific goals. Deriving its academic aspirations for a positive science of behaviour from the tradition of natural sciences, it deliberately opted for the laboratory as the site for investigations and experimental observation under controlled and artificial conditions as the most cherished method. Human nature was believed to be the same everywhere and for all times. Against this background, a vigorous search for a generalisable and replicable body of psychological knowledge fabrication played a pivotal role in shaping the growth of the discipline's texture (Morawski, 1988). The prime concern of a psychologist was to make psychology a "science" and science was identified with objectivity and experimentation, pregnant with the ideology of modern self. The consequent commitment to positivist-empiricist metatheory, reductionism, and operationalism led to the emergence of a *decontextualised science of behaviour of the other*. The adoption of this orientation dictated the terms and conditons for not only the mode of inquiry, but also the objects of inquiry.

The historical construction of psychological research (Danziger, 1990) reveals that the selection and choice of research problems were guided by methodological and several extrascientific considerations (Jain & Misra, 1991; Leary, 1987). The prescriptions pertaining to the form of knowledge products were socially determined. The pursuit of academic activities was also related to market forces. This led to two related consequences: (*a*) those problems that were not within the scope of experimentation were diagnosed as non-problems, and (*b*) the available methods were not only overused but often misused. The main focus of this endeavour was on tapping transcendental reality by using the strategy of goal directed hypothesis testing. Also, this provided a model of human beings which was necessarily reactive in nature and projected them as *atemporal* and *ageless organisms disembedded from* their *contexts*. Like machines or physical objects, they were assumed to respond to the incoming stimuli administered by the experimenter. Also, it was assumed that the variables maintained their identity irrespective of the context. The contexts of investigation and application were often very different. The machine metaphor, as Weiner (1991) indicated, has parts (structures) which interact to reach an end. Behaviours are largely treated as involuntary actions or reflex-like (i.e., fixed, routine) performed without conscious awareness and are predetermined by the activating stimuli. This could not create dissonance because psychological processes were reified as entities and behaviours were their expressions. The machine metaphor directed the search for explanations of behaviour in mechanical ways. This, however, has been continuously portrayed and impressed upon as the most desirable and dependable framework for the study of behavioural phenomena. In this way, psychological reality was constructed by observing the empirical reality. This was consistent with the ideas of progress and enlightenment. As Gergen (1991) argued, "rationality, observation, progress and essentials—all of them modernist leitmotifs—were congenial companions to the increasingly potent and pervasive image of the machine" (p. 36). The aim was to predict behaviour by controlling the extraneous variables and manipulating the desired ones. The role of the sociocultural context had little scope in this format of knowledge generation, as it was treated as a source of error, and more so because it resisted the attempts of experimental control. In order to include the sociocultural context, the design of study demanded its reduction to a stimulus, and conversion into an independent variable. For instance, needs, values and other such factors became stimuli in the guise of "central determinants" in the celebrated "new look" studies on perception. Similarly, in social psychology, attitudes and beliefs became responses. It may not be out of place to mention that in social psychology, "social", which in certain ways comes close to "cultural", became social stimuli, and the individual remained the unit of analysis as in other branches of psychology. In an analysis, Pepitone (1989) and Triandis (1988) questioned the assumption of "acultural, intrapsychic, associative mechanism of information processing" which had been adopted as an apriori model for autonomous individual minds. They argued that the normative (value/belief) structures emanated from culture. The meaning constancy of various concepts across cultures cannot be assumed. Also, the observed variations across cultures may be superficial and the underlying mechanisms may be similar. The present state of social psychological knowledge provides little evidence of

the supposition that mechanistic theories are universal. While studying the nature of human beings psychologists overlooked the fact
that they are self-defining and hold certain conceptions of themselves rooted in the culture outside the laboratory and the experimenter's constructions.

The use of method, however, did enable psychologists to maintain and exploit the illusory image that they had of themselves as
capable of valid and, more or less, universal generalisations. The
scientistic practice of psychology encouraged a detached pursuit of
abstracting the relationships between reified variables, and *observers*
(individuals) were treated as *subjects* (or objects) providing data. The
rhetoric involved in it was grounded in the use of statistical techniques, characterisation of the individualist notion of psychological
processes, and the style of scientific writing. The rectification of constructs through quantification played a major role and, despite the
disjunction of conceptualisation and measurement procedures, intelligence and personality testing proliferated. The tools served as heu-
ristics for inventing theories (Gigerenzer, 1991). The institutionalisation
of inferential statistics which supplied the metaphor of "mind as an
intuitive statistician" clearly illustrates this point. The metaphors of
"scientist" and "judge" in the domain of motivation (Weiner, 1991)
also reveal the fascination with the positivist view.

On the whole, psychological researchers in mainstream psychology
continued to practice a *culture-free* psychology. The immunisation
against culture, cherished and prescribed by psychologists, however, could not help them much in maintaining the illusion of brute
data representing an objective reality. The strategies of deception,
debriefing, and detachment could not free them from the methodological trap. A growing body of research demonstrated that there
were limits to psychological knowledge, that the methods chosen
created artifacts, that the findings lacked ecological validity, and
that psychologists had been engaged in unproductive and repeti-
tive research without any sign of reasonable progress in understanding. It became obvious that scientific certainty could not be achieved
through the rigorous derivation of scientific laws from a base of
research operations and sense data (D.T. Campbell cited in Overman,
1989). All this reflected a pathology of knowledge which Koch (1985)
diagnosed as "*a meaningful thought syndrome*".

Culture in Psychology:
Doing Cross-cultural Research

The focus on culture as a target variable for psychological investigation received an impetus following the emergence of cross-cultural psychology. This field purports to examine the range of variability in psychological processes in cultures (and ethnic groups) differing along some variable using a comparative method. Its unit of analysis and concerns are individualistic. However, being preoccupied with treating *culture* as an *experimental treatment*, it questions the presupposed universality and conducts an empirical inquiry by searching for variations in behaviours across cultures. It is generally held that the boundaries of the psychic sphere vary across cultures. Being a branch of scientific psychology, it aims to test the generalisability of theories by identifying the similarities as well as differences in behaviours across cultures and by establishing or demonstrating *"etics"* (cultural universals) and *"emics"* (cultural specifics). Using a concept/measure from an alien culture leads to *psuedo-etics*. What is needed is *empirically derived etics*. Beginning with the notion of *manmade part of environment* (Herskovits, 1948), cross-cultural psychologists have extended their domain to include *material* as well as *subjective* aspects of *culture* (Triandis, 1972). In a debate on the nature of culture, Rohner (1984) proposed the view that "it refers to the totality of equivalent and complementary learned meanings maintained by a human population or by identifiable segments of a population, and transmitted from one generation to another" (pp. 119–120). This, however, appeared to be too inclusive and the debate remained inconclusive (see Segall, 1984). A comparison of cultures, however, presupposes comparability because things which are totally different do not warrant any comparison. As a result, considerable research effort has been invested in the search for *equivalence* and developing appropriate measures for tapping variables in different cultures. The difficulties inherent in such an endeavour have prompted researchers to examine the degree of *invariance* in behaviours across different cultural groups.

The domain of cross-cultural psychological studies characteristically emphasises the influence of *culture* as an *independent* or antecedent *variable* on individual differences and variations in behaviours across cultures, rather than on social variations. In this sense, culture is deemed as a set of "social stimuli" or "a composite of treatments" waiting to be unpackaged by researchers. It is not a single variable (Segall, 1983). It has often been argued that this perspective contributes towards the refinement of empirical general psychological propositions and findings in many ways (e.g., unconfounding of variables, extension of the range of variability, study of the context, inclusion of new variables). Since "cultures (groups) are supposed to cut the pie of experience somewhat differently" (Triandis, 1980), researchers expect to find a greater magnitude of cross-cultural differences. The focus of study ultimately is on the co-variation between cultural and (individual) behavioural variables.

The *handbook of cross-cultural psychology* opens with the remark, "Cross-cultural psychology is concerned with the study of behavior and experience as it occurs in different cultures, is influenced by culture or results in changes in existing cultures" (Triandis, 1980, p. 1). While this explication does not exclude a reciprocal relationship between culture and human behaviour, it construes determining the influence of culture upon behaviour as its primary concern. A properly accomplished cross-cultural psychology would yield local variations in the universal laws of behaviour. Another aspect of this field is that the term "cultural" subsumes "ecological" as well as "societal", whereas behavioural variables are inferred (Berry, 1980b, p. 5) and constitute dependent variables. To enable a better comparison, assessing the extent of variation in the repertoire of action reflecting the underlying attributes of behaviour has been advanced as a methodological strategy (Van de Vijver & Poortinga, 1982).

The main strategy of cross-cultural psychologists, however, has been to dimensionalise cultures along some hypothesised dimension, usually a psychological one, and then to observe variation in some related behavioural phenomenon with a focus on the individual. The study of individualism and collectivism (Triandis, 1989; 1990) exemplifies this strategy very well. However, the delineation of the structure of culture and its reciprocal relationship with behaviour is yet to be achieved. Strictly speaking, culture as a collective human product in its own right falls beyond the domain of cross-cultural psychology. Reviews of research in this area (Brislin, 1983; Kagitcibasi & Berry, 1989; Price-Williams, 1985; Segall, 1986) and a recent volume on *Human behavior in global perspective* (Segall, Dasen, Berry, & Poortinga, 1990) and the *Nebraska symposium 1989* (Berman, 1990) provide evidence that the database of psychological studies has been extended and some concepts and practices have been studied in non-Western cultures as well, but the issue of conceptualising culture remains unresolved (Eckensberger, 1979; Malpass & Poortinga, 1986). Also, the orientation of the whole enterprise continues to be Western in its emphasis so far as the theoretical stance is concerned.

Cultural Psychology: Transcending the Disciplinary Boundaries

In recent years, efforts have been made to bridge the gap between anthropology and psychology. These attempts have largely been initiated by anthropologists who share a relatively global view of culture. In anthropological analyses, culture has been diversely viewed as an adaptive/cognitive/structural/symbolic system. Despite differences in the respective conceptual emphases, all these perspectives are unanimous in their view that culture is traditional, institutionalised, and acquired. Being holistic in nature, it involves some degree of organisational structure and is oriented towards value systems. In an analysis of the diverse perspectives on culture, Lett (1987) noted "there are two main approaches: adaptive and ideational. The *adaptive* approaches regard culture as a socio-cultural system composed of behaviors and their attendant beliefs, while the *ideational* approaches regard culture as a symbolic system composed of beliefs and their attendant behaviors" (p. 58).

With the emergence of the hermeneutic-interpretive movement, the recognition of dialectics, and the change in the conceptualisation of scientific paradigm, notions of knowledge and reality have undergone considerable change (Manganaro, 1990). Developments in symbolic anthropology have responded to these changes in a constructive way. As Geertz (1983) argued, the "interpretive study of culture represents an attempt to come to terms with the diversity of the ways human beings construct their lives in the act of leading them" (p. 16). For him, culture denotes "an historically transmitted pattern of meanings embodied in symbols, a system of inherited conceptions expressed in symbolic forms by means of which men communicate, perpetuate and develop knowledge about and attitudes toward life" (Geertz, 1973, p. 80).

The interface between psychological and cultural domains has been pursued in several subfields of anthropology. In *psychological anthropology*, previously known as *culture and personality study*, efforts were made to discover "the ways in which personality systems enable social and cultural systems to serve their function" (Spiro, 1972; p. 605). While early studies in this area had a predominantly psychoanalytic orientation (Hallowell, 1953), in recent years the focus has shifted to cognition (D'Andrade, 1990). This field of study has explained the aspects of culture using underlying, perhaps transcendental, psychological functions. The idea of psychic unity was dominant and sociocultural environments were assumed to be shaped by psychological functioning. Cultural data were treated as expressions of individual needs and motives. Another related field is that of *ethnopsychology* which attempts to unravel ethnic variations in folk theories of mental life. Folk beliefs are investigated and the cultural significance of social and psychological events as they are interpreted in the social context is sought. Being indigenous in orientation, it takes specific cultures and societies as frames of reference (Rosaldo, 1980; White & Kirkpatrick, 1985).

In recent years, some attempts have been made to develop *indigenous psychologies*. Heelas and Lock (1981), for example, considered them as "cultural views, theories, conjectures, classifications, assumptions, and metaphors — together with the notions embedded in social institutions — which bear on psychological topics" (p. 4). The notion of *indigenous anthropology* (Hussain, 1982; Wright, 1988) has also been advanced with an emphasis on the indigenous perspective and aimed at new identities, particularly in decolonised nations. Marriot (1990) developed an *Indian ethnosociology* using the Samkhya Yoga system of philosophy. Psychology in the Philippines (Enriquez, 1987), Japan (Hoshino & Umamato, 1987), and India (Neki, 1973; N. Pandey & Naidu, 1986; Paranjpe, 1984; 1988; D. Sinha, 1990; J.B.P. Sinha, 1980; Tripathi, 1988b) also showed a trend of developing indigenous ways of looking at psychological phenomenon. Non-Western countries are developing indigenous paradigms to deal with their problems from specific sociocultural perspectives (Atal, 1981; Dube, 1988; G. Misra, 1990; Moghaddam, 1987; J. Pandey, 1988a; Pederson, 1979; D. Sinha, 1981a).

The most recent development in this area is that of *cultural psychology*. Its aim, according to Shweder (1990), "is to study the ways subject and object, self and other, psyche and culture, person and context, figure and ground, practitioner and practice live together, require each other, and dynamically, dialectically, and jointly make each other up" (p. 4). It focuses on intentional things and intentional worlds. Intentional things have no "natural" reality or identity separate from human understanding and activity. It imaginatively conceives of "subject-dependent objects (intentional worlds) and object-dependent subjects (intentional persons) interpenetrating each other's identities or setting the conditions for each other's existence and development, while jointly undergoing change through social interaction" (p. 25). In *Thinking through cultures*, Shweder (1991) elaborated upon this field and demonstrated the efficacy of this perspective in the study of person concepts and other issues. Cole (1990), following the Russian sociohistorical school of thought, attempted to demonstrate how history, ontogeny, and microgenesis were related to the development of psychological functions.

Rethinking Culture–Psychology Interface

It is evident from the preceding account of the prevailing analyses and uses of "culture" in psychology and related discourses that with a few exceptions, most of the perspectives have been limited in their account to either the subjective side of culture or its materialistic indicators. Second, their methodological approach has been predominantly a positivist-empiricist one. They have endeavoured to discover culture and/or its human consequences from the vantage point of an observer recording objective phenomena. They have been confined to the scientific practice of looking for neutral data, proceeding through inductive logic. This exercise, however, presupposed the object of study to be static and its behaviour invariable irrespective of the observer. In other words, the investigator tended to assume a high degree of control over the objects of study. Unfortunately (or fortunately), cultural (and human) phenomena defy these presuppositions. They are dynamic, context-dependent and have relational functioning. Therefore, the empirical strategy falls short of the demands of the phenomena under study. However, the linkages of power, authority, and image that accompany this kind of scientific practice have proved to be very attractive. Moreover, researchers were convinced that they were on the right track and hoped that gradually sufficient facts would accumulate to enable control over the world of affairs in the desired direction. This dream, however, was shattered.

Developments in the philosophy of knowledge, sociology of knowledge, and sociology of science have shaken these convictions. The lessons which have been learned have led to the realisation that "there are no value free facts", "knowledge does not grow cumulatively", "observations are theory laden", "social forces are internal to science", "knowledge is socially constructed", "there is not a fixed way of doing science", and "objectivity of science is secured by the social character of inquiry" (Feyerabend, 1987; 1988; Gergen, 1985; Hanson, 1958; Kuhn, 1970; Longino, 1990; Ravetz, 1990; Rouse, 1987). Studies of laboratory life (H.M. Collins, 1985; Latour, 1987; Latour & Woolgar, 1986), the development of disciplines (Barnes & Shapin, 1979; Henriques et al., 1984; Hull, 1988; Leary, 1987; Rose, 1985; Wagner & Wittrock, 1990), and analyses of scientific discourse (Gilbert & Mulkay, 1984; Potter & Wetherell, 1987; Woolgar, 1988) have seriously questioned the authority and dependence on empiricistic-positivistic knowledge, and have shown its applications to the human domain as problematic and flawed.

Knowing human phenomena entails an understanding of human made worlds. As Shotter (1990) stated, "its aim is to try to understand the *nature of our own human making of our own human nature*" (p. 11). This is *the* problem of all human sciences. Here, "culture" comes to the rescue. According to Shotter (1990), "man is a being in a culture in nature.... People deal with nature in terms of their knowledge of the part their actions play in relation to the part played by other people's actions in maintaining (or progressing) the culture" (p. 13). He termed acting from within a position in culture as

> knowing of the third kind — a two way process of *formulation* in which feelings related to socio-cultural things are "given" or "lent" a form "from within" an occasion or situation that arises within the flow of activity constituting a discourse. This kind of knowing is developmental in nature. It involves processes of testing and checking, of justifying and warranting, of accrediting and legitimating, which bears upon its "hook up", so to speak, to the realities within which it is used (Shotter, 1990, p. 14).

Thus, culture, in its broadest sense, of which psychology may be viewed as a part, provides the tools for understanding, and sets the limits of the range of possible knowledge.

This assertion, in consonance with post-empiricistic approaches to knowledge, is very relevant. It proposes that knowledge is socially situated, linguistically constituted, and is a product of historically anchored communication among people. Gergen (1989) described reality as is (*a*) embedded within an elaborate linguistic code, (*b*) dependent on social communities able and willing to share these conventions, and (*c*) interdependent with an array of practical activities which are facilitated and supported by these conceptions. Pointing to the linkages between material, mental, and inferential worlds, he argued that these realities refer to differences in ways of talking and writing or linguistic construals and relating to them is more like discourse. In this sense, empirical data have rhetorical power for persuasion rather than that of supplying the criteria for the validation of reality.

It is accepted that reality does not exist for individuals in some predetermined readymade form. Rather, they construct it. This goes against the received (objective) view of knowledge. This involves an explicit acknowledgement of values influencing the research process, which increases the burden of responsibility. But, it simultaneously increases the range of choices and, instead of maintaining the status quo, opens up the possibility of new or innovative options for social action. This change involves liberation as well as commitment. Thus, viewing knowledge/understanding not as an ontological reality but as a *functional fit* emerging out of social transaction locates knowledge in the relationship, collectivity, usage, and culture. The explanations posited are propositions presented as reformulations of experiences that are accepted as plausible accounts in response to a question that calls for an explanation. The criteria of acceptability of such a proposition may be diverse depending on the community (or culture) involved.

Exploring culture and related phenomena in this changed epistemic context is liberating as well as puzzling. It is liberating because of its emancipatory potential for accommodating diverse versions of reality. The realities of "others", "primitives", and "savages" who were objects of study would be as authentic as ours (Fabian, 1983; Pandian, 1985; Wolf, 1982). Developing empathetic sensitivity to other cultures requires, what Kukla (1988) envisaged as *ethnophenomenology* in which knowing other cultures is "immersing in that culture's worldview in order to observe in oneself the effect of such an immersion" (p. 151).

Studying cultures in their own terms is important, not only for the study of culture, but also for psychology. As Bruner (1990), talking about *the proper study of man*, remarked, it is man's participation *in* culture and realization of his mental powers *through* culture that make it impossible to construct a human psychology on the basis of the individual alone.... Our culturally adapted way of life depends upon shared meanings and shared concepts and depends as well upon shared modes of discourse for negotiating differences in meaning and interpretation (p. 13).

Culture is relevant to psychology because of the inherent power of folk psychology or everyday understanding of people. It is

a culture's account of what makes a human being tick. It deals with the nature and consequences of intentional states and dominates the transactions of everyday life. It alters with the cultures' changing responses to the world and to the people in it.... A culturally sensitive psychology is and must be based not only upon what people actually *do*, but what they say they do and what they *say* caused them to do, what people say their worlds are like (Bruner, 1990, p. 16).

In a culturally-oriented psychology, saying and doing represent a functionally inseparable unit. There are agreed upon canonical relationships between the meaning of what people say and what they do in given circumstances, which guide their conduct.

In fact, psychological phenomena occupy a central place in real life and are the main components of day-to-day language use and its conventions. In the study of cultural phenomena, the use of the traditional empirical perspective creates more obstacles than facilitates the study. Understanding the meaning of a behaviour, which is context-dependent, requires an interpretive and constructive approach. This involves understanding the other, which may be pursued more as a joint action or relational coordination than focusing on intersubjectivity (Gergen, 1990b). The use of interpretive analysis has attracted considerable attention following the work of Geertz (1973) who viewed the task of a student of culture as one of "*guessing meanings*". In this, patterns of interaction in concrete situations are emphasised. The relational nature of meaning and forms of culture suggest that the process of investigation should transcend the dualism of subject and object and opt for a more dynamic stance. Much of the meaning depends on the discursive forestructure supplied by the culture which already exists before the commencement of any behavioural episode. However, the positivist programme of research proceeds along the lines of modernist thought and idea of progress and prescribes a range of human functioning by adopting metaphors from outside the academic domain and dictates what a human is like. The computer model, for instance, has led to a view of man as a "physical symbol system". As such, the postulated behaviours (e.g., encoding, storage, and retrieval), in accordance with the model, are predictable and controllable. Thus, in this system, what a human being is like, and his ontology, are critically defined by the method.

The problem with "culture" is that it is an open-ended system. As Geertz (1973) pointed out, it is the product of human beings' trafficking in signs, mainly symbols. The study of culture, therefore, has to be carried out with the tools (e.g., signs, objects, and interpretant) supplied by the culture itself. This is best reflected in the changing metaphors used in understanding social behaviours. Gergen (1990a) demonstrated that social life has been conceived diversely as "animal laboratory", "network of meaningful relations", "market place", and "stage with changing time". These metaphors are divergent from the logical positivistic philosophy and indicate the emergence of a post-empiricist trend which, among other things, is also marked by different forms of intelligibilities, thus expanding the range and forms of understanding. Cultures with differing world-views, thus, may co-exist with different images and metaphors of mind and behaviour. Diversity and pluralism in one's perspective does not in any way obstruct one's understanding.

From the present perspective, culture may be taken as a social expression of a constant search for values and in this endeavour human beings transform the nature and, thus, engage in history making (Godlier, 1986; G.C. Pandey, 1972). The experience of nature's transformation is embodied and articulated in terms of concepts, symbols, and attitudes which are not only determined by (earlier) cultural tradition, but also determine its future course. In this continuous process, both individual and social are engaged in a constant and creative interplay. The focus on the material or external components of culture would fail to perceive the meaning of the symbols and signs. Since creative activity is relational, the world of culture should be appraised by interpreting the way (its) participants relate to it.

The premise that cultures provide ways and means to interpret behaviour and experience gives rise to the attempt to see how cultural differences lead to diverse conceptualisations of psychology. Against this background, it is important to examine the Western and non-Western cultural perspectives and their implications for psychology.

The Western Point of View

Man is the measure of all things.
Protagoras (*c.* 500 BC)

In recent years, numerous analyses have been undertaken which vividly illustrate the Western perspective. Lasch (1991), in *The true and only heaven*, argued that capitalism due to its dependence on consumerism, promotes hedonism and thus undermines the traditional values of thrift and self-denial. He located the problem in the idea of an economic man inherent in the model supplied by Adam Smith which implicated that satisfaction of needs through production led to comfort. This led to *acquisitive individualism* fostered by liberalism. Thus, insatiable desire came to be viewed as a powerful stimulus to economic development. The denial of natural limits on human power, and freedom and physical resources have now created problems. According to Lasch (1991), a more equitable distribution of wealth cannot be achieved under an advanced system of capitalistic production.

The work of Bellah et al. (1985) also highlights the significance of utilitarian calculus and devotion to self-interest as a major theme in Western society. Freedom from the demands of others, and justice for equal opportunity (not distributive justice) have led to a utilitarian and *expressive individualism*. Referring to Tocqueville, these authors opined that people have the habit of *thinking of themselves in isolation and imagine that this whole destiny is in their hands*. Life has been divided into a number of separate functional sectors (e.g., home, workplace, leisure, public, and private) and success has been treated in professional terms. The authors further noted that with the emergence of psychology as an academic field and, even more importantly, as a form of discourse, the purely subjective grounding of expressive individualism has become complete. The voice of the people revealed that most of them "imagine *an autonomous self exist-ing independently, entirely outside any tradition and community and then perhaps choosing one*" (Bellah et al., 1985, p. 65). The right to self-fulfilment has given rise to the viewpoint that "acts are not right or wrong in themselves, but only because of the results they produce, the feelings they engender or express" (Bellah et al., 1985, p. 78). Thus, self and its feelings have become the only moral guide. The institutions of family and marriage have become optional and mat-ters of choice. The belief that the individual is the only firm reality — *ontological individualism* — constitutes the dream of the people.

Schwartz (1986), in *The battle for human nature*, noted that in the academic domain, the change from moral philosophy to social sci-ence, from *should* to *do, ought* to *is,* represents the struggle between scientific language and the language of morality for hegemony in describing the meaning of "person". This is reflected in the internal-isation of individualism as a matter of principle or right. The pur-suit of privacy, and the choice to be free — solidified in individual-ism, results in the pursuit of self-interest in the public arena also. The image of the rational economic man, the roots of which lie in evolutionary theory, behaviour theory, and economics have resulted in an economic imperialism and the self-interest has been nour-ished by the different cultural practices.

These notions of the individual in the Western context have been articulated by Sampson (1988) in terms of the construct of *self contained or possessive individualism* which emphasises an extreme form of individualism which accords priority to individual over society. It maintains an autonomous structure which has fixed boundaries and an independent ontology with an internal locus of control. In brief, the model of human science inquiry rooted in the Western cultural tradition may share the following features.

1. A logocentric view which recognises that the rational pro-cesses form the basis of understanding and action.
2. Anthropocentrism in which man is the centre of all the worldly activities and happenings. This monotheistic tradi-tion has led to an individualistic perception of the world.
3. Belief in dualism leading to dichotomy between mind and matter, subject and object.
4. Control over nature and ideas of progress and modernisation.
5. Linear perspective on time, and history as chronological.

6. Egocentricity and contractual nature of human relationships.
7. Thinking as context free and predominantly rational.
8. Idea of autonomous and bounded self with fixed boundaries between self and others.
9. Idea of progress, materialism, and hedonism.
10. Systematic thinking emphasising putting things together in composition.
11. Knowledge is amoral and secular.
12. The subject of study is considered a static entity and a dynamic approach is employed for exploration and understanding.

Although this tradition has not been static and has changed in course of time, the emphasis has largely been the same since long and has informed the modalities of academic enterprise by supplying an anthropocentric world-view. Concepts to understand human phenomena are rooted in the related images of the order of things, and have supplied working hypotheses to people (Gergen, 1991). The notions of "human behavior as a response to stimuli", "reinforcement", "personality dispositions", "human existence as individual", "knowledge as power", "(internal locus of) control", etc., originated in this culture and were adopted by academic practitioners and again fed back into the cultural repertoire. In this way, a point of view emerged which is only *one* of the various possible point of views. Unfortunately, this came to be considered as the *only* point of view which was sustained by practices within the disciplines. Since point of views are constructions, their tenability and legitimacy are derived from the convictions of those who subscribe to them rather than any external or objective criteria of validity. Theories and paradigms do not change or get rejected merely on the basis of contrary or insufficient data. Rather, the reverse is true: an established paradigm compels to view a given set of data in a particular way. This tendency is often overlooked and people continue with their suppositions. The history of scientific revolutions supplies many instances when theories have changed while the facts have remained the same.

In this context, other points of views encompassing different sets of presuppositions and world-views become significant as far as understanding human phenomena is concerned as they open up new dimensions. The narrative of knowledge and metaphors of life processes in different cultures are not the same as noted in the Western tradition. The Indian point of view will be discussed here, which offers a somewhat contrasting panorama of life. In undertaking this exercise, the intention is to unravel the possibilities of different and equally (or more?) plausible theoretical forestructures which may eventually supply more viable and legitimate accounts. In any case, acknowledging this perspective on human existence would at least make psychologists aware of other routes and ways of doing humanly things. It is, indeed, possible to offer different but legitimate construals of reality.

Constructing Reality: The Indian Way

This Atman (the vital essence of man) is the same in the ant, the same in the gnat, the same in the elephant, the same in these three worlds... the same in the whole universe.

Brhadaranyaka Upanishad I, 3, 22 (*c*. 1000 BC)

India has a very rich, complex but continuous tradition in which little (folk) and great (*shastric*) traditions have grown along side. Living in a tropical zone, the history of these people had a different rhythm and tempo of social change. Here, plurality and multiplicity of forms and types have prevailed. In its intellectual history, religious background and spiritual emphasis were comprehensive enough to allow the pursuit of knowledge. The conceptual analyses pertaining to personal–existential concerns were evolved with practical goals. For instance, yoga was a system of knowledge as well as a system of practical training. As G.C. Pandey (1972) stated,

> the Indian mind... has sought to govern social relations not by an abstract reason but by intuition and compromise. It has met new challenges by modifying rather than recycling older solutions.... Instead of the conquest of Nature, it has upheld the ideal of adjustment to Nature at one level and that of emancipation from it at another.... Instead of seeking freedom through power, it has sought freedom through self-control.... The older and the newer forms have continued side by side and this continuity and heterogeneity within the ambit of overall progress and unity (p. 86).

The Hindi word which comes closest to culture is *sanskriti* derived from the root which means to purify, to transform, to mould. It also implies association in which positive qualities become dominant. The nature of this rich tradition is difficult to summarise satisfactorily. Many attempts have been made by scholars to reconstruct the philosophical–psychological perspectives of Indian culture (Coomaraswamy, 1943; 1957; Guénon, 1945; Heesterman, 1985; Heimann, 1964; Hiriyanna, 1932; Klostermaier, 1989; Murphy & Murphy, 1968; Organ, 1990; G.C. Pandey, 1972; 1984; Paranjpe, 1984; Radhakrishnan, 1927; Raju, 1985). Its philosophical traditions are diverse and share different assumptions. However, some of the salient features common to most of the traditions and relevant to the practices are as follows.

1. Indian mode of thinking is *context sensitive*. In this metonymic kind of thought everything is placed in context (Ramanujan, 1990). Space, time, and person (*desha, kala, patra*) are important in determining the course of action. Things are perceived in terms of concrete contextual features (Shweder, 1990).

2. There is an emphasis on harmony or coherence rather than unity. Civilisation (*sabhyata*) means living together in harmony. Urbanity is subjugated to higher cultural values. Village, the social unit, is referred to as *grama* meaning harmony which is used in music as well to denote the quality of harmony in tones.

3. Things derive their existence and nature by mutual dependence and are nothing in themselves (Nagarjun, cited in Murti, 1955, p. 138). Man is part and parcel of the great Whole. Thus, the person is one aspect of a broader sociocentric organic (holistic) conception of the relationship between the individual and society. The units are necessarily altered by the relation in which they enter. Social roles are the fundamental building blocks.

4. Worldly existence is believed to have a rhythmic character. All the world processes are organised or determined by various antitheses (e.g., subject/object, spirit/matter). The interplay of pairs constitutes the whole. The intrinsically dynamic nature of the universe represents an organic view with interconnected and interdependent entities. This kind of conceptualisation closely approximates newer developments in quantum physics and the behaviour of subatomic particles (Capra, 1983).

5. The attitude towards time transcends historicity. Being is

    neither merely an atemporal visualization of itself nor an absolute separation from time and space, but is the realization of itself as separable on one plane, and the potentiality of being involved in time and space on the other. The Indian view does not reject history, it transcends it. Human existence is simultaneously atemporal or timeless and temporal or placed in time (V.N. Misra, 1971).

6. It asserts cosmic plurality and cosmic interchangeability. Initially, *Rta* was the immanent dynamic order or inner balance of the cosmic manifestations themselves. Subsequently, *dharma* was considered as the immanent principle of order in nature as well as social and moral life. Social institutions and interactions were organised around this principle. It represents a system of values to bring the lower into harmony with the higher (G.C. Pandey, 1972). It organises life at every level in this universe.

7. Knowledge is for emancipation from suffering, and liberation. Philosophy and life are intimately linked. Instead of seeking truth or knowledge for its own sake, truth seeking is supposed to make man free. Truth involves wellbeing of everybody.

8. An introspective or contemplative attitude, and looking inwards is emphasised. The use of reason is preferred but intuition is perceived as the only method for access to the ultimate knowledge. Knowing reality needs actual experience. The process of realisation or *darsana* is more crucial. The authority of people who have realised (*darsana/apt*) is accepted as a valid basis for knowledge (G.C. Pandey, 1984). On the other hand, the contemplative attitude leads to a passive forbearing attitude toward the objective or the natural world. People adapt themselves to nature without any reconstruction (Nakamura, 1964).

9. The recognition of a multiplicity of world-views is emphasised and respected. The *Rg Veda* mentions: God is one, but men call him by many names (*Ekam Sad Vipra Bahudha Vadanti*). This has led to a synthetic tradition and a high degree of religious and intellectual tolerance.

10. Human beings are not only agents or doers (*karta*) but experiencers (*bhokta*) as well. They experience the consequences of their actions. Egoism, considered as a part of human life, is due to ignorance of the true human nature. This view leads to an emphasis on self-sacrifice rather than aggrandisement (Paranjpe, 1984). Humans are capable of being rational or wise but occasionally become irrational because of desires

and involvements. Desire is never extinguished by the enjoyment of desired objects.

11. The law of *karma* or action is the principle governing everything. It is the cause and effect both. It incorporates the whole universe and extends from the past through the present to the future. Reincarnation is also a part of this principle of cosmic justice. Attaining individual perfection through *sadhna* is emphasised. The idea of *karma* continues to operate as a very important component of the contemporary system of thought and behaviour in India (Keyes & Daniel, 1983; Neufeldt, 1986; O'Flaherty, 1980; Reichenbach, 1990; Srinivas, 1952).

12. The four ends of life (*purusharthas*), namely, duty (*dharma*), enjoyment (*kama*), earning of wealth (*artha*), and liberation or release from the eternal cycle of birth, death and rebirth (*moksha*), are to be pursued according to one's station in life.

13. The significance of unity of all life forms as the expression of an unseen and transcendent reality is the core of this tradition. This has led to minimisation of individuality and specific particulars. As Coomaraswamy argued, "the heart and essence of the Indian experience is to be found in a constant intuition of the unity of all life, and the instinctive and ineradicable conviction that the recognition of this unity is the highest good and the uttermost freedom" (1957, p. 4). The changing manifestations of the phenomenal world are considered as illusory. The universal being behind these manifestations is the ultimate source of reality.

14. The "person" is situated in a social, physical and cosmic web of relationships. He is not "dividual" rather than individual (Marriot, 1976). He is indebted to gods, ancestors, and teachers and is expected to perform sacrifices (*yajnas*) for people, ancestors, and organisms. The boundaries between self and other are not fixed and the person is embedded in the group (Tripathi, 1988b).

The propositions outlined here represent a mix of text as well as context. Despite social change and modernisation (Westernisation), these propositions reflect the world of Hindus (Srinivas, 1952) and in various forms constitute their operative culture, in terms of Goodenough's (1989) distinction which refers to the particular system of standards in a person's propriospect that he selects to interpret the behaviour of others or to guide his own behaviour on a given occasion. Studies by anthropologists, sociologists, and other social scientists have yielded a wealth of information on the behavioural/ psychological world of Indians. For want of space, only some of its salient aspects will be discussed here. To a large extent, the worldview of Indians is organised around the notion of *dharma* and they subscribe to a belief in the inherent order of the universe (Roy & Srivastava, 1986; D. Sinha, 1969). The Indian cultural tradition is alive in not only the life rituals (*samskaras*) that are performed and celebrated, but also in the structure of society. Family, community, and social considerations play an important role in regulating the behaviour of people. Also, a number of practices require engagement in certain activities for the sake of those activities (e.g., *sandhya*). The principle of *karma* constitutes an important explanatory category for different groups of people. The relationships with trees, soil, environment and ecology are maintained with a sacred value of sharing on an equal footing (Sengupta, 1965). Although the pattern of family is changing, yet joint families are substituted by extended families and relationships are maintained. Industrialisation, migration, and mobility have led to many changes but the overriding trend points to order and coherence in the forms of life activities and organisations.

Religious life attaches importance to the human relationship and local as well as great traditions of worship of gods and goddesses occupy a large part of the life space of people. Pilgrimages, *vratas*, listening to the *Purans*, especially the *Bhagwat* and the *Ramayana*, are major religious and social activities in villages as well as cities. Many families have *gurus* who are treated as spiritual leaders and are held in high esteem. In addition, holy persons or *sants* have their own organisations and their own disciples (Gould, 1987). The relationship between the teacher and the disciple (*guru–chela*) has proved to be an effective indigenous therapeutic model (Neki, 1973). The belief in a disciplined life as the good life persists (Madan, 1987).

A look at the patterns of child rearing and patterns of interactions among family members reveals that interdependence and reciprocal expectations and obligations are important. The child is considered as an extension of the parents (*santati*). Marriages are largely arranged in which the relationship between two families is the primary consideration in decision-making. Wife–husband relationships are of identity and complementarity rather than of equality. It is interesting to note that several religious ceremonies necessarily require the presence of the wife and there is a God whose body is part male and part female (*Ardhanarishwar*). The functional organisation of caste groups has deteriorated but on occasions the rituals in various *samskaras* demand the cooperation and participation of people of different castes such as goldsmiths, blacksmiths, and potters. The hierarchically organised caste groups have other patterns of relationship and exhibit a close relationship between text and context (Das, 1977). Incidentally, the patterns of joint activity noted in these spheres have considerable local variation and constitute the little tradition which at times becomes stronger and prevails over the great tradition (*Shastras*). The ritual practices largely embedded in the actions and performances of the people and their practices are transmitted from generation to generation. The life cycle ceremonies, agricultural rites, protecting godlings of the village, festivals with local colourings, and social adaptations (Ostor, 1980) indicate an intimate relationship between people and the different components of their habitat.

This scenario puts a person in his context and defines his position in terms of the features of the context in which he is embedded (Daniel, 1984). The person's identity is constitutive and things are more fluid in terms of their configuration. This demands a construal of analytical categories of a different kind than those operative in the Western world-view. The adoption and imposition of an alien frame of understanding would yield an incoherent rendering. Unfortunately, this has happened for the most part in psychology in India.

Modern Psychology and Culture's Account: The Indian Experience

As a modern discipline, psychology in India was established during the 1920s as an extension of Liepzig's tradition. This transplant was nourished during the preindependence period and continued as such for a long time, and it was only recently that attention was directed towards indigenisation (D. Sinha, 1986). The way in which the cultural suppositions of researchers bias the psychological observations can be observed in the psychological accounts of Indians during the British period. Referring to the work of British psychoanalysts in colonial India, Hartnack (1987) argued that the psychoanalytic concepts served as labels to reinforce British feelings of self-satisfied superiority over the colonial wards, extended their supposed expertise to the colonial administration as an aid in the 1920s. The political and scientific ideologies were mapped onto one another. Berkeley-Hill, one of the analysts, wrote: "British rule is justified, since the Hindus are neither interested in responsible leadership nor do they have a psychological disposition for it, since they are, in addition to being *obsessive-compulsive* also *infantile...*" (Hartnack, 1987, p. 242). The *Indians' behaviour* was compared with that of *dependent* people, with *women, infants,* Irish and European *neurotics.* This analysis reveals that reading the psychology of the people was neither objective nor unbiased.

However, this (scientific) lens was used throughout the latter period also. Subsequent characterisations of the Indian people by Indian as well as Western researchers led to almost similar conclusions. Durganand Sinha's (1988a) review of *basic* Indian values and behaviour dispositions revealed that "fatalism", "passivity", "dependence", "paranoid reaction", "narcissism", "insecurity", "anxiety", "authoritarianism", "submission", and "indifference to contradiction" were the main features of the Indian psyche. This cluster of characteristics diagnosed the Indian culture as dysfunctional and hopeless. The roots of this diagnosis lay in the external orientation of Hindu philosophy, natural ecological conditions, researchers' bias, and methodological limitations of the tools used. The dilemma is complex. The (scientifically) produced findings (or stereotypes) created a (myth or) fact (God knows) about the people of a culture who, because of these characteristics, did not deserve to live in this world. The flaw lies in the reading of the culture.

Doing Psychology in a Culturally Informed Way

Studying the psychology of a particular group or culture can be justifiably undertaken in terms of culturally provided categories. The problem is not merely of equivalence of concepts and measures. The various concepts and symbols used in a culture form a whole or gestalt. Using an alien concept would not fit into the whole and would result in a patchwork with little or no meaning and a lot of confusion. It is somewhat like groping in the dark and either confusing onething for something else or saying that the "given thing" is not there. In both cases, one is bound to draw erroneous conclusions and miss the reality.

Concepts are expressed through the medium of language. While transaction across languages is possible, it does not serve the entire purpose. Conceptualisation of concepts and their spectrum demands more than that. The concepts and categories of Western cultural moorings are embedded in a different set of ontology of the person. As such, their use, as seen in the characterisation of the traits of Indians, would be disastrous. As Marriot (1990) argued, all social sciences develop from thought about what is known to particular cultures and in the present practice only Western type ethnosocial science is used and its application is fraught with the risk of imposing an alien ontology and an alien epistemology. The situation in Indian psychology is lacking in this respect (G. Misra, 1988; J. Pandey, 1981; 1988a; 1988b; D. Sinha, 1986). Trained in the Western modes of thinking and practice and treating the same as universal-like, a considerable effort of Indian psychologists has been confined to replicating Western psychological research and consequently their work has been largely unproductive and socially irrelevant.

In recent years, however, reinterpreting the categories of observations (J.B.P. Sinha, 1988) and searching for indigenous concepts and theories have attracted the attention of researchers. In fact, being sensitive to the cultural context and its underlying premises enrich the psychological discourse. However, the current practice in psychology is largely *culture-blind* and rigid in its conceptual categories on account of their presupposed scientific credibility. Thus, Western categories assumed to be scientific, become culture fair and ready to be used elsewhere, whereas categories from other cultures, being cultural, are treated as nonscientific. This situation is alarming and calls for critical rethinking and reflection. To illustrate, attention will be drawn to some of the recent studies which reveal that incorporating the cultural context and related theoretical suppositions drastically changes both knowledge and understanding. A few studies dealing with aspects of moral reasoning, achievement, dependence, and conceptualisation of self will be discussed here.

MORAL REASONING Several studies on Indian samples have shown that "immanent justice" was invariably very strong in moral judgements of children as well as adults and, in general, their reasoning was not so developed as that of the Western samples. This shows that the level of moral maturity, in Piagetian–Kohlbergian sense, is very low. Studies have also reported that attribution for positive and negative outcomes for moral responsibility was greater for persons than situations, reward allocation was more on the basis of need which indicated a lower level of distributive justice (see Jain, 1991; G. Misra, 1991a; Shweder, 1991). However, viewing moral development within the cultural context changes one's understanding. The work of Shweder, Mohapatra, and Miller (1987) has challenged the prevailing notion. They contended that a culture's ideology and world-view have a significant bearing on the ontogenesis of moral understanding. The idea of conventional obligation prevails in those cultures in which social order is separated ideologically from the natural moral order. Thus, the terms of a contract are decided by those who enter it. More specifically, cultures emphasising social arrangements as secondary formations adhere to the conventional model. In contrast, cultures where the natural moral order is accepted, society is not separated conceptually from nature. The natural order is the moral order and vice versa (Shweder, 1991). Using a large number of practices, the distinction between moral and conventional was investigated by Shweder et al. (1987) and culture specific aspects of moral code in Indian and American children and adults were identified. It was found that while conventions did matter, the pattern in Americans tended towards more pluralistic or relativistic judgement while among Indians it moved towards viewing the practices as universally binding and unalterable. The results implicated the possibility of alternative rationally based moral codes rooted in a conception of natural law, justice and harmony, yet not founded on individualism and social contract. In this kind of post-conventional morality, the factors of consent, voluntarism, and free contract are discretionary.

ACHIEVEMENT Ever since McClelland proposed the linkage between n-Ach and economic development, substantial efforts have been made to exploit this human property for national development in many parts of the world. However, the concept rooted in the Protestant ethic and culturally specific individualistic competition and independence was not of much help. Despite this, the same scale of motivation continued to be used across the world. Subsequent work has revealed that the meaning of achievement is constructed differently in diverse cultures. Terms such as success, failure, risk, and aspiration have their meaning in a given context adopting diverse goals and means of achievement. Fyans, Salili, Maehr, and Desai (1983) noted that there were multiple perspectives on achievement and different forms of achievement motivation were associated with the goal that was held. The Indian sociocultural context emphasises a relational view of the individual, and familial concerns are more salient than personal. Following this reasoning, the development of achievement goals and means using open-ended measures was studied (Agarwal & Misra, 1986; 1989; G. Misra & Agarwal, 1985). The results revealed that social concern (e.g., being a good person, well-being of others, fulfilling one's duty, helping others, and getting affection from elders) was the predominant part of achievement goals. On the other hand, social skills (e.g., respecting elders, good behaviour, helping others, elder's blessings, and observing rules) constituted the cluster of predominant means of achievement. An attributional analysis by Dalal, Singh, and Misra (1988) confirmed these observations. Results from Japan also indicate an affiliative character of achievement. Recognising the culturally relevant patterns of achievement facilitates a more realistic understanding of the problems.

DEPENDENCE Viewed from a different perspective, the term dependence means sensitivity, affiliation, and a specific expectation-obligation relationship. Thus, in an individualistic frame of reference, dependence becomes an unwanted and undesirable trait. In contrast, in a sociocultural setting in which people have dependency need as well as dependency expectation, the relationship (Neki, 1976) takes a different turn, and the attempt to manage people through individualistic, self-determining ways fails. Keeping in view this feature, J.B.P. Sinha (1980) approached the problem of leadership in the organisational context. He observed that dealing with people with dependency need required care, affection, and a mutually supportive leadership, which he called *nurturant task master*. Such leadership closely approximates a father in the Indian family who takes care of the needs of children and, at the same time, strictly enforces the rules and standards of behaviour. The interpersonal transaction in the Indian setting is typically structured in terms of affectively loaded and personalised understanding.

SELF In recent years, self and related concepts (e.g., self-determination, causality orientation, competence, self-concept, self-esteem, and self theories) have gained currency as explanatory constructs in mainstream psychological discourse. In all these attempts, self has generally been considered as a separate, distinct, bounded unit with a fixed boundary and internally localised control. This Western notion in the monotheistic tradition is structured around an individualistic perception of the world. Sampson (1988) termed it self *contained* individualism which differs from non-Western or *ensembled* individualism which is characterised by variable self–other boundaries, field control, and inclusive self. The work of Triandis (1989; 1990) illustrated the cultural–behavioural dimension of *individualism–collectivism* which contrasted Western and non-Western perspectives. He noted that both included certain subcomponents and differed in predicting various behaviours. More recently, Markus and Kitayama (1991) systematised cultural differences in terms of *independent* and *interdependent* categories which emphasised autonomous and connective construals of persons, respectively.

In all these conceptualisations, the major differences between the two categories are the location of perceived control and relative separateness from the context. However, they fail to capture the sense of the Indian self-concept. Bharti (1985) attempted to tap its spiritual underpinnings. In this context, a distinction is made between *real self*, *empirical self*, and *material self*. *Atman* is the non-material realisation of the real self as opposed to the material, experiential self involving sensation, desires, and thought. It is dividual and not an individual. The empirical self in the Hindu tradition is interiorised as a state of being which is hierarchically lower than the self of the religious ultimate. The material self is related to behaviour, it is situational in nature and does not need reconciliation, since it is less than the true self. Rawlinson (1981), following the *samkhya-yoga* model of consciousness, argued that the act of awareness implicated three levels of consciousness: *manas* (lower mind), *ahamkar* (ego), and *buddhi* (intellect). The *manas* picks up input and passes it to *ahamkar* which organises the input. Finally, *buddhi* evaluates the categories. *Ahamkar* works as the central processor and may turn away from the input and engage in *raga* (passion), *dvesa* (hatred), and *moha* (delusion). The three *klesas* (defilements) refer to the tendencies of consuming the world, compulsion to destroy, and confusion and lack of discrimination, respectively. In general, they avoid reality. Yoga teaches that these defilements are endemic to all experiences at the normal level. The practice of yoga involves focusing attention on one's inner states correctly.

Paranjpe (1984; 1988) worked out a Vedantic model of *jiva* (person) or a living being. It consists of five layers like the concentric sheaths of an onion. These layers are made of "food" (*annamaya kosa*), "vital breath" (*pranamaya kosa*), mental (*manomaya kosa*), cognitive (*vijnanamaya kosa*), and joyous (*anandmaya kosa*). Thus, it is an hierarchical and structural model. The material world, or *prakriti*, is always in a state of flux on account of the continual interaction of three qualities (*gunas*), i.e., inertia or mass (*tamas*), movement or energy (*rajas*), and *sattva*, which may be translated as intelligence-stuff. The dominance of one of these *gunas* may lead to imbalance and contingent change. Their interaction involves the principle of *karma* and God has no role to play. Paranjpe (1984) compared these three qualities with mass, energy, and information. The persistent dominance of one of these qualities produces individual differences. The qualities are persistent as well as transitory. Human behaviour is regulated by the law of *karma* which states that all actions have consequences which yield traces and become the cause for future action. The human condition is viewed as consisting of suffering (*dukha*) of material, mysterious, and self-construed types. The true self or *atman* transcends the *jiva* and ego, accounts for the experience of self-awareness, has the capacity to witness, and is blissful in nature. According to Sankara (cited by Paranjpe, 1988, p. 196),

> The misconstrual of the nonself as self ties a man to egoism, and it is the tie (*bandhan*) which leads to the suffering of the cycle of birth and death. Having considered the body to be real and constructing it to be the "me", the Jiva nurtures it and protects it by following its desires. The ego thus becomes trapped in a reality of its own (misconstrual — like a moth in its cocoon) (*Vivekchudamani*, v. 137).

Discussing the training of a Vedantin, Hiriyanna (1952) clarified that man has a mixed nature. On the one hand, he is a member of the animal world with its instincts and desires, on the other, he has the potential for spirituality. The training involves transformation of man into a wholly spiritual being by transcending his animal nature. Hiriyanna added that this process passed through four stages:

(*a*) social morality, (*b*) duty (*nishkam karma* and meditation), (*c*) renunciation, and (*d*) communion. Social morality enjoins that a person must perform certain deeds (*karma*). These include life activities or *nitya karma* as well as *naimittika* or obligatory ones. After discharging one's obligatory *karmas*, the person should pursue worldly activities and should not shun society. Civic cohesion and *varnashramdharma* should be observed. As it is impossible to pursue both, the person should transcend obligatory *karmas* and pursue *nishkam karma* or duty for duty's sake. This leads to self conquest, and the deeds have specific outcomes. Doing one's duty leads to *duritksya* or *sattva sudhi* (purification of heart and cleanliness of mind) and to spiritual growth. In this context it may be relevant to note that *nishkam karma* has been found to mediate the stress–strain relationship. N. Pandey and Naidu (1986) observed that people who were strongly inclined toward *nishkam karma* experienced a lesser degree of strain than those who were less inclined toward it. Similarly, G. Misra (1989) found that effort orientation led to greater intrinsic motivation, incidental learning, and a higher level of performance.

It may also be noted that deeds may be transformed into duty provided that the thoughts are not focused on specific results. The intention of the doer is crucial. Thus, *kamya karma* may become *nitya karma*. Meditation (*upasana*) is the next step in the process. In particular, *ahamgrahopasna* is very important. This involves "a process of mentally identifying oneself with the object mediated upon. It is a process not merely thinking about it but actually becoming it in imagination" (Hiriyanna, 1952, p. 7). This leads to identification with the universe. It is a habit of deep concentration and by practising it continuously one is able to overcome the anxiety which is usually experienced while performing deeds. The next stage is *renunciation*. At this stage, one realises the part–whole relationship. Knowledge of the ultimate reality occurs as intuition and revelation. As Hiriyanna (1952) remarked,

> reason is adduced only for indicating probability but does not serve the purpose of demonstration. Intellectual appreciation leads to mediate knowledge with intuition results in immediate realization in experience. Finally, a person experiences *communion*. By constant practice one experiences unity that can bring about final freedom. This kind of experience yields no other result except establishment of a habit to repeat it.

On the whole, a moral view of the universe is upheld and an attitude reflecting hope for the future and resignation towards the past is promoted. In such a frame of reference, each person constitutes his own fate. Personal egotism as well as egotism of the species are kept in check. Spiritual experiences constitute an important part of wellbeing. Referring to *sushruta*, D. Sinha (1990) remarked that the Indian concept of health involves a state of delight or a feeling of spiritual, physical, and mental wellbeing.

Roland (1988) attempted to analyse self from a civilisational perspective within the framework of psychoanalysis. He showed considerable sensitivity to cultural peculiarities by introducing the notion of spiritual reality within everyone which is realised and experienced in varying degrees. He rightly asserted that while Indian culture emphasises pure consciousness and gradual dismantling of mental phenomena in consciousness, Western cultures are engaged in the pursuit of mentation, unification of reality, and objectification of all phenomenan. The concept of familial self refers to a basic inner psychological organisation that enables people to function properly within the hierarchical intimate relationship of the extended family, community and other social groups. Its suborganisations include reciprocity, empathy, we–self regard, narcissistic configurations of we–self regard, and socially contextualised ego ideal. Roland (1988) contrasted the subject–object duality of the West with the Indian monistic view and contended that this leads to transformation of the subjective in Indians while control of the objective is stressed in the West. The impact of urbanisation and Western modernisation has led to many changes (for instance, introduction of the Western social ethic, nuclear family, and competitive individualism) but the maintenance of tradition and cultural continuity remains a strong factor.

Contrary to the popular myth, Roland (1988) observed, "Hindu culture not only recognises the particular proclivities of a person, but also accords a remarkable degree of freedom in feeling, thinking, and maintaining a private self, while greatly encouraging the cultivation of one's inner self, in counterpoint to the considerable constraints on behavior in the social hierarchy" (p. 240). He added that the psychological make-up of Indians has been misunderstood. Oriented around *dharma*, it is highly developed. The familial self operates through contextualising and engages in metonymic thinking. This reflects an orientation of working with destiny and not a passive attitude toward fate.

Marriot (1976) observed that the notions of actor and action and of the divisibility of the person require a different model of behaviour. He argued that in Hindu transactions "those who transact as well as what and how they transact are thought to be inseparably 'code-substance' or 'substance-code'" (p. 110). These codes may be relatively gross or subtle and particulate (divisible). They are basically particles which are constantly moving from one aggregate (body) to another. In this scheme, persons are aggregates of particles of substance-code of various kinds, and their nature is constantly changing, owing to the addition or subtraction of these particles. Persons are thus "dividual" rather than "individual", and they are constantly exchanging some of themselves with what is in their environment, including other persons.

Marriot (1990) attempted to construct an alternative general theoretical system for the social sciences in a non-Western civilisation, using that civilisation's own categories. He isolated three constituent processes in the Indian personality, i.e., the three *gunas* of Samkhya in terms of marking (*sattva guna*, goodness), mixing (*rajas*, the passionate) which is active, and matching (*tamas*, the dark). He contended that Hindu thought explains events as the product of at least three independent variables operating in concert. This is depicted through graphs on three axes at right angles to each other. They consist of humours (*dosas*), elements (*mahabhutas*), strands (*gunas*), and human aims (*purusarthas*). The substance-code is one, and it "flows" through society and the world without impermeable boundaries or absolute distinction of kind. Thus, each person is a transitory moment in these ongoing processes. This analysis has been criticised for being limited in dealing with the entire range of phenomena and some of the important suppositions of Samkhya (Larson, 1990).

Collins (1991) made an effort to develop an Indian self psychology based on Marriot's framework and psychoanalytic concepts. He concluded,

all inter and intra-personal relations are reflections and replications of the creative self-recognition and *Purusa* and the partial refusal of his object-selves to remain only his self objects. Beings at all levels, from the Emanator himself to the lowest blade of the grass or rock are seeking to find themselves mirrored (which is identical to finding their desires fulfilled) in "downstream" self objects. Like *Purusa*, they are frequently disappointed by the disinclination of self objects to the mirroring role. Although moments of partial self-satisfaction occur when "willing" and appropriate self-objects are found, the greatest happiness comes from inversion (*nivrtti*) towards the emanating self. Paradoxically, through this "upstream" move persons recreate (remark) themselves and their world, making it (once more, and momentarily) an apt self object. When one knows oneself as god's self object, everything becomes one's own self object (pp. 177–178).

It is contended that marking, mixing and matching of *gunas* cannot be understood in their own terms since they do not employ any motivational principle. To this end, cosmogenic selfhood and its reflex in persons can explain the purpose of transactions.

Using textual analysis in the contemporary context does provide insights but needs to be supplemented by the shared everyday understanding of people. Based on a critical analysis of the assumptions in non-Western traditional thinking and contemporary observations, Tripathi (1988b) suggested that the crucial and distinctive features of the Indian mind lie in the construal of its boundaries. While in the Western mind, the boundaries are relatively more fixed in the case of self and environment, they are constantly shifting in the Indian mind. The boundaries are variable. Tripathi noted that in the case of the Indian, the self sometimes expands to fuse with the cosmos but at another moment it completely withdraws itself from it. For the Western mind, the dichotomies between self and other, man and nature, subjective and objective are complete. This is not true of the Indian who does not consider such dichotomies. To illustrate this point, Tripathi (1988b) analysed the relationship between individual and group in the Indian and the Western contexts. Thus,

> in the West the self and group are taken as two different entities each having its own fixed boundaries. The self then gets *related* to the own-group by forming links with the group. In the case of Indian, the self does not *relate* to the own-group but is *included* in it (Tripathi, 1988b, p. 322).

This, however, does not mean that Indians are pure collectivists. Self-realisation is also important. It depends on the nature of occasion or context whether the individual will be the focus or the collectivity.

The concept of person was approached by Shweder (1991) from another but related perspective. He noted that person concepts are often structured using a concrete, contextualised, nonabstractive, apparently undifferentiated thinking. His work in Orissa revealed that personal accounts are concrete and relational. Persons are described with reference to objects, occasions, places, and other persons. Such a concrete behavioural context is not found in American person accounts which are largely behavioural. This does not implicate that Indians have lesser processing capacity but reflects a different world-view which attaches little value to differentiation and abstraction. Shweder (1991) proposed that "the metaphors by which people live and the world views to which they subscribe mediate the relationship between what one thinks about and how one thinks" (p. 148). He identified holism as a mediating world premise which primarily subscribes to a sociocentric conception of relationships. Thus, the Indian *person is located in society* and regulated by strict rules defining interdependence which is context-specific and particularistic. The social construction of person as studied by Shweder (1991) indicates that the natural order and moral order are identical and the person is placed in this order.

The Emerging Perspective

The preceding descriptive account of the various efforts to place psychosocial understanding in a cultural perspective gives the flavour of the diversity of approaches adopted by individual scholars. In general, both the text and context have been utilised, though the degree of reliance on these sources has varied according to the orientation and goal of the scholar. They do, however, go a long way in unravelling the background assumptions for an alternative account of human action which locates its regulation in a differently organised system of concepts. An articulation of such a possibility seems to be more relevant in the present context.

Recent years have witnessed a resurgence of interest in understanding human phenomena from a new perspective emphasising the rehabilitation of the human mode of thought, and initiating dialogues on subjectivity, metatheory, narratives, meaning and recognition of cultural embeddedness of thought and action (Bruner, 1990; 1991; Clifford, 1988; Drefyus & Drefyus, 1986; Fiske & Shweder, 1986; Geertz, 1973; Gergen, 1982; 1989; Harré, Clark, & DeCarlo, 1985; Hermans, Kempen, & van Loon, 1992; Kruglanski, 1989; Semin

& Gergen, 1990; Shotter, 1990; Shweder, 1991; Shweder & LeVine, 1984). This signifies the possibilities of a more coherent and plausible account employing a situated and shared conception of reality. This new orientation goes beyond the positivistic view of knowledge and proposes that knowledge claims, particularly in the human domain, are relative to the setting in which they are grounded and it is neither pertinent nor possible to make context-free generalisations with a reasonable degree of legitimacy.

Against this backdrop, it is important to reorient the human psychological discourse to incorporate the Indian world-view. In doing so, the belief in some natural/universal human psychological principles is unwarranted. Instead, there should be a model of conceptualisation that emerges from the language and practice of real people in real/concrete interactional or transactional situations. This reflects the following preferences: (*a*) there is no objective reality out there which psychologists have to map, and examine the accuracy of that mapping (representation) with the objective reality; (*b*) psychologists should not engage in reductionism; (*c*) they should respect the construals of phenomena by the people which have earned legitimacy in the conventions shared by them; and (*d*) the focus of attention should be on practical activities, activities in which people engage in real life encounters. There is no inherent basic conflict between commonsense, everyday understanding, and scientific understanding. In fact, commonsense understanding is more strongly grounded in the history and culture of the people. Since there is no foundational rationality (Kruglanski, 1989) underlying efforts to test and understand some statement or phenomena, it seems more plausible to approach the experiences and actions in their own terms. The preceding review of studies, which were sensitive for deriving their concepts, tools, and propositions from the culture under study, reveals that they freely relied upon the culture specific ontologies and metatheoretic suppositions. Their freshness and legitimacy derives from the fact that they were open to the possibilities of dialogue with the modes of thought and action shared in the culture. Thus, despite the apparent but unwarranted threat of cultural relativism, univocal psychological discourses have limited value. With the growing recognition of the limits of scientism and an increasing inclination of modern scholarship towards rhetorical, narrative and interpretive approaches to human understanding, the discursive mode is found to be more congenial.

This mode of inquiry would be more suitable in the Indian socio-cultural context where text and context exist side-by-side and influence each other. As a student of culturally constituted behavioural phenomena, the tool box containing research instruments as well as the dimensions of academic discourse would require innovative reconstructions. In particular, different forms of linguistic products and activities would require greater attention, not as representations of some underlying mental phenomenon, but as real activities constituting behavioural activity. This would not only expand the repertoire of analytical tools, but also add new dimensions to the theoretical and conceptual arena of the discipline. Of course, such an effort would be transdisciplinary and would utilise resources from allied disciplines as well.

❦ FOUR ❦

Is Abnegation a Basic Experiential Trait in Traditional Societies?

The Case of Mexico

❦ Rogelio Diaz-Guerrero ❦

Introduction

I t is, and perhaps it should not be, a surprise that in the background, philosophers, sociologists, anthropologists, psychologists, and perchance historians and economists arrive at a number of similar theoretical conceptions, each, nevertheless, incrementing one's understanding.

It is generally agreed that a traditional society is one where modes of activity or belief are handed down (transmitted) from one generation to the next and perpetuated over and above the facts discovered by the social and physical sciences.

> The forces of imitation are so much more potent... the child's receptivity to its surroundings... so much more important (Bandura, Ross and Ross, 1963) demonstrate this type of learning and that power is what provokes imitation in the U.S.... that as long as every adult with whom he comes in contact is saturated with the tradition, he cannot escape a similar saturation (Mead, 1931, p. 195).

Nisbet (1966) argued that it was none other than the French Revolution, which quoting Taine he said was the single most important event in Europe's history after the fall of Rome, that must be credited with the first successful onslaught on tradition: reason versus tradition, religion versus state, the nature of property, the relation of social classes and above all equalitarianism. He has added, "Everywhere in the modern world, the clear direction of history seemed to be toward the separation of individuals from communal or corporate structures: from guild, village community, historic church, caste or state and from patriarchal ties in general" (Nisbet, 1966, p. 42). It is cross-cultural psychology that quantifies individualism versus collectivism across cultures (Triandis, 1988).

It is important to note that early scholars like Tocqueville and J.L. Talmon perceived tradition as the accumulation of pragmatic experience and sharply contrasted this to rationalism or ideologies that in their view would end up destroying the most important human values: honour, loyalty, friendship, and decorum.

According to Epstein (1994), nearly 100 years ago Freud introduced a dual theory of information processing. The primary process which operates through wish fulfilment, displacement, condensation and provides the latent content that explains the manifest, as distinguished from the more logical, rational, realistic mode of the secondary process.

All these in turn appear to foreshadow important aspects of the modern psychology of cognition. Bruner (1986) talked of propositional thought which is abstract, general, theoretical, and public. But, more importantly, there exists narrative thought which covers most of one's personal life, it is story-like, personally convincing, imaginative, dreamy, includes feelings and emotions, characters, settings, and biographies.

In a comprehensive and importantly programmatic paper, Epstein (1994) characterised what may be the two fundamental and inter-related modes of cognitive processing: the experiential and the rational systems. Some of the contrasts are: holistic versus analytic; affective, pleasure pain-oriented versus logical, reason-oriented; association-istic connections versus logical connections; behaviour mediated by "vibes" from past experiences versus behaviour mediated by conscious appraisal of events; encoded reality in concrete images, metaphors and narratives versus encoded reality in abstract symbols, words and numbers.

Cross-cultural psychologists may ask: Where does enculturation fit? Bruner (1990) provided an answer to this question, "the folk psychology of ordinary people is not just a set of self assuaging illusions, but the culture's beliefs and working hypotheses about what makes it possible and fulfilling for people to live together.... It is where psychology starts..." (p. 32).

Where do cultural beliefs, for instance, what Diaz-Guerrero called historic–sociocultural premises (HSCPs) (Diaz-Guerrero, 1967a) and personality traits tally within the new cognitive nomenclature? He proposed that the HSCPs are propositional-narrative and that there are at least two types of personality traits, propositional or rational such as conscientiousness and others singularly experiential such as abnegation. The last, discovered after much cultural exploration in Mexico, may lie at the very centre of what has been called a traditional society. It is plausible that as long as it maintains experiential characteristics, particularly unconsciousness or semiconsciousness in other traditional societies, as it does in the Mexican, modernisation will be difficult.

Antecedents

In the spring of 1989, *Excelsior*, the Mexican New York Times acceded to publish eight long articles under the title: "Our cousins and ourselves, the personality of Mexicans and Americans". The last of these articles — after reiterating the transcendental importance of culture in the psychological and social development of the individual — argued:

> It appears indispensable, before ending this contrasting of the behavior of Mexicans and Americans... to refer to a dichotomous dimension, that may, in a deeper fashion underscore...the differential aspects previously described. We refer, in the case of the Mexicans to abnegation with its deep historical roots and in the American case to egocentrism, to center power, freedom, every thing that human nature can give, in the individual (Diaz-Guerrero, 1989a, p. 16-A).

> It is pointed out that the histories of both nations appear to explain this. In the case of Mexicans, abnegation, even that of life, was a requirement for the social life of the prehispanic cultures. Abnegation is central in the religion introduced in Mexico by the Spaniards and besides "the historic load of the predisposition to abnegation in the Mexicans becomes larger when the Indian women whose social status was lower than that of the men... ended up being the undervalued wives or concubines of the invaders" (Diaz-Guerrero, 1989a, p. 16-A).

In the 1960s, the Pancultural Semantic Differential (Diaz-Guerrero & Salas, 1975; Osgood, May, & Miron, 1975) was utilised to study the self-concept of adolescents in 19 culture languages. In self-evaluation, the young Mexicans ranked 19th, in the potency of their self 17th, and in the total meaning of their self they ranked 19th only above the Hindu sample. It was impossible to avoid the conclusion that comparatively they possessed a very diminished self. In the same cross-cultural study 600 other concepts were evaluated. While Mexican adolescents devalued their self, they highly evaluated and considered highly powerful the father, the mother, the family, friends, relatives, etc. It was argued,

The value and the potency that Mexicans give to themselves, appear to be inextricably linked to persons and symbols that in their affect or in their faith are miraculously good and powerful. The Mexican... out of humility has imposed upon himself this insufficiency, scarcity and reduction with the goal of better life, highlighting the greatness and immensity of the symbols in which he believes: God, the Virgin Mary, the saints, the churches, the pyramid, and the persons and institutions that are almost everything for him: the mother, the father, the older brother, the friend and, particularly, the family (Diaz-Guerrero, 1982, p. 236).

In effect, in this study, an enormity of symbols and persons *are before him.* There was already a part of what later was to be defined as abnegation.

According to the article in the *Excelsior,*

The Mexicans, in the average have grown up with a tendency to abnegation, the negation of their self and their needs in favor of others and of society. This explains, at least partially, their way of understanding respect, the form in which they bestow power, their ease for preferring love over power, the cultural, particularly the folkloric over the material, harmony with friends and family over money, to cope with problems by self modification rather than by self assertion, to be sensitive to the field rather than independent from it, to develop feminine aspects within machismo, to be flexible rather than severe, to cooperate rather than to compete and to consider obedience as a great virtue. But we have seen once and again, that the inflexible command of culture collides frontally with reality's versatility and its opportunities to confuse love with power, obedience with servility, self-modification with passivity, flexibility with corruption, and also, when crude reality takes over, to provoke cynicism towards and distrust of everything, particularly authority and secular power (Diaz-Guerrero, 1989a, p. 16-A).

This is not the first time that self-denial in Mexico has been used, if only narratively, to explain other behaviours of Mexicans.

The Research Seminar in Ethnopsychology

In 1987, Rolando Diaz-Loving and Diaz-Guerrero organised within the graduate division of social psychology at UNAM, a seminar under the title of "Research seminar in ethnopsychology". Initially, everything written since the beginning of the twentieth century about the psychology of the Mexican was reviewed and discussed. Years later several sessions were dedicated to analyse the hypotheses that could be derived from the postulates of Mexican ethnopsychology (Diaz-Guerrero, 1989b). On the basis of the postulate, and the conceptualisation (Diaz-Guerrero, 1979), that personality is the product of a culture–counterculture dialectic, the following hypothesis was proposed: From the dimensions discovered for the Mexican culture, the most important is one termed affiliative obedience. If Mexicans are going to be, following these commandments, obedient by affect, they will have to develop at least two personality traits: one of abnegation and the other of flexibility. Avendaño-Sandoval, a participant at the seminar and Melgoza-Enriquez, in search for a theme for her professional thesis, expressed interest in testing this hypothesis.

The procedure adopted first provided a conceptual definition of abnegation and flexibility, and then developed items consistent with that definition. A questionnaire comprising these items was administered to subjects and factor analysed to determine the construct validity of each trait, that is, the existence of the hypothesised dimensions in the cognition of the subjects. It is not the objective of this paper to provide methodological details that led to the confirmation of the hypothesis (see Avendaño-Sandoval & Diaz-Guerrero, 1990; Melgoza-Enriquez, 1990; Melgoza-Enriquez & Diaz-Guerrero, 1990).

The essential aim was to determine the extent to which the trait of abnegation was a basic trait of the Mexican personality, that is, to what extent it explained other traits and dimensions of his psychology, and if it could predict the existence of other traits yet to be discovered.

Conceptual Definition and the First Operational Definition of Abnegation

The original study defined abnegation as the behavioural disposition in which others are placed before oneself or to sacrifice oneself in the service of others. The contrary disposition was self-assertion. The intention of using the term "to sacrifice" was to provide a synonym of abnegation, which it is, but has greater intensity.

Initially, Avendaño-Sanadoval and Diaz-Guerrero developed the items. The test format was forced choice between a statement of abnegation and one of self-assertion. It was ensured that each item portrayed a real life situation. A total of 41 items psychometrically cleared on the average gave 50 per cent of answers for each option. The test was administered to 410 subjects. Factor analysis of principal components with varimax rotation yielded four factors with eigen values greater than 1. Consistent with the definition, the first factor was labelled personal abnegation. Situations portrayed ranged from severe to minor stress. For example, "In the hospital, they leave a gauze in my stomach and it becomes infected". For this, the self-assertion option was "I change doctor and I sue him". This was mentioned by 46 per cent of the subjects. The abnegation option was "I ask the doctor to operate me immediately", this was the preferred option of 54 per cent of the subjects. "The bus conductor does not stop where I signal". The self-assertion option was "I yell at him" and the abnegation option "I just get out at the next stop". It was noted that 75 per cent endorsed the option of abnegation, 25 per cent of self-assertion. The items determined up to what point self-assertion was avoided. In the other three factors the context was changed. The second factor was not personal but social, the third one about health, and the fourth had existential tonalities. Thus, for the item: "I was told of my fatal diagnosis", 25 per cent chose resignation and 75 per cent preferred self-assertion: "I have other tests done, I consult other physicians". It is contended in this paper that;

Beyond its behavioral origin in the culture-counterculture dialectic, it is important to develop hypotheses about the psychodynamics of abnegation in the individuals. There are at least two aspects to be considered:

1. Its relation to the experimental analysis of behavior. What is it that reinforces abnegation? It is hypothesized that the reinforcer can be the intrinsic pleasure of doing it....

2. Its dynamic relation to the cognitive economy of other traits and needs of the person. Two possibilities are proposed:
    The individual abnegates because the action pleases or satisfies him psychoculturally, or behaves this way fearing the reaction of the other. This fear can be explained in three ways:

    (a) Not to abnegate, not to put the other before one, breaks with the cultural command.

    (b) The individual is in a rather uncomfortable psychocultural situation of forcing himself above the other. He has bothered, he has offended the other.

    (c) The individual besides the above and more importantly, fears the attack of the other or a hostile interpersonal reaction... (Avendaño-Sandoval & Diaz-Guerrero, 1990, p. 13).

It is important to discuss what appears to be a strong tendency to avoid self-assertion. Diaz-Guerrero firmly believed that underlying it, in the case of Mexicans, is abnegation, a trait or a concept that they sometimes do not accept. On the other hand, they happily accept the description of themselves as amiable, generous, and "aguantadores" (steadfast forbearance). The study cited earlier (Avendaño-Sandoval & Diaz-Guerrero, 1990) mentions a finding by Flores-Galaz, Diaz-Loving, and Rivera-Aragon (1987). When trying to validate the Assertivity Scale of Rathus for Mexicans, the first factor they found was one of no-assertivity. They explained the result on the basis of the self-modifying coping style of Mexicans. Can self-modification be another behavioural expression of abnegation?

In 1988, La Rosa and Diaz-Loving published the results of an extensive study to determine the self-concept of 1,083 university students. They identified nine factors. The first factor accounting for almost 50 per cent of the variance (La Rosa, 1986, p. 98), was defined by the following adjectival scales: courteous–discourteous, and well brought up–badly brought up. As may be recalled, the first part of the definition of abnegation, demands placing others before oneself.

In the pilot studies that were undertaken for the construction of the first questionnaire of abnegation, the problem was to develop items that were not answered in an abnegated fashion, and there was a doubt whether the results were not just verbalisation. In a laboratory experiment (Avendaño-Sandoval & Diaz-Guerrero, 1992) it was demonstrated that 84.7 per cent of males ceded a present to a confederate that was desired, but was gained through personal effort. In the case of women, only 30 per cent ceded it and 70 per cent remained undecided. When the reason for their behaviour was elicited, women indicated that they felt embarrassed (*les habia dado "pena"*). The type of behavioural abnegation manifested by males closely approximated the two parts of its conceptual definition: the others were placed before them and without doubt, they sacrificed so that others may benefit. In the case of women, however, there was another expression of abnegation: embarrassment at self-assertion (*que le dé a uno pena de autoafirmarse*).

The Second Operational Definition

Under the direction of Reyes-Lagunes and Diaz-Guerrero, Avendaño-Sandoval operationalised abnegation with the support of distinguished professors and colleagues. She obtained 85 items coherent with the original conceptual definition. In this case, statements such as "It embarrasses me to say no" could be answered as true or false or as a question mark, i.e., "When the item refers to a situation that you have not experienced or when you cannot remember exactly" The questionnaire was administered to 850 males and females in three age groups, and pursuing diverse occupations. The methodical form for the realisation of the psychometric analysis can only be derived from the reading of the resulting dissertation (Avendaño-Sandoval, 1994). Out of a total of 20 factors, three were accepted. The first one, abnegation centred in the family, was defined by items such as: "I enjoy working overtime if it is for my family" and "Even if I am tired I will do things for my family". This factor showed a high congruence with the definition. It is possible that in the only context where it is highly acceptable to be abnegated is in relation with the family.

The second factor, labelled abnegation centred in social behaviour, was reflected by such statements as: "I am generally very amiable", and "Generally, I am polite". Interest in this factor is intensified when one observes that the third and the fourth items in factor loading are: "I am a well brought up person", and "Almost always I am courteous". This factor was a hybrid of the first factor in the self-concept of La Rosa and Diaz-Loving (1991) and of the first factor in the flexibility scale of Melgoza-Enriquez and Diaz-Guerrero (1990). The three constructs were very similar in content; in Avendaño, the accent was on amiability, in La Rosa, on courteousness, and in Melgoza-Enriquez, on tolerance. In the last case, together with tolerance Mexican style, there was the wish to please and the wish to cooperate. The question is: are all these different facets of abnegation?

The third factor, termed sensitive abnegation or cautiousness, was characterised by statements such as: "I am embarrassed to say no", and "It is difficult for me to complain". This is almost identical to the no-assertivity factor of Flores-Galaz et al. (1987), where the key statements were: "It is often that I have difficulty in saying no", and "I am embarrassed if I am to reject personally an invitation". The young women in the abnegation experiment indicated that they did not try to get the present because "they felt embarrassed" (*les daba pena*). Is it possible that no-assertivity and this kind of sensitive abnegation are the most stressful expressions of abnegation?

Is There a Depth Psychology of Abnegation?

Often during the course of his lectures in north, south and central Mexico, after discussing how psychological studies of Mexicans in terms of cultural dimensions were initiated and after describing what is known about personality traits, Diaz-Guerrero asserted that these studies indicate that Mexicans are abnegated. Often he is told that the trait should be labelled amiability or generosity. This and other more extreme reactions bring to mind Shakespeare's observation: "The Lady protests too much" and, in consequence, that there was something rotten in Denmark. The word *pena* is derived from the Latin *poena* which means punishment. The *Dictionary of the Royal Academy of the Spanish Language* dedicates nearly 500 words to the connotation of *pena*. The first connotation is "punishment imposed by a legitimate authority", another is "affliction", the third is "pain, torment", and the last is "difficulty, onerous work". Of course, there are other expressions: *alma en pena* (soul in pain), and *pena capital* (capital punishment).

The *Pequeño Larousse Ilustrado* points out that in Venezuela, Columbia, and Mexico, the word *pena* has acquired another connotation, that is, shyness and shame. The *Diccionario Basico del Español de Mexico* adds another meaning: "sadness or compassion that produces in a person the pain, poverty, sickness, etc. of another". This is exemplified by the sentence: "Abandoned old people produce great pena in me!". Perhaps, there is a common thread underlying the empathic compassion factor with its high load item: "I am moved by the suffering of other people" discovered by Diaz-Loving, Andrade-Palos, and Nadelsticher (1986), sensitive abnegation and no-assertivity. The *Pequeño Larousse* includes the subsense of shyness and shame in the expression: *Me dá pena molestar* (I feel shamed when I bother others). It is this last sense, that the term *pena* has been used in the questionnaires of abnegation and assertivity, but the cognitive net of the word *pena* would encompass all the other connotations.

What is evident, nevertheless, is that on the one hand, Mexicans are not pleased to hear that they are abnegated, and on the other, that factorially, abnegation is linked to the meaning of *pena*.

How Conscious are Mexicans of Abnegating?

During 1992 and 1993, Diaz-Guerrero and Rodriguez-Velasco carried out an extensive study on the meaning of abnegation and its synonyms, and their relation with self-concept, in 100 Grade 9 and 100 Grade 12 high school students, half males and half females in state institutions in Merida, Yucatan, Mexico.

The first number of the *Revista de Psicologia Contemporanea*, edited by "El Manual Moderno" of Mexico City, carries a paper entitled "The subjective meaning of abnegation and its synonyms". According to this paper, "As it has been reported (Avendaño-Sandoval & Diaz-Guerrero, 1990; 1992), the discovery of the existence of a trait of abnegation bestirs the need to relate it, on the one hand to the culture-counterculture dialectic and on the other to the laws of learning and to psychodynamics". Beyond this, there is the question as to the degree of consciousness with which abnegation is engaged in by Mexicans. It is postulated that the frequent response of abnegation in most Mexicans is given in an automatic, unconscious or semiconscious way. Moreover, it is considered that once realised, and depending upon the different situations, the next reaction can vary from rejoicing at having abnegated to considering oneself stupid and getting mad or depressed for having done so. It is, therefore, necessary to probe into the consequences for both normalcy and psychopathology of the existence of this trait in individuals.

On the basis of this applied, clinical interest, it was decided to apply the Semantic Differential (SD) technique, to determine the subjective meaning of the concept of abnegation and its synonyms. This technique, as is well known (Diaz-Guerrero & Sals, 1975; Osgood, Suci, & Tannenbaum, 1957), provides the affective, subjective meaning of concepts in three fundamental dimensions: evaluation (E), potency (P), and activity (A), and also the intensity of the total meaning: EPA, that is, simply the aggregation of E, P, and A. The SD also includes a scale to determine the degree of familiarity with the concept.

Diaz-Guerrero (1959) opined that what is unconscious is not verbalised or not adequately verbalised and, consequently, the greater the meaning provided by an idea the more it will advance from the unconscious to the semiconscious and to the conscious. Thus, it was assumed that the degree of familiarity and the EPA would indicate the level of consciousness of the concepts in this study. The evaluation would indicate how good is the concept, its potency, its standing in power and its activity, its level of dynamism.

It was hypothesised that the concept of abnegation would be the least valued, potent and active of the synonyms and the most unconscious, that is, the least familiar and the one with the lowest EPA (Diaz-Guerrero & Rodriguez-Velasco, 1994, p. 17).

A sample of 200 subjects responded to the Pancultural SD of the Spanish Language (Diaz-Guerrero & Salas, 1975) for the following 10 concepts: I as a person, tolerant, sacrificing, amiable, flexible, abnegated, disinterested, resigned, forbearer (aguantadoe), and generous.

There were few statistical differences among the four groups: generous, amiable, and forbearer, in that order, received the highest evaluation. Almost 2 SDs below the evaluation of generous were abnegated and resigned. In potency, forbearer followed by generous and amiable received the highest scores, and very significantly below, the lowest were abnegated and resigned. Forbearer followed by amiable and generous received the highest scores in dynamism and as in the previous cases, abnegated and resigned received the lowest scores. In familiarity, amiable received the highest score followed by forbearer and generous. Resigned and abnegated were the least familiar; in fact, abnegated was the least familiar. In the total affective meaning of these concepts in cognition, forbearer, amiable and generous appeared in the first place. The last ones, very significantly below 0 of the semantic space, were abnegated and resigned. Surprisingly, there was complete congruence between the stated hypotheses and the obtained results.

Perhaps as important and surprising, as the confirmation of the hypotheses, was the finding that the psychological meaning of abnegated is a subjective synonym of resigned. This concept along with its synonyms — submissive, patient, meek, lamb-like, enslavable, passive, conformist, docile, and of extreme externality — explain why the concept of abnegated is not very acceptable and it tends to be repressed.

The results clearly showed that the terms generous, amiable and forbearer were the most acceptable, familiar and had greater meaning. Forbearer was perceived with greater power and activity than the other two. These results indicated that Mexicans can accept that they are forbearers.

If the hypotheses that the unconscious is what cannot be verbalised, and that the SD, through the intensity of meaning and the degree of familiarity, measures levels of conscientisation are valid, it is evident that abnegated and resigned are contiguous with unconscious.

Conflicts arising from unwanted automatic abnegated behaviour could be resolved by cognitive behavioural psychotherapy, desensitising it in progressive steps through acceptable synonyms. Psychodynamic psychotherapy can do so by liberating the repression of the concept, getting close to it through its conscious synonyms, that is, the manifest content of the latent abnegation (Diaz-Guerrero & Rodriguez-Velasco, 1994). This "abnegation complex" of Mexicans can be clinically managed just as Freud managed the Oedipus concept, and Adler, the inferiority complex.

Studies on Assertivity

In the initial study on abnegation (Avendaño-Sandoval & Diaz-Guerrero, 1990), it was implicit that abnegation and self-assertion (*autoafirmacion*) formed a bipolar dimension. The word assertivity (*asertividat*) does not exist in the Spanish language. This explains that when Flores-Galaz et al. (1987) tried to operationalise it, they found a first factor of no-assertivity. Here, there is some kind of confirmation of Whorf's hypothesis that people cannot think beyond their language.

With uncommon persistence Flores-Galaz (1994), under the direction of Diaz-Loving, completed a number of studies with the aim of searching for a Mexican meaning of assertivity. Her efforts to study the cognitive net of the word assertivity led to cognitive nets of the Spanish word *asercion*: action and effect of *asseverating* and its derivatives *asertivo* and *aserto*, for affirmative and affirmation. Thus, the highest semantic loads of her cognitive net were: correct, to hit on the spot, security, certainty, truthful.

Inspired by the results of her first study (Flores-Galaz et al., 1987), Flores-Galaz propounded a complex and refined definition of assertivity. Assertivity, according to her, in the most positive American sense, may be seen in Mexico in (*a*) everyday interactions and services, (*b*) assertivity in the affiliative area, and (*c*) in school interactions for students and in occupational interactions for workers.

Congruent with her definition, she developed a questionnaire comprising 95 items and administered it to 439 students equally divided by gender and educational level (junior high school, senior high school or university). A principal component factor analysis with varimax rotation produced 28 factors with eigen values greater than 1. Only the first four factors had alphas above .62. In view of this, the items were clustered according to the theoretical areas: affiliative, school, and cotidian areas. The internal consistency of the grouped items was calculated and it was found that the alphas were above .84. A second, identical factor analysis of the items remaining in each area after determining the internal consistency, yielded 18 factors. Only the first seven were theoretically clear and since there was a high degree of redundancy, by permissible procedures they were reduced to five. Psychologically, these five factors were coherent.

Factor 1, labelled indirect assertivity, included items like: "It is easier to tell a classmate things that may offend him by telephone than personally". Factor 2 was denominated no-assertivity in the affiliative area. It was represented by items like: "It is difficult for me to express openly my feelings to my parents", and "It is embarrassing for me (*me dá pena*) to tell the children of my friends to stop being noisy". The third factor, labelled assertivity in cotidian situations, was defined by statements similar to "If a couple close to me in the theater or in a conference is noisy, I ask them to keep silent" or "I complain when there is bad service in restaurants or in any other place". The fourth and fifth factors were merely situational expressions of no-assertivity and of indirect assertivity when facing several types of authority in the school.

In an attempt to overcome the limitation of her study being based only on students, Flores-Galaz applied a parallel questionnaire where, for instance, she substituted classmates by working companions, to 432 employees in the City of Mexico divided equally on the basis of gender and with approximately one-fourth with the following levels of education: primary, junior high, senior high, and professional.

In the same doctoral dissertation Flores-Galaz (1994) reported correlations among employees for three dimensions of assertivity, that is, locus of control, achievement orientation, and self-concept. Her most important observation, one that should be replicated, was that assertivity in cotidian situation in Mexico was the only one that reproduced, or at least approximated, the positive US assertivity. This assertivity that Diaz-Guerrero labelled assertivity in power relations, correlated positively and significantly with internality (.51), mastery (.51), competition (.29), work (.47), and in a less significant way with self-concept on the La Rosa and Diaz-Loving (1991) scale.

This finding provides the first Mexican measuring device hardly susceptible to falsification that would permit an adequate appraisal of the results of other measuring devices in the selection of internal, capable, and hardworking individuals with a positive self-concept.

Abnegation and Assertivity

Again, during the course of his lectures in different regions of Mexico, Diaz-Guerrero asserted that Mexicans are fundamentally, apparently in an automatic form, abnegated; questions arise about what would happen when as a result of NAFTA, the egocentric and assertive Americans and the abnegated Mexicans collide with each other. The only thing that is important is that Mexicans must differentiate between the universe of love, affect and friendship, and the universe of power, economics and politics. In the first universe Mexicans should follow the directives of abnegation, and in the second, those of self-assertion.

Flores-Galaz's (1994) results support this advice. To compete with the most positive form of American assertivity, Mexicans should behave in accordance with the trait that underlies cotidian assertivity, i.e., self-assertion, dignity, integrity, and modesty in the face of achievement. The scale of cotidian assertivity with its various correlates measures a valuable form of Mexican style, i.e., productive, hardworking and *no dejado* (never let the other abuse you).

Abnegation, Self-Assertion and No-Assertivity

Occum's razor: "Entities should not be multiplied without need", would lead to the conclusion that the factors of no-assertivity and indirect assertivity are facets of abnegation. In fact, as already discussed, no-assertivity includes items related to sensitive abnegation and one can maintain the hypothesis that indirect assertivity correlates highly with factors of abnegation. However, to say that cotidian assertivity is a facet of self-assertion is not easy. As already discussed, there may be something deeper, related to the concept of dignity and integrity.

It must be emphasised here that Flores-Galaz and Diaz-Loving resolutely tried to find in Mexican subjects the equivalent of assertivity the way it is defined by American authors. It is no less interesting and significant that when Diaz-Guerrero first spoke of coping styles (Diaz-Guerrero, 1965; 1967a; 1967b), he attributed the passive, self-modifying style to Mexicans, and the active, the one involving modification of the environment and of others, i.e., the self-assertive style to Americans.

Ethnopsychology

Inspired by the large number of correlates of those beliefs with psychological, social, economic and even political dimensions and by the observations of colleagues, particularly those in the graduate department of social psychology at UMNAM, Diaz-Guerrero posited a new scientific discipline: ethnopsychology.

Setting off from postulates of this new science, an attempt has been made to determine the typical personality traits of Mexicans.

The first trait identified was abnegation and flexibility. Abnegation appears to be crucial. It must be borne in mind that in the original study it was measured as the avoidance of self-assertion. In the second experiment, it was expressed behaviourally and beneficially by giving to another something gained through personal effort. In the second factorial study, there were both forms of abnegation: the family and social behaviour centred abnegation factor measured "giving apparently through love", whereas the sensitive abnegation factor measured "avoiding to offend".

In several writings Diaz-Guerrero contrasted the Mexican and the American cultures arguing that the Mexican culture is one of love and the American one is a culture of power. It has been pointed out that in both cultures love and power are important, but in the Mexican culture love is more decisive, whereas in the American culture power is more significant. Much has been made of the fact that in the areas of power such as technology, economy, and politics Americans are better endowed, whereas Mexicans are better placed in the areas of love, friendship, folklore, humanities, and arts.

Nurturing this culture of love is a trait of abnegation. Thus, for all that has been said, it appears more to be the result of enculturation than of socialisation, or stated differently, the empire of culture has prevailed in the culture—counterculture dialectic.

Because it is a product of enculturation, automatic and apparently unconscious, its less unconscious and more acceptable manifestations have usually been studied: affiliative obedience, and coping style of self-modification. Thousands of adjectives obtained by La Rosa and Diaz-Loving (1991), in their brainstorming sessions with hundreds of students, had to be conscious and plausibly acceptable. Consequently, as in the case of the most acceptable and conscious synonyms of abnegation: amiable, forbearer and generous, courteous, well brought up, attentive, amiable, decent, friendly appeared as the first factor in their self-concept. Incidentally, this first factor was in perfect agreement with "the others before me" and with the loving aspect, much more conscious and acceptable of abnegation.

While the procedure used in the study by La Rosa and Diaz-Loving was rational, establishing first the categories of the self, in a recent study by Valdez-Medina (1994), under the direction of Reyes-Lagunes, the procedure was free association. In this case, there was less constriction on what is acceptable and what is conscious. This piece of intensive and methodologically trend-setting research, comparable to that of La Rosa and Diaz-Loving, confirmed what has been discovered about the psychology of Mexicans and also supported the existence of different levels of cognition.

The Stressing Aspects of Abnegation

Abnegation has been measured both for its prosocial features of giving, sacrificing for and obeying out of love, and for its plausible stressing facets to avoid self-assertion and to develop *pena* of being assertive. Behind this, it is evident that there is a "psychodynamics" of abnegation: not to abnegate may break with the cultural command, not to abnegate may offend the other, not to abnegate may provoke violence from the other.

To abnegate is, therefore, a complex disposition. It may be referred to as the abnegation complex. It has already been suggested that it is an automatic disposition, possibly unconscious, one that is not accepted and may be desensitised and creates problems when it is replaced by any of its synonyms. What other possible consequences can be derived from this complex? In Mexico, socially, everybody expects that the others will be equally abnegated: amiable, courteous, well brought up, accommodating, affectionate, and this leads to the first hypothesis. Mexicans feel hurt when these encultured expectations are not fulfilled. It is possible to hypothesise the existence of a trait of susceptibility in Mexicans. This may vary from being sensitive, delicate, touchy to being suspicious. Because of this, and because of the dilemmas resulting from the use of abnegation in power transactions such as in work, economy, politics, it is hypothesised that there exists in Mexicans a trait of distrust, which may range from misgiving and suspicion, to malice, dissimulation and even paranoia.

It may not be difficult to understand that if Mexicans are susceptible because of being abnegated, they should feel great *pena*, almost fear in offending or hurting other Mexicans who are equally abnegated and susceptible. This explains the delicacy of social relations in Mexico.

Of course, it is difficult to deny that abnegation, in terms of giving and loving as well as avoiding offending others, sometimes proves successful and at other times disastrous to soften the power relations between humans. It is you first, and then I but if you do not respond the same way, and specially if in spite of this you are offended, you are telling me that for you, power is more important than love. To hypothesise, even in this rather rustic manner, but as in Mendeleiev's table, the existence of the traits of susceptibility and mistrust permits one to understand the negative correlations that Flores-Galaz (1994) found between indirect assertivity and no-assertivity and self-concept. On these two traits subjects scored below the theoretical mean, which means that perhaps only a minority of Mexicans prefers indirect ways of self-assertion or, particularly, develops much *pena* when it is a matter of self-assertion. It is hypothesised that such Mexicans are more susceptible and distrustful than others, perhaps the only ones.

Epilogue

There is probably far more to what is called the psychodynamics or cognitive processing of abnegation. Its characteristics, as studied in the Mexican population, permit one to call it an experiential personality trait. Since this may be the first time that personality traits are classified as either propositional rational or experiential narrative, it may be maintained that as with other experiential contents, abnegation should prove persistent, even across situations, and more difficult to change.

According to Diaz-Guerrero, this trait would be found in all traditional societies. It is likely to be the cornerstone of what has been called a traditional society. It diametrically opposes the selfish gene of the sociobiologists. On the basis of the arguments presented here, it may be said that its Darwinian functions would be to soften power relations, a much needed function in a world tilted towards power.

Ethnopsychology, it is obvious, has a responsibility and, as Kurt Lewin once said of psychology, a vast territory, an immense continent full of fascination and power and great realms and lands where nobody ever has set his foot.

❧ FIVE ❧

Psychology of Language Acquisition and Bilingualism in India

The Cultural Input

❧ Ajit K. Mohanty ❧

Since the 1970s, many psychologists in India have expressed concern about making psychology more relevant for society and Sinha (1984b; 1986), a pioneer among them, repeatedly pleaded for culture embeddedness and contextualisation of psychological research as necessary steps towards relevance. This concern is reflected in the growing literature on *indigenous* and *indigenised* psychology in India (Adair, Puhan, & Vohra, 1993; Puhan & Sahoo, 1991; Sinha, 1986; 1989; 1997). Sinha (1997) distinguished between *indigenous* and *indigenised* approaches in the following words: "The former refers to psychology that is generated and develops in a particular culture and utilizes its collective creations, constructs and categories. The latter refers to a process of transformation of imported elements of modern psychology to make them appropriate to the sociocultural setting" (p. 133). The march towards an indigenous approach as well as indigenisation in psychology in India has been characterised by concern about Western dominance (Mohanty, 1988) and a rejection of such dominance (Sinha, 1981b) and "has now assumed almost the shape of a 'movement'" (Sinha, 1997, p. 135). Rejection of Western dominance, however, need not be construed as an end in itself nor as a movement away from the goals of a universal psychology. The East–West dichotomy itself is often defeating, but it symbolises the need for theory, problems and methodology of psychological research to be contextualised in the immediate social reality without which an understanding of psychological processes is necessarily incomplete. While this is equally true of all areas of psychology, in some it is much more obvious. The study of linguistic processes and language acquisition, with its focus on language which is a cultural phenomenon having unique formal and structural properties, is one such area. Since language is an integral aspect of culture, the process of its acquisition is hard to distinguish from the process of enculturation. In fact, cultural transmission occurs predominantly through language and the acquisition of language is culturally conditioned. Children learn to use language in a socially appropriate manner through their participation in social interactions (Ochs, 1986; Vygotsky, 1978) which provide the contextual framework for communication. Apart from transmitting sociocultural knowledge, language also acts as a potent medium of socialisation. "Verbal behavior, speech acts and communicative functions are culturally conditioned, contextually embedded and linguistically coded. Use of language, therefore, has to be viewed in a holistic framework in which cultural context and the form and function of language are necessary parameters" (Mohanty, 2000). The relationship between culture, language, and verbal behaviour has been depicted in Figure 5.1.

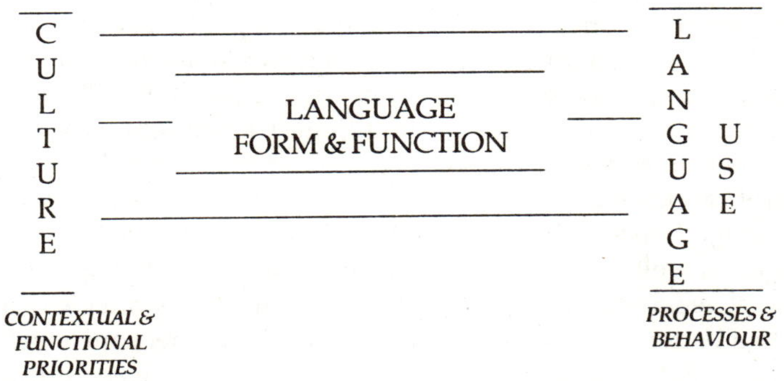

```
C  ————————————————————————  L
U  ————————————————————  A
L  ————      LANGUAGE      ————  N
T           FORM & FUNCTION       G  U
U  ————————————————  U  S
R  ————————————————————  A  E
E                                  G
   ————                            E  ————
CONTEXTUAL &                    PROCESSES &
FUNCTIONAL                      BEHAVIOUR
PRIORITIES
```

Figure 5.1 Relationship between Culture, Language and Language Use

Sociocultural factors such as the degree of acceptance of pluralistic norms, dominant monolingual or multilingual nature of society, linguistic policy and planning, sociolinguistic conditions and social norms of language use, and other social psychological considerations set the communicative goals and functional priorities in all forms of communicative interaction. These priorities, in turn, influence the process of acquisition, language socialisation, nature of bilingual or multilingual functioning of the individual, linguistic identities and preferences, etc. In a complex multilingual society like India, with diverse cultural norms regarding the use of languages, verbal communicative behaviour must be understood in the sociolinguistic and cultural context (Mohanty, 1991). Thus, it is imperative that studies of language acquisition and processes adopt an indigenous framework based on culture and context specific generalisations. This paper seeks to provide a general overview of Indian research on language acquisition and bilingualism, and to examine the extent to which the field of developmental psycholinguistics in India has been responsive to the need for such a cultural and indigenous framework.

Language Acquisition Studies in India: An Overview

While examining Indian research, it must be remembered that the field itself is interdisciplinary in nature bringing in the perspective of linguistic theories including the changing Chomskyan (1957; 1965; 1986) paradigms along with a rich cross-cultural and cross-linguistic methodology (Mohanty & Perregaux, 1997). The cross-linguistic data, particularly from non-English languages, have called for a reexamination of the existing assumptions, and the diverse theoretical perspectives of different disciplines made such conceptual integration possible. Broad categorical differences between languages as well as the unique features of specific languages have been related to different processing and acquisition strategies leading to a better understanding of the underlying mechanisms. For example, Slobin (1982) pointed out the differences between subject–object–verb (SOV) languages like most Indian languages and Turkish, in which object inflection plays a major role in the identification of different semantic relations, and subject–verb–object (SVO) languages like English, in which the word order serves as a reliable marker of grammatical and semantic relationships. The linguistic diversity in India has made it possible to collect acquisition and processing data from different languages. But, in the absence of an interdisciplinary and indigenous perspective, it has not led to any significant integration and conceptual development. Psychological studies of processing of different Indian languages have failed to be truly cross-linguistic without an appreciation of the linguistic view of the typical structural features of these languages. As has been pointed out (Mohanty, 2000), structural features such as a flexible word order and the use of reliable case markers to indicate semantic relations play a significant role in linguistic processing which has not been adequately understood.

Language acquisition research in India has also suffered from a cleavage between the linguistic approach and the psychological approach each bringing in an independent perspective unaffected by the other. Mohanty (2000) referred to this problem of a clear lack of an interdisciplinary approach:

> ...a general lack of interdisciplinary perspective is characteristic of the Indian work on language development. While psychological studies have sought to examine environmental and contextual conditions of acquisition mostly using cross-sectional methodology with almost a complete neglect of the formal properties of language, the linguistic studies, usually based on longitudinal small sample data, have primarily focused on the form and structure of language with little emphasis on the underlying psychological processes of development. As a result, phonological and syntactic development have been favoured topics among the linguists. Psychologists, on the other hand, have studied more global aspects of language acquisition such as the conditions of individual differences in general use of language in communication.

Indian studies of phonological development have primarily focused on the formal aspects of the sound system of language. Despite studies of various languages such as Hindi (Sharma, 1969), Tamil (Thirumalai, 1972), Kannada (Kumudavalli, 1973; Sridevi, 1976), Telugu (Nirmala, 1981a; 1981b), and Urdu (Beg, 1991), meaningful cross-linguistic comparisons remain confined to the sequence of acquisition of specific sound features of languages and the approach is purely linguistic rather than psycholinguistic (Vasanta, 1992). Studies on morphological development in India have generally indicated the gross stages of development comparable to the findings of Brown (1973) with English-speaking children. Devaki (1987; 1992) noted broad cross-linguistic similarities in Indian studies with respect to the order of morphological acquisition and the process of inflections and derivations. However, the extent of such comparability of findings, within Indian languages as well as with studies on English-speaking children, can be attributed to the use of common and borrowed grammatical categories in the analysis of children's language use protocols needs to be carefully examined. The concern is pertinent since the rich Indian tradition of scholarly study of grammar following Panini has hardly influenced linguistic studies of morphosyntactic development in India. Some Indian studies have concluded that in morphological acquisition children do show evidence of rule awareness through overgeneralisation errors in plural marking (Nirmala, 1983/1984) and generation of verb forms given unfamiliar forms by adding functors like *karna* in Hindi (Varma, 1979), *maaDu* in Kannada, and *cai* or *paNNu* in Tamil (Devaki, 1987; 1992). However, the possibility that such rules could be somewhat different from those borrowed from the dominant Western theories is yet to be seriously considered.

Regarding syntactic development and the development of semantic categories related to various syntactic devices, studies have been undertaken in several Indian languages covering a broad range of syntactic and semantic features such as case relations (Lakshmi Bai, 1983/1984; 1984; Nirmala, 1981a; Sailaja, 1989), negation (Lakshmi Bai, 1986; Usha Devi, 1990; Vaidyanathan, 1984), and interrogation (Vaidyanathan, 1988). These studies have focused on the sequence of development and have highlighted trends at variance with each other as well as with Western studies (reporting data from English-speaking children). In the absence of an indigenous theoretical or problem orientation, these studies do not enhance one's understanding of the process of language acquisition in the Indian linguistic and cultural context.

To the extent that these studies of language acquisition have not succeeded in exploiting the unique characteristics of Indian languages and the diverse sociolinguistic conditions of such languages, it appears that they are pale copies of Western studies somewhat indigenised to the context of specific Indian languages without much weightage given to their special characteristics. One typical feature which is an exception in leading to some interesting studies is the flexible word ordering of Indian languages. With this feature, subject–object–verb positions in the sentences are relatively free unlike English and similar other languages. The free word ordering feature gives rise to some interesting questions: "Is there a preferred word order which takes a developmental priority?" or, "What is the psychological basis for choice among the different permissible word orders?". Indian studies of different languages (see Mohanty & Mohanty, 1981, for Oriya locative sentences; Vasanta, Sastry, & Ravi Maruth, 1994, for grammaticality judgement of Telugu sentences) have shown that developmentally the use of the SOV word order is preferred over the other possible orders. Studies of word order preference in bitransitive sentences, however, have not yielded any consistent finding; some studies (Mishra, 1994; Vasanta & Sailaja, 1993) have noted a preference for subject–indirect object–direct object–verb order while others (Mohanty & Mishra, 1985) for subject–direct object–indirect object–verb order. As has been pointed out earlier, because of flexible word ordering in Indian languages, case makers and object inflections are much more reliable indicators of the sentence level syntactic/semantic relationship between words compared to the word order cues. A study by Mohanty and Mishra (1982) revealed that in the production of Hindi locative propositions children followed a pragmatic topic–comment strategy. When two objects (nouns) were presented in a certain locative relationship with each other, children's descriptive utterances followed a word order in which the noun topicalised by the prior context appeared earlier. For example, when a picture card showed a cat under a table, children described it as *billi/mej ke niche/baithi hai* (the cat/under the table/is sitting) when the prior context cards focused on "a cat". The same picture was described as *mej ke niche/billi/baithi hai* when "a table" was topicalised by the focus in prior context cards. These results were replicated by Mishra and Dubey (1987) for Hindi locative propositions with the adverbial *on*. Word order studies have demonstrated a successful focus on the typical linguistic features of Indian languages as well as a clear interdisciplinary approach to understanding the process of language development.

Numerous studies have been undertaken on the factors affecting language development of Indian children. Unfortunately, most of these studies barely go beyond a simple demonstration of a relationship between some characteristic variables like SES, deprivation and disadvantage, caste, and home environment and various measures of language development. As such, they do not contribute to an understanding of the process through which the conditions of language development operate in the case of Indian children. In contrast, a study by Anjali Singh (1987) assessed the development of linguistic skills such as grammar comprehension, word meaning, and expressive performance of 2- to 3-year-olds in Indian joint families of different social classes and in orphanages. On the basis of her findings, Singh observed that language development was not affected by social class as such but by the quality of linguistic environment to which members of the joint family — mother, father, grandmother, grandfather and siblings — contributed. The study revealed a strong positive influence of grandparents, particularly grandmothers, on language development of children in Indian joint families. The study is striking for its indigenous approach in analysing the factors of language development in the context of the Indian culture and the joint family system. Some intervention studies (Mohite, 1983; Sahu & Swain, 1985) have shown application orientation while also contributing to unveiling the role of gross cultural variables in language development.

It is fairly evident that the current Indian research on language development is not theoretically grounded in an indigenous framework which is yet to emerge despite a rich tradition of scholarly study of language and grammar. Culture and context sensitivity of these studies remain confined to a focus on the linguistic form and structure of Indian languages and to some gross cross-linguistic comparisons. At the level of identification of problems and selection of appropriate methodology, Indian researchers have shown a clear reluctance in trespassing the boundaries of disciplines; linguists have focused on phonological, morphological and syntactic development emphasising the acquisition of formal features, and psychologists have largely studied the environmental correlates of acquisition. This lack of an interdisciplinary perspective is unfortunate because, in the absence of it, research problems become narrow, methodology limited and, consequently, theoretical integration — indigenous or indigenised — remains elusive. The findings of language specific patterns of development are quite interesting and should lead to more purposeful and conceptually driven cross-linguistic comparisons. With the exception of a few studies dealing with training and intervention for augmentation of linguistic skills and the study by Singh (1987) on language acquisition in joint families, other studies on the relationship between gross environmental conditions and language development offer little practical insight into how linguistic skills are acquired. Understanding the processes of influence of environmental variables is essential for a comprehensive view of acquisition of Indian languages. Such a view is needed to reconcile cross-linguistic similarities and differences as well as differences between Indian and Western findings. For example, observations of no gender difference or differences in favour of boys are typical of Indian studies of language acquisition which are in sharp contrast to Western findings showing a clear feminine advantage. It appears that language acquisition must be understood in the context of the gender bias in socialisation of the Indian child and, possibly, in the process of language socialisation, an area which has attracted the attention of Indian scholars only recently.

Language Socialisation

Language socialisation is defined as the process of "socialisation through language and socialization to use language" (Ochs, 1986, p. 2). In acquiring a language, a child has to learn the linguistic code as well as sociocultural conventions for its appropriate use. It is through repeated participation in social interactions, which provide the context for language and act as transmitters of sociocultural knowledge, that children develop culturally appropriate communicative competence. In different cultures, social interactions have predictable patterns and routines or set of sequences of exchanges, providing practice in specific linguistic structures and, at the same time, transmitting cultural norms particularly in respect of language use. Thus, in language socialisation, language is both the object as well as the medium of socialisation. Mohanty and Perregaux (1997) discussed several cultural devices in language socialisation. In most cultures, language socialisation has some common goals such as transmitting affect and values in communication, orienting towards status and role appropriate use of language, setting functional priorities in social communication, and developing stylistic preferences. However, in multilingual societies like India, a child is also socialised into multilingual modes of communication. Norms of communication in such societies, as Mohanty (1994a) argued, are characteristically different from those of the dominant monolingual societies of the West. Therefore, the goals of language socialisation in such societies have to be viewed as different. In a multilingual context, the language user has to meet the additional demands of communication in multiple languages by developing special awareness of language variations and strategies to deal with the same through functional separation of languages into different social domains of communication. Thus, languages get differentiated into a variety of situations as well as a variety of hierarchy of domain and interlocutor specific sociolinguistic preferences. For example, one may prefer using one's mother tongue for communication in the family and ingroup domain, English for formal workplace communication, Hindi for choice of movies and entertainment and for outgroup communication in public places (with the knowledge that sometimes one may get better compliance by using English), and Punjabi or Urdu in market places. The process of socially appropriate language use in multilingual situations is further complicated by social norms regarding switching from one language to another and mixing linguistic codes in the course of a single communicative event primarily to enhance the effectiveness of communication. Thus, the Indian multilingual context requires the language user to develop complex cognitive strategies for effective language use. In such a society the goals of language socialisation include development of awareness of language variations, domain appropriate use of language, code-switching and code-mixing rules, domain specific differentiation of languages into a hierarchy of preferences, and functional allocation of languages in communication (Mohanty, 1994a). In his observational study of 2- to 7-year-olds growing up in multilingual environments, Mohanty (1994b) analysed the process of language socialisation as these children achieved multilingual communicative competence and suggested a sequence of six stages of development in this process. In a later analysis, Mohanty, Panda, and Mishra (1999) grouped these stages into three periods, viz., period of language differentiation, period of awareness of languages, and period of multilingual functioning. The observational data in Mohanty's (1994b) study show the sequence of stages in socially appropriate use of communicative devices in multilingual settings regardless of the levels of bilingual competence of individual children, but the processes through which the norms of multilingual functioning are transmitted in social interactions remain to be analysed.

Studies of language socialisation in the Indian context are interesting and highlight the emergence of a new trend of research which is rooted in the context of the sociolinguistic realities of Indian multilingualism. These studies have demonstrated that effective functioning in a multilingual society requires special adaptive strategies which Indian children seem to develop quite early through the process of language socialisation. The mechanisms of social transmission in multilingual socialisation, however, remain to be fully understood.

Early socialisation into multilingual modes of communication encourages tolerance of diversity and pluralistic norms which, in addition to the cognitive aspects of multilingual functioning discussed earlier, contribute to making individual bilingualism or multilingualism a positive phenomenon. In this respect, Indian studies of bilingualism stand apart in their theoretical as well as methodological orientation from Western studies.

Bilingualism in a Multilingual Society

The field of bilingualism in India has developed a clear interdisciplinary and indigenous perspective. Indian studies have attempted to view the phenomenon of bilingualism in the context of a multilingual society and to examine its role in terms of the sociolinguistic realities of multilingualism. The field has been enriched by significant contributions from linguists, psychologists, and speech pathologists, all motivated by the dominant multilingual character of Indian society. Indian studies have focused on a conceptual analysis of bilingualism, its cognitive and social consequences, and related pedagogical issues of medium of instruction and mother tongue education. Few studies have dealt with the development of bilingualism, the nature of speech pathology associated with bilingualism, and the development of secondary linguistic skills (reading and writing) among bilinguals.

Issues pertaining to the definition and classification of bilingualism have been addressed by Mohanty (1994a) who defined bilingual persons or communities as "those with an ability to meet the communicative demands of the self and the society in their normal functioning in two or more languages in their interaction with the other speakers of any or all of these languages" (p. 8). Mohanty also grouped the numerous classifications of bilingualism into three broad categories based on (a) social context and pattern of language use, (b) level of skill in the languages, and (c) context of development of bilingualism (Mohanty, 1994a). In his analysis of the phenomenon of Indian bilingualism, Mohanty (1994a) proposed an indigenous framework by conceptualising individual and community level bilingualism in India as the first incremental step in the direction of societal multilingualism. Such a conceptualisation is necessary to differentiate between individual bilingualism in the multilingual

Indian context and bilingualism in the dominant monolingual societies of the West. The characteristics of Indian bilingualism have also been discussed by several linguists (Annamalai, 1990; Dua, 1986; Khubchandani, 1986; Pattanayak, 1981; 1990; Srivastava, 1977). Mohanty (1992/1993) discussed the problems and issues in the measurement of bilingualism in the Indian context.

The early empirical findings led to a negative view of the bilingual person as one whose mental capacity was divided between two languages making bilingualism a handicap. Most of the later studies, however, dispelled this myth leading to "the emergence of a positive perspective in bilingualism research" (Mohanty & Perregaux, 1997, p. 232) to which Indian studies have made significant contributions. Given the linguistic diversity and the complex sociolinguistic realities of Indian society, there is a clear methodological advantage of Indian studies in which it has been possible to draw comparison samples of bilinguals and monolinguals from among the same cultural groups. In contrast, Western studies have invariably drawn bilingual samples from among immigrants who are culturally different from the dominant monolinguals. Thus, Western studies have generally confounded cultural differences with bilingualism. A series of studies (see Mohanty, 1994a, for details) conducted among the Kond tribals in Phulbani district of Orissa has utilised a sort of frozen language shift phenomenon resulting in a complete language shift from Kui to Oriya for some Konds and Kui–Oriya contact bilingualism for others. As a result of the history of language shift process, it was possible in these studies to draw comparable samples of Kui–Oriya bilinguals and Oriya monolinguals from the same cultural group for assessment of the impact of individual bilingualism on cognitive, linguistic, metalinguistic, and academic skills. The Kond studies have a clear methodological advantage over their Western counterparts in which bilingual samples, invariably drawn from among the immigrants and/or cultural and linguistic minorities, were compared with the monolingual majority groups. The findings of the Kond and other Indian studies (Southworth, 1980) have been integrated to propose a model of the relationship between bilingualism, metacognitive process, and cognitive skills in the context of plural multilingual societies (Mohanty, 1994a; 1994b).

The metalinguistic and metacognitive hypothesis of bilinguals' intellectual and scholastic advantage has been widely supported in Indian as well as Western studies. As pointed out by Mohanty and

Perregaux (1997), "it would be too simplistic to assume that the relationship is independent of the cultural context of bilingualism" (p. 235). As discussed earlier, Indian children are socialised into multilingual modes of communication quite early in their development. Consequently, multilingualism is accepted as part of the Indian lifestyle making it a positive phenomenon. "The social norm influences the individual in favor of many languages and not one, making bilingualism a positive force in his or her life. Thus, when other factors are controlled, social psychological and cognitive consequences of bilingualism can be expected to be positive in pluralistic and multilingual cultures" (Mohanty & Perregaux, 1997, p. 236). The phenomenon of bilingualism in language contact situations can be viewed from the social psychological perspective of intergroup and intercultural relations in plural societies (Berry, 1990). Berry analysed the outcome of culture contact in terms of the acculturation attitude of individuals or groups in contact along two dimensions: maintenance of one's own identity, culture, language, etc., and establishing a relationship with the other group. Depending upon the positive or negative choices with respect to these two dimensions, Berry identified four outcomes, viz., assimilation, integration, separation, and marginalisation. Using this cross-cultural model, Mohanty (1994a) argued that language contact situation of stable bilingualism and language maintenance is an instance of integration. Assimilation type of orientation is associated with language shift and transitional bilingualism, whereas separation can be characterised as linguistic divergence and linguistic nationalism. A negative contact attitude on both the dimensions, characterised as marginalisation, is an instance of double semilingualism. Based on empirical studies in bilingual and monolingual situations of contact among the Konds and non-tribals, Mohanty (1991; 1994a) demonstrated the validity of such an analysis and concluded that bilingualism promoted social integration at the individual and community levels.

Studies on bilingualism have pedagogical implications for issues relating to bilingual education and medium of instruction. In a series of studies, Srivastava and his colleagues (Srivastava, 1990; Srivastava & Khatoon, 1980; Srivastava & Ramaswamy, 1987) compared children from mother tongue medium schools with those from other language and English medium schools on school achievement and self-concept measures. When the effect of intelligence was partialled out, there was no difference between the instructional media groups. They also observed that the advantage of children from English medium schools was due to school climate related variables such as selection and admission criteria, teaching methods, and use of teaching aids and materials. Based on these findings and conceptual analysis of the issues in respect of the question of medium in schools, it has been suggested that initial education should be provided in the mother tongue with provision for English language teaching in the last four years of schooling. Similar recommendations have been made by many other scholars (Krishnamurti, 1990; Mohanty, 1994a; 1994b; Srivastava & Gupta, 1990) including linguists as well as psychologists. Mohanty (1990) defended the goal of maintenance of minority mother tongues pleading for language-shelter-type bilingual education with initial literacy in mother tongue followed by the use of multiple languages as the media of instruction. In the absence of any systematic programme of bilingual education and controlled evaluation of mother tongue medium schools vis-à-vis English medium schools, it may be premature to draw any definite conclusion about bilingual education and mother tongue literacy. However, the primacy of mother tongue and the role of multiple languages in Indian education is undeniable and it is clear that the so-called advantages of English medium schools are due to the quality of schooling and school climate rather than the effect of the medium itself. It is, indeed, unfortunate that educational planners in India have not taken serious note of the implications of the findings of studies on bilingualism and medium of instruction.

The preceding brief sketch of language acquisition and bilingualism research in India is neither exhaustive nor fully representative. The purpose here is to outline some major trends in psycholinguistic studies and to assess the level and scope of cultural input into theory, problem and methodology of research in these areas. It is clear that Indian psycholinguists have not taken into account the rich body of knowledge of the nature of languages in the ancient Sanskrit texts. Panini's classic study of grammar is the most prominent work recognised by Western scholars as the forerunner of modern transformational generative grammar. The traditional analysis of language in the ancient texts has been studied largely by Sanskrit scholars and linguists. Without an interdisciplinary perspective, psycholinguists have remained unaffected by the rich heritage of language studies in India. However, in general, Indian researchers working in the area of language acquisition and bilingualism have conceptualised their research problems and analyses of the findings in the context of the features of Indian languages as well as the sociolinguistic characteristics of multilingual communication. By and large, Western theories and approaches have prompted the questions that Indian studies have focused on, but there have been conscious attempts at contextualisation. Application and problem orientation are not visible trends in Indian developmental psycholinguistic studies as much as in bilingualism studies. Studies on gross sociocultural and characteristic variables of development of linguistic skills fail to unveil the processes by which the relations are mediated. Even the few available training studies do not go far in enhancing understanding of the underlying processes. In contrast, studies on bilingualism as well as those on language socialisation are sensitive to the sociolinguistic and cultural realities and they reveal a clear tendency on the part of researchers to go beyond the boundaries of their disciplines. As a result, the problems addressed by these studies are broad based, relevant and have practical application value. They not only challenge Western views and models, but also provide new insights and directions.

In conclusion, it may be said that there are clear indications of contextualised research in India in the field of language acquisition and bilingualism. Studies in other areas of psycholinguistics such as reading processes and development and speech pathology, which have not been covered in this analysis, also reflect similar trends (Mohanty, 2000). In its present state, psycholinguistics in India does not have an indigenous framework but the area is contextualised, relevant and problem-oriented and, in that sense, it seems to have been indigenised fairly well. In an area which takes language as its focal theme, contextualisation and culture embeddedness are inevitable. Even when the goals may be towards a universal psycholinguistics, the approaches must be rooted in the cultural context because in studies of language acquisition and processes, the indigenous framework is not an alternate paradigm, it is the only paradigm.

❧ SIX ❧

Disadvantaged Children's Deficiency in Learning to Read

What's the Remedy?

❧ Jerry S. Carlson ❧ J.P. Das ❧

Introduction

This paper deals with disadvantaged children in California who fail to acquire reading skills, and reports an effective method of remediating their failure and improving their reading ability. In both ways, the paper pertains to Professor Sinha's core interests — the amelioration of cultural disadvantage and a restless search for empirical evidence.

The so-called Chapter 1 children are disadvantaged academically and many of them belong to the lower socioeconomic status (SES). Lower SES is equivalent to having severely limited access to wealth, power, and social status. Yet, these children are neither mentally handicapped nor is their reading level so low as to give them a label of learning disabled. Their cognitive and academic needs may often go unrecognised. Even when recognised, they acquire appropriate remediation, not the more-of-the-same classroom instruction. But how does one select an appropriate remedial programme for them?

The basic approach is through understanding the children's cognitive difficulties and identifying the underlying intellectual deficits that make them poor readers. Their cognitive processes have to be understood within a theoretical context, which in this case is a neurocognitive framework. The major processes are planning, arousal–attention, and the two information coding processes, simultaneous and successive (PASS processes). The processes are operationalised and assessed through specific tests. The logical path is to examine the processing strengths and weaknesses of the children, and to implement a remediation programme based on the PASS theory, a programme that is rationally derived from the theory.

The studies reported here determine the efficacy of a programme to remediate decoding and word reading deficiencies in reading disabled, Chapter 1 children. The programme is based on Luria–Das model of information processing and specifically addresses those elements of information integration that underlie the difficulties faced by non-retarded dyslexic children in decoding and word reading.

The focus on Chapter 1 children was motivated by the fact that these children constitute the single largest group of reading disabled youngsters in American schools today. On average, elementary grade students entering Chapter 1 programmes are at the 29th percentile on standardised reading tests; students scoring below the 25th percentile are usually not included in these programmes (Birman et al., 1987).

Most of the investigations on the Chapter 1 entitlement programme have been descriptive, focusing primarily on the demographic characteristics of students (Kennedy, Birman, & Demaline, 1988), the relationships between financial expenditures and academic achievement (Carter, 1984; Hanushek, 1981), teaching practices (Brophy, 1988), and classroom variables (Rowan & Guthrie, 1988). Surprisingly, little research has been done on student achievement and the efficacy of particular remediational or other educational programmes to improve targeted curricular areas.

The most notable exception to the paucity of research in this area is the sustaining effects study (Carter, 1982). Data from this study reveal that Chapter 1 programmes are effective for improving the reading abilities of only a small group of students. Factors that account for the gains in reading achievement are less related to the Chapter 1 experience than to the children's initial level of performance and their mental abilities (Carter, 1984). If a child's initial level of performance is relatively high, the child makes substantial gains and soon leaves Chapter 1. However, this is not the case for the majority of students. Indeed, the group of students for whom Chapter 1 funding is targeted is precisely the group that does not improve as a result of Chapter 1 intervention.

This conclusion was substantiated by Walberg (1984). On the basis of a review of literature on the effects of Chapter 1 programmes on educational achievement, he concluded, "On balance Chapter 1, (sic) appears to have done little good for students: it has neither raised the achievement of the educationally-deprived and poorest students, nor reduced the gap between them and other students" (p. 17).

Cognitive Factors Underlying Reading Difficulties of Chapter 1 Children

The model of information integration applied here (Das, Kirby, & Jarman, 1979; Naglieri, 1992) comprises four elements: planning, attention, and simultaneous, and successive processing (PASS). Planning and attention represent the processing elements primarily involved in the selection of information to which the individual chooses to attend. Through planning and attention, an individual can select from his or her repertoire of prior knowledge that which is relevant to particular problems, and at the same time, design operations to solve those problems. Successive integration occurs when information is coded in a temporal sequence. For example, successive processes are involved if one spells a word, commits a poem to memory, or analyses a word by breaking it into its sequential phonemes. Simultaneous integration is involved when information is coded holistically such as when one concurrently perceives the relationships among the constituent parts of a problem.

In a recent investigation (Little, Das, Carlson, & Yachimowicz, 1994), the PASS model was applied to determine (*a*) the cognitive similarities and differences between Chapter 1 and non-Chapter 1, and (*b*) which of the PASS variables underlay the decoding and word reading difficulties experienced by these children. The sample comprised 69 Chapter 1 and 65 non-Chapter 1 Grade 3 children. Seven tests from the PASS were used (Das & Naglieri, 1989; Naglieri, 1992): Planned Connections, Selective Attention, Expressive Attention, Sequence Repetition, Word Series, Sentence Repetition, and Speech Rate. Three reading tests were administered: two from the Woodcock Reading Mastery Test — Revised (WEMT — R), Word Attack and Word Identification, and the SAT.

Principal factor analysis of the PASS measures revealed two clearly differentiated factors: successive processing (sequence repetition, word series, sentence questions, and speech rate), and planning and attention (planned connections, expressive attention, selective attention, and speech rate). The reason that speech rate loaded on both factors is because it requires successive processing and has substantial attentional demand.

The two PASS factors were regressed on each of the three reading measures. Successive processing was the highest correlate of both Word Attack and Word Identification (Rs .49 and .51, respectively). When planning and attention was included in the analysis, the result was multiple Rs of .62 and .63, respectively. Planning and attention was the highest correlate of SAT Reading (R .45). When successive processing was included, it yielded a multiple R of .60.

The relationships between reading variables, PASS performance, and Chapter 1 status were analysed further by structural equation modelling. The analysis, depicted in Figure 6.1, revealed that Chapter 1 status alone did not have any direct relationship with either of two outcome factors: SAT Reading or Word Skills (a composite of the two Woodcock tests). This implied that the individual difference relations associated with the identification of achievement deficits were mediated by the two higher-order factors: planning and attention and successive processing. In addition, no direct path from the Chapter 1 status variable to either SAT Reading or Word Skills was found: deficits in achievement associated with group differences in SAT Reading Skills were mediated by deficits in the abilities represented by the planning and attention variable; deficits in Word Skills were mediated mainly by deficits in successive processing but also by deficits in planning and attention.

Remediation of Word Reading Deficiencies

Research (Share & Stanovich, 1955; Stanovich, 1988) has identified a phonological core deficit as the primary problem of the majority of dyslexics. Siegel (1989) noted that the "garden variety poor readers" were deficient in pseudoword recognition, short-term and working memory, and syntactic awareness. Carlson and Das (1992) provided data discussed in this paper that indicated that deficits in phonological coding were related to deficient successive processes.

It has been observed that reading disabled children have difficulty learning incidentally and transferring acquired skills to new tasks (Lovett et al., 1989). This may be a primary reason why direct teaching (see Chall & Curtis, 1990) of reading materials has met

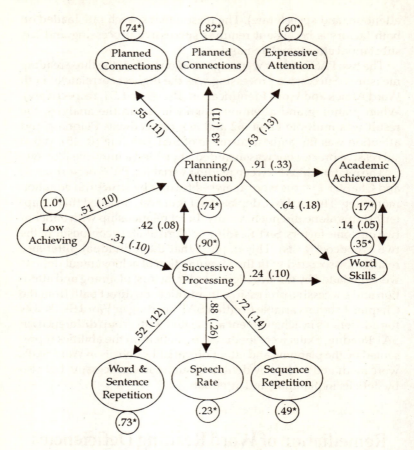

Figure 6.1 Relationships between Reading Variables, PASS Performance and Chapter 1 Status

with only partial success. It also poses a major obstacle to the alternative to direct teaching: teaching processes or components that underlie reading ability.

Although often criticised, the process of training has increasingly attracted the attention of applied cognitive psychologists. Furthermore, it is consistent with our view that reading disabled children require a method of instruction that is based on elements of information integration that are fundamental to reading and constitute a main source of their reading difficulties.

While Chapter 1 children may be able to read familiar words using visual coding, they have difficulty reading unfamiliar words that require phonological coding. From our theoretical perspective, the cognitive processes underlying these two types of coding are simultaneous and successive information integration. Pronunciation of the word requires the sequencing of the sounds, assembling pronunciation, and programming speech output. The latter two functions involve the planning element of the PASS model.

The Reading Remediation Programme

The PASS Reading Enhancement Programme (PREP) was designed to improve selected aspects of children's information processing skills and increase their word reading and decoding abilities. Since it is based on the notion that the transfer of principles can be facilitated through inductive rather than deductive inference, it stands in sharp contrast to direct training of strategies for the remediation of reading skills. The programme is structured in a way that inductive inference and internalisation occur spontaneously rather than through deductive rule learning (Campione & Brown, 1987; Vygotsky, 1962).

Procedures such as rehearsal, categorisation, monitoring of performance, prediction, revision of prediction, and sounding and blending are an integral part of each task. Rather than being explicitly taught by the tutor, children are encouraged to become aware of the use of the underlying cognitive processes through discussion of what they did during the tasks.

The programme comprises eight tasks, each with a global processing training form and a curriculum related bridging form. The global form has no reading content. It provides a structured series of exercises that require the application of successive strategies as well as planning and attentional resource allocation. The bridging form has the same cognitive demands as its matched global form. However, it employs letters and their combinations.

Each task has three levels of difficulty: the easiest level allows the child to have initial success with the materials, become familiar with the task and expectations of the training programme. The more difficult levels build on the easiest level through added complexity. Depending on the progress made by the child, instruction typically requires 15 to 18 hours spread over approximately 12 weeks.

Effectiveness of the Remediation Programme

In order to evaluate the effectiveness of the remediation programme two studies were conducted. The first study focused on the effects of remediation on decoding and word reading skills. The second study was designed to replicate and extend the results of the first study by (*a*) employing larger sample sizes, and (*b*) focusing on the extent to which the cognitive processes underlying decoding and word reading skills were affected by the remediation programme.

Study 1

Method

SAMPLE

A sample of 50 children was randomly selected from the Chapter 1 programmes serving two schools in a middle sized southern California community: one school served a middle class neighbourhood; the other school served a lower middle class neighbourhood. Assignment to Chapter 1 was based on low SAT scores and teachers' recommendation. The children were assigned randomly to either the remediation group or to the comparison group (N 25 in each group). There were approximately equal number of males and females from Anglo or Hispanic ethnic backgrounds in the sample. Due to attrition over the course of the remediation, the final sample upon which the analyses were based was 22 in the remediation group and 15 in the comparison group.

The subjects in the remediation and comparison groups were given identical tests at the beginning of the intervention as well as at the end. Both groups received regular instruction, including Chapter 1 services, over the time span of the intervention.

Measures

THE WOODCOCK READING MASTERY TEST — REVISED The WRMT — R was used to obtain a standardised measure of reading ability (decoding and comprehension). Two subtests of the test were used: Word Attack and Word Identification.

Norms for the WRMT — R are based on 6,089 subjects from various parts of the US and controlled for race, community size, and socioeconomic status. Internal consistency reliability measured by the split-half Spearman–Brown formula yielded a median full score reliability of .98. The Word Attack subtest had a reliability of .97. Equivalent forms of the WRMT — R were used for the pretests and posttests to reduce practice effects.

DECODING PROBES Three times during the remediation, decoding probes were used as a measure of improvement and transfer of acquired skills to decoding. To measure the direct effects of training on decoding skills, pretests and posttests were administered assessing the speed and accuracy of reading a list of 30 words chosen randomly from the pool of words used in the remediation. Ratio scores for these probes were calculated by dividing the time taken to read all the words by the number of words read correctly. This yielded a score in terms of seconds per correct word.

A pretest list of words was presented three times during remediation (Probes 1, 3, and 5). These words were then used in bridging tasks in the next three remedial sessions. After three sessions the probes were again presented. Since the words in all the probes, as in the remediation tasks, were already known to the subject, this test was not susceptible to practice effects due to repeated exposure to the words. Instead, improvement noted on these probes was an indication of direct improvement in decoding skill with words which were used in training during these sessions.

A second set of probes (Probes 2, 4, and 6) was given at the same time as the posttest of Probes 1, 3, and 5 to measure transfer of decoding skills to new material. These probes were not used in remediation, they comprised lists of 30 different words at the same level of phonetic complexity as the previous probes. Thus, if the scores on Probes 2, 4, and 6 approximated the posttest performance on Probes 1, 3, and 5, transfer of decoding skills acquired in the intervention could be inferred.

INTERVENTION

Remedial instruction was carried out with pairs of children. Each child had his or her own set of materials. The children sat next to one another facing the instructor. The intervention consisted of 15 hours spread over 8 weeks. Each session usually involved training on two global and two corresponding bridging tasks and lasted approximately 50 minutes. The tasks were presented in the following order: Related Memory Set, Joining Shapes, Transportation Matrices, Connecting Letters, Serial Recall, and Window Sequencing. This order of presentation was used to maximise the variety of materials and maintain the subjects' interest.

RESULTS

Tests such as t-tests and multivariate analyses of variance were used for statistical analyses. The dependent variables were reading probes, word identification, and word attack.

The means and standard deviations of the remediation of comparison groups are presented in Table 6.1. An initial comparison of pretest and posttest means using t-tests revealed significant improvements ($p < .05$) for children in the remediation group on all measures. None of the contrasts for the comparison group were statistically significant.

Table 6.1 Remediation Results: Means and Standard Deviations

Measure and Group	Pretest		Posttest	
	Mean	SD	Mean	SD
Reading Probes				
Remediation	31.4	7.7	38.8*	4.6
Control	30.2	9.2	30.4	8.8
Word Identification				
Remediation	51.0	7.5	58.1*	7.9
Control	50.5	9.9	50.8	8.6
Word Attack				
Remediation	16.7	7.3	25.1*	8.2
Control	13.7	7.4	17.3	7.8

*Statistically significant/t ($p < 0.05$).

When the word identification and word attack scores were converted into grade equivalent scores, the improvement was especially impressive for word attack, the pretest–posttest change was from 2.57 years to 4.38 years. For the comparison group, the pretest–posttest change was 1.99 years to 2.36 years. Word identification pretest–posttest changes were from 2.94 years to 3.58 years for the remediation group and from 2.97 years and 2.92 years for the comparison group.

A 2 (groups) × 3 (tests) × 2 (occasions) (pretest–posttest) multivariate analysis of variance (MANOVA) was carried out. The results of this analysis revealed (*a*) a nonsignificant group effect ($F_{3,33}$ = 1.99, ns), (*b*) a significant time effect ($F_{3,33}$ = 41.5, p < .01), and (*c*) a significant group × time interaction ($F_{3,33}$ = 17.3, p < .01). Group × time interaction was accounted for by all the dependent variables: Reading Probes, Word Identification, and Word Attack (Decoding). The univariate F values were $F_{1,35}$ = 49.6, p < .01; $F_{1,34}$ = 20.8, p < .01; $F_{1,34}$ = 11.03, p < .01, respectively. These results confirmed the statistical equivalence of the comparison and remediation groups on the premeasures as well as the significant improvements on the Reading Probes and Word Identification postmeasures resulting from the intervention.

The relatively small sample size and high attrition rate notwithstanding, the results of Study 1 are encouraging. They stand in sharp contrast to the majority of the reported attempts to improve reading abilities of Chapter 1 children. If the results of Study 1 could be replicated and extended to provide evidence of the effects of the remediation programme on the cognitive processes underlying decoding and word reading difficulties, the conclusions of the efficacy of the remediation programme would be substantially enhanced. Accordingly, Study 2 was carried out.

Study 2

Method

SAMPLE

An initial sample of 100 Grade 4 Chapter 1 children was selected from two elementary schools serving the same southern California community as in Study 1. Ss were randomly assigned to either the remediation or comparison group. Attrition was approximately the same for both the remediation and control groups over the 5-month period of the study. This provided complete data for 41 Ss in the remediation group and 37 Ss in the comparison group. Boys and girls were approximately equally represented. Representation by ethnic group in the sample was 54 per cent Anglo, 45 per cent Hispanic, and 1 per cent Afro–American.

MEASURES

WOODCOCK READING MASTERY TEST—REVISED All the children in the sample were pretested and posttested on the Word Attack and Word Identification subtests of the WRMT—R.

INTERVENTION

The PREP materials described earlier were used again. The only change in procedure from that followed in Study 1 was that the student–teacher ratio was modified from two students to one teacher to four students to one teacher.

RESULTS

The means and standard deviations for the remediation and control groups for the reading and cognitive measures are presented in Table 6.2.

Table 6.2 Remediation Results: Means and Standard Deviations

Measure and Group	Pretest		Posttest	
	Mean	SD	Mean	SD
Word Identification				
Remediation	37.9	8.9	45.1*	11.5
Control	31.8	10.4	35.0	13.1
Word Attack				
Remediation	9.7	4.9	15.5*	7.1
Control	8.2	7.1	9.1	8.2

*Statistically significant/t (p < 0.05).

The scores on both the Woodcock Reading Mastery Tests were converted into grade level comparisons. The group receiving the remediation improved from 2.6 years to 4.4 years on Word Attack and from 2.9 years to 3.6 years on Word Identification. The control group did not improve on either of these measures.

Discussion

The results of these studies stand in contrast to the majority of the reported attempts to improve the reading abilities of Chapter 1 children. The conclusions drawn from the sustaining effects study exemplify the problem: for the most part, Chapter 1 services have been ineffective in improving the reading abilities of the target population.

In these studies, both the experimental and control groups received the regular Chapter 1 reading instruction provided by the school district. The experimental groups received the "add-on" of PREP. An examination of the pre- and posttest scores for the control groups revealed that only minimal and nonsignificant gains were made over the 12-week period of the study: a result that comports with Carter's rather disheartening conclusion. In contrast, the gains achieved by the experimental groups on both the Word Identification and Word Attack subtests were substantial — around over 1 standard deviation in each case.

The approach here focuses on the first of the four fundamental components of reading: decoding, assigning meaning to a word, sentence comprehension and paragraph comprehension. The reason for this is that it is necessary to translate the printed word into a pronounceable form before language processing can occur at the lexical, syntactic, and semantic levels.

Several interrelated factors explain why the group receiving PREP improved in decoding skills and word reading ability. These include memory enhancement, increased knowledge base, expanded attentional capacity and/or deployment, and greater efficiency in successive processing.

With some exceptions, Torgesen recognised that the majority of reading disabled children had shorter memory spans than those who were not reading disabled (Torgesen, 1995; Torgesen & Houck, 1980). Although research on the cognitive bases of memory span has substantiated Baddeley's (1986) theory of working memory to some extent, the relationships between working memory, memory span, naming time, and articulation, on the one hand, and reading competence, on the other, need to be elaborated and understood in order to account for the gains brought about by PREP in Chapter 1 children (see Baddeley, Eldridge, & Lewis, 1981).

It has been observed that reading disabled children with average or higher intelligence experience difficulty with both articulatory and phonological coding processes (Torgesen, Kistner, & Morgan, 1987). Das and Mishra (1991) reported weak correlations between memory span and naming time as well as between these two variables and speech rate, which is a measure of phonological coding and articulation. This, coupled with the results of such studies as those by Bowey, Cain, and Ryan (1992) that observed rather weak connections between working memory and reading disability, suggests that many poor readers have average or even good memory spans and it may be uneconomical for remedial programmes to focus mainly on memory enhancement.

Within the context of successive processing, the PREP involves tasks that require both phonological coding and articulation. Many of the tasks demand overt articulation, especially in bridging tasks words were actually named and articulated. It is obvious that reading requires overt articulation involving the motor programming of speech. At the same time, naming words also requires phonological coding. Therefore, it is not surprising that a remedial programme aimed at facilitating both phonological coding and articulation, within successive processing tasks, would yield better results than an attempt solely to enhance memory. In fact, as has been shown in previous research (Das & Mishra, 1991), the path proceeding from memory span to reading must pass through a latent variable created by both naming time and speech rate.

Torgesen, Wagner, Simmons, and Laughon (1990) asserted that a combination of reliable measures of word span and of articulation rate may provide a good index of phonological coding processes in young children. The PREP programme comprises several tasks that involve a combination of the two requiring successive processing of the information provided.

In our judgement, the PREP will be optimally successful in cases where the cognitive profile of children matches the emphases on successive information integration and the planning and attentional processes in the programme. Thus, Chapter 1 children who are deficient in their ability to process information successively and have deficits in attentional resource allocation are most likely to benefit maximally from the intervention.

❦ SEVEN ❦

An Ecological Perspective on Mental Health Problems of Tribal Children

❦ R.C. Mishra ❦

Introduction

While addressing the mental health problems of tribal children I am reminded of a Chinese saying that my teacher, Professor Durganand Sinha, had told me when I was a graduate student: "If you are planning for one year sow crops; if you are planning for ten years plant trees; if you are planning for a hundred years plant men". This saying captures the essence of all the efforts directed at the wellbeing of children in the last few decades. A child has been regarded as the most valuable asset everywhere. Gunatilleke (1985) pointed out that a child's wellbeing constitutes a very important and reliable criterion for evaluating a society's concern for quality and human content of its development. Hence, the promotion of healthy child development is one of the most important national and international goals (World Bank, 1993). Various child development programmes and activities sponsored by organisations like the UNESCO, the UNICEF, and the WHO for the Third World countries aim at achieving this particular goal.

The constitution of a National Policy for Children in India is one of the most significant events in this context. The policy considers children as supremely important, and their nurture and solicitude as the responsibility of the nation. It states that children's programme should form a prominent part of the national plans for the development of resources so that children can grow up to become robust citizens, physically fit, mentally alert and morally healthy, endowed with skills and motivations needed by Indian society.

In formulating various child welfare programmes in India the physical needs of the "weaker sections of society" have particularly been the focus of attention. It is believed that children from these sections are exposed to a variety of experiential deprivations and sociocultural disadvantages (Sinha, 1977b; 1982). General poverty seems to characterise the life of these groups, and this largely prevents the fulfilment of children's nutritional, health, and educational needs (Sinha, 1975). Consequently, in various child development programmes (e.g., the Integrated Child Development Scheme or ICDS) in India, efforts have been made to organise early childhood services specifically in these directions. On the contrary, the schemes covering relatively wider aspects of psychosocial wellbeing of children have not received adequate attention. Paucity of resources and widespread physical health problems among these groups seem to be the major reasons for the greater concentration of programmes on physical aspects of life of the deprived sections of society.

It is against this background that the mental health problems of tribal children should be examined. However, before attempting to do so, a few words about the concepts of "mental health" and "social disadvantage" are in order. The global concept of health includes not only physical wellbeing, but also mental, social and spiritual wellbeing of individuals (WHO, 1988). It is regarded as the most essential and inseparable component of public health and social welfare programmes (Shah, 1982). The emphasis is on the prevention of disease as well as maintenance and promotion of health in the community (Michael, 1982; Taylor, 1990). However, attempts to define and study "mental health" are biased in favour of pathology (Russo, 1985), and there is evidence of a variety of "mental healths". Nevertheless, in keeping with the WHO definition, mental health professionals are at least unanimous that mental health is not the mere absence of mental illness (Eichler & Parron, 1987; Nagaraja, 1983). At the same time, however, there is no consensus on the definition of positive mental health. A perusal of literature on mental health in India provides evidence only for the existence of an operational definition of the concept. Carstairs and Kapur (1976) viewed the concept of ideal social functioning as the social equivalent of positive mental health. According to Wig (1979), mental health is the other name of quality of life.

Similar difficulty surrounds the conceptualisation of "social disadvantage". It has been used as a hypothetical construct as well as an empirical variable to account for a variety of behavioural characteristics. Its meaning, operations and connotations vary considerably. On the one hand, it is used to refer to a state of "dispossession or loss of social opportunities or privileges", on the other hand, it is also used to refer to "a lack of basic necessities for the survival of individuals". Thus, a large number of variables of environmental and sociocultural nature are considered, either singly or in combination, as referents of social disadvantage. Ranging from nominal descriptions such as those based on caste, socioeconomic status, residential area, and ethnic or cultural group membership, social disadvantage has been defined in terms of the extent of presence or absence of a large number of variables of sociocultural nature (Mishra, 1990; Misra & Tripathi, 1980). Factor analyses have yielded "physico-economic" and "experiential factors" as constituents of a deprivational environment (Misra & Tripathi, 1980).

Research using different variables of social disadvantage separately or a composite measure of it (such as a standard scale) has revealed the negative effects of adverse socioeconomic circumstances on the development of various cognitive abilities/skills and personality structure. Reviews of the effects of social deprivation/disadvantage (Misra, 1983; 1990; Misra & Tripathi, 1980; D. Sinha, 1982; D. Sinha, Tripathi, & Misra, 1982) have focused on the development of linguistic, cognitive, motivational, and personality dimensions. In general, the findings indicate that social disadvantage is a great curse for the child. It not only interferes with the growth of cognitive potentials and motivations, but also produces a personality characterised by greater conformity, anxiety, introversion, alienation, shyness, depression, emotional instability, and lowered self-concept (Bhargava & Aurora, 1981; S. Sharma, 1978; 1988; Singh, 1981), thereby revealing the pathological condition of the child.

In studies of disadvantaged children researchers have often focused on the psychological differences between samples drawn from mainstream society. Only a limited number of them has paid attention to such differences in tribal communities, though subsistence economy, level of income, parental education, parental occupation, and residence have often been used as indicators of social disadvantage of tribal children (Singh, 1981). Included here are not only ecological and sociocultural variables, but also a number of acculturational factors (such as education, urbanisation, and industrialisation).

While this strategy appears to be a convenient device for the study of social disadvantages faced by individuals or groups, there are a number of inherent assumptions involved in this approach when the same is applied to tribal children. In the first place, the approach seems to be biased in favour of those who have moved away from their traditional lifestyle as a consequence of the general programme of social and cultural change. Second, it lacks sensitivity to the ecocultural experiences of children in their natural environments to characterise sociocultural privileges or disadvantages.

The problem is serious when one takes into account the mental health of these children. A mental health problem exists when a person fails to cope effectively with the realities or demands of his or her life. The diagnosis, prevention and treatment of difficulties associated with an individual's coping with his or her environment are the basic ingredients of the psychology of mental health. Therefore, the role of psychologists in the assessment of childhood problems and delivery of services for children suffering from mental health problems needs to be examined in the light of locally appropriate approaches to a series of issues. These include the kind of theory and technique of assessment that will be locally appropriate, the nature of information required for validating the theory and assessment outcomes in that setting, the people in a society who may be used as key informants about various mental health problems and who may be later engaged in delivering mental health services, providing feedback to psychologists, and chalking out the needs of the community from time to time. The latter aspect is of special importance as it brings out the needs of children for mental health services that may be addressed at a given point of time (Serpell, 1982).

Issues in Assessment

The test technology developed by psychologists is one of the most widely known and publicly recognised application of their science. The uses and abuses of psychological tests have been the subject of serious debate in all parts of the world (Irvine & Berry, 1983; 1988; Poortinga & Van der Flier, 1988). However, their application has been universal in attempts to identify the nature and severity of mental health problems. Increased reliance on the behavioural model of mental health or psychopathology in recent years has provided an impetus to the use of psychological tests. According to Howarth (1980), the principal value of psychological tests lies in discovering "the nature of psychological resources available to a client" and in understanding "his or her habitual strategies of lifestyle". The ultimate goal of this exercise is to propose an action plan to promote an individual's behavioural autonomy and acceptance in the community. Thus, the effectiveness of a specific action programme will depend not only on the empowerment of a particular individual, but also on the overall resources of his or her family, neighbourhood, and society (Nakajima, 1994).

The application of standard psychological tests, especially intelligence tests, has been the most popular approach to understand the mental health problems among children. In very few instances have the behaviour ratings of children been attempted. The general strategy has been to select a standard test of general intelligence (modelled on Binet or Weschler) or a few of its subtests, and administer it to groups of children, perhaps after making changes in language but hardly any modifications in its contents. Differential test scores of the groups are then taken as indicators of good or poor mental health status. Whether the test contents and the operations necessitated by them are matched with the experiential background of children or with the behavioural repertoires that are fostered among them in their respective environments is hardly considered important in this context. The experience of those working with children from different cultural backgrounds has brought out several non-cognitive dimensions (such as familiarity with the contents and operations of test, test taking attitude, and ease in test situations involving interaction with a strange tester), which significantly influence a child's performance on tests. Such "test sophistication" effects have often been offered as an alternative explanation for higher scores of groups on intelligence or ability tests (Nerlove & Snipper, 1981; Rogoff, 1981). These non-cognitive dimensions of test performance are greatly encouraged in schools. The degree to which children have exposure to schooling determines the level of their success on various tests.

Some mental health professionals are aware of these and other variabilities in test performance of children contingent on differences in their opportunities of learning. Thus, several alternative strategies have been adopted in the assessment of their psychological status. These include: (*a*) setting a variable criterion for scores relative to the sociocultural background of the child; (*b*) allowing some extra practice on the initial items relative to the degree of the child's disadvantage;

and (c) modifying selected items to make the test contents appropriate to the prior experiences of disadvantaged children. These strategies have often been criticised for violating the essential assumptions of test standardisation (Newland, 1980). It has been argued that such changes render the findings of tests inappropriate for diagnosing psychological disabilities.

Alternative Developments

Owing to the difficulties associated with standard tests, many researchers and mental health professionals have resorted to the use of learning ability tests. However, the empirical validity of these tests has not been found to be higher than that of "inappropriate" intelligence tests (Hegarty & Lucas, 1979). In more radical strategies adopted in recent years, attempts have been made to abandon the use of tests by relying completely on observations of cognitive behaviours of children in daily life activities in natural settings, or systematic adaptation and restandardisation of foreign tests for use with local populations, or innovations of new tests using concepts, methods and materials derived from the child's own cultural setting. However, in the light of years of unsuccessful experience with the practice of adaptation and restandardisation of foreign tests for use with test naive and culturally different populations, there has been a gradual preference for the strategy of developing new tests from an indigenous perspective (Serpell, 1988; D. Sinha, 1983; D. Sinha & Mishra, 1993).

The development of new tests provides an opportunity for the search and accommodation of those dimensions of behaviour that are highly valued in a particular society. Without the inclusion of these dimensions into tests, the psychological assessment of children, though statistically reliable, is likely to remain culturally insensitive. Learning disabilities and lower academic achievement that are often reported among the majority of tribal children (Rath & Patnaik, 1979; Singh, 1981) may simply reflect inconsistencies between culturally valued abilities and those measured by psychological tests. Berry (1986) argued that the result of the pursuit of such culturally insensitive testing programmes has been that people in all parts of the world have been leading their lives in a competent manner, whereas psychological tests of cognitive abilities have yielded evidences of stupidity. Goodnow (1980) and Serpell (1982; 1988) discussed these inconsistencies in detail. These observations draw one's attention to those demands that children's ecology, society or culture places on them, and because of which their competencies may develop to a particular extent or in a particular direction (Berry, 1988). Most of the studies have attempted to analyse the extent to which children belonging to different groups exhibit various psychological abilities or competencies. Little has been done with regard to the study of the direction the abilities of children in the course of development may take as a function of the demands of their ecology and culture. This situation warrants an analysis of the ecocultural settings in which children carry out their day-to-day activities in order to understand their cognitive abilities as well as their overall psychological make-up. Psychological tests must be developed in tune with these activities if they have to serve any meaningful purpose.

Reference may be made to studies of psychological differentiation for which EFT and CEFT have served as popular measures. When the same tests were used with tribal children in Bihar (Mishra & Sinha, 1985; D. Sinha, 1979) they failed to elicit any meaningful response among them. Such difficulties prompted Sinha (1979; 1984a) to develop two new tests—the Story–Pictorial EFT (SPEFT) and the Indo–African EFT (IAEFT). These were based upon the rationale of earlier tests, but instead of presenting stimuli in the form of abstract geometrical designs (which did not make sense to tribal children), stimuli such as birds, snakes, vegetables, butterflies, and dogs were drawn from their local contexts, and these were embedded in the complex background of familiar pictures of trees, forests, and gardens. In the SPEFT, a story was also added to each picture to describe the circumstances which led to the hiding of objects. This not only stimulated the interest and involvement of the children, but also a kind of motivational set to search for the objects embedded in the pictures. The strategy has been quite fruitful, and the test has been successfully used in many research endeavours (Mishra, Sinha, & Berry, 1996; D. Sinha, 1979; D. Sinha & Bharat, 1985; D. Sinha & Shrestha, 1992; G. Sinha, 1988). The IAEFT, which requires a triangle (often called an arrowhead) to be disembedded in familiar pictures of basket, pitcher, hut, tree, and flower, etc., has also been successfully used with test naive samples of tribal children (Mishra, 1996) and adults (Mishra, 1988) as it provides a familiar context in the test.

Differentiation and Categorisation Among Tribal Children

For the last one decade Mishra has been engaged in research aimed at analysing the psychological adaptation of children and adults of Birhor, Asur, and Oraon tribes of Bihar in collaboration with Professors Durganand Sinha and John Berry. Birhors, a nomadic tribe, pursue their subsistence economy primarily through hunting and gathering activities in the forests. Oraons are a fully settled agricultural community. Asurs, pursuing a mixed economy of hunting–gathering and agriculture, occupy an ecological position between the Birhors and the Oraons. Studying high and low acculturated samples of children and adults in each group, an attempt has been made to examine the relative contribution of ecological condition, contact-acculturation, test-acculturation and some socialisation variables to a variety of cognitive behaviours. Drawing materials and test contents from the local contexts, 11 measures of cognitive abilities (for example, pictorial perception and interpretation, psychological differentiation, memory and category clustering, and classification and intermodality transfer) were developed and used. These encouraged the involvement of children as well as adults.

The findings broadly suggest that children belonging to even the most traditional group of Birhors (who would be regarded as highly deprived on various criteria of social disadvantage) do not manifest any cognitive deficiency. In fact, on some of the tests (such as psychological differentiation, and intermodal perception and classification), their performance was better than that of the other groups (Mishra, Sinha, & Berry, 1996). Minor differences in their performance as compared to the other groups on some tests may be attributed to their differential experience of acculturation (such as of schooling and urbanisation) rather than to differences in cognitive capacity. On the test of perceptual differentiation in an earlier study, Sinha (1979) found that nomadic Birhor children scored significantly higher than children of transitional Birhors and sedentary Oraons. These findings point to a congruence between the ecocultural characteristics of people's lives and the psychological characteristics that are developed and maintained among them.

Such differences in cognitive functioning of children are well illustrated by a study (Mishra, Sinha, & Berry, 1990) in which the performance of Birhor and Oraon children on an object sorting (categorisation) task was compared. Using a measure of "contact-acculturation", which comprised ratings on such objective indicators of acculturation as knowledge of languages, nature of household items (utensils, ornaments, etc.), style of dressing, means of liveli-hood, use of technology, travel experiences, and exposure to movies, children were selected to represent both high and low acculturation levels in Birhor as well as Oraon tribes. Children were presented 29 familiar and locally salient objects which apparently (as judged by the researchers) belonged to the categories of clothes, animals, cere-als, school objects, household goods, and women's adornments. After naming each object, the children sorted them into as many categories as they considered appropriate, placing all those objects that could go "together" in groups. The reasons for clubbing vari-ous objects into one category were solicited. Children were also asked to reclassify them. The sortings were scored according to a number of features, such as number of categories, categories conforming to expected categories, subcategories, shifts in the basis of grouping, and the nature of grouping (i.e., conceptual, functional, perceptual or idiosyncratic).

Findings revealed that Birhor children produced significantly greater number of general or unified categories than the Oraons, and these were largely maintained in resorting of objects. More con-forming categories and subcategories were associated with a higher level of acculturation. Function (use of objects) was the dominant basis of categorisation in both the tribes. Conceptual categorisation was more evident in the sorting of high acculturated Oraon children than others. These findings clearly point out that the cognitive func-tioning of children cannot be examined without analysing their eco-logical and acculturational contexts.

Daily Life Activities and Cognitive Functioning of Tribal Children

In the study discussed earlier, the operations required on the task were not a regular part of children's daily life activities, yet the per-formance of Birhor children provided evidence of their cognitive competence. What would happen if there was a congruence between the psychological processes involved in the performance of daily life activities and those tapped by a test?

This issue was examined by Mishra (1996). In this study 8–13-year -olds of the Birjia tribe (a traditional tribe of Bihar like the Birhors) were administered the Indo–African EFT (Sinha, 1984a) and Kohs' Block Design Test. One group of children represented those who spent the major part of their time in the forest (called forest children) grazing their cattle. The other group (called village children) stayed at home performing domestic chores. An analysis of the performance of the groups revealed that on both the tests, the scores of the forest children were significantly higher than those of the village children, although in a general classificatory scheme, forest children could be easily placed in the disadvantaged category. Greater demands of visual exploration and discrimination on the forest children compared to the village children were cited as reasons for the high level of performance of the former group.

Effect of Training on Test Performance of Tribal Children

Several studies have examined the effect of training on the performance of disadvantaged children on perceptual and cognitive tasks (Patnaik & Rath, 1982; Rath & Patnaik, 1979). These studies have observed considerable improvement in the performance of children on perceptual, cognitive and intellectual tasks/tests. However, whether or not such effects are stable over time is not known.

The issue of improvement in performance following training and the maintenance of training effect was addressed in a study (Mishra, 1990) which compared the performance of 5–6 year old children of Scheduled Castes and Scheduled Tribes with that of the high caste (Brahmin) group. Comparisons were made (a) prior to training, (b) soon after training, and (c) approximately 16 weeks after training. Children were administered the Pictorial Interpretation Test (Sinha, 1977b), the Sequential Perception Test (Sinha, 1977b), and the SPEFT (Sinha, 1984a). The Pictorial Interpretation Test requires interpretation of interposition cues in pictures. In the Sequential Perception Test, the subjects are instructed to arrange a set of randomly presented pictures in the proper sequence so as to constitute a story. The

SPEFT requires disembedding familiar objects embedded in a complex set of pictures.

After initial testing, each child was shown a large variety of pictures which involved psychological operations almost similar to those demanded by the criterion tests administered to the children. The training sessions continued for 4 weeks, each weekly session was of 40 minutes duration with 4 to 5 children. Children were also given Kohs' Block Design Test as a game of house-building, and the IAEFT (Sinha, 1984a) as a game of catching the hidden thief (the triangle).

After this exposure and training, the children were again assessed on the three tests given earlier. The third test was administered after an interval of about 16 weeks. On the two tests, the pretraining scores differed significantly with the Brahmin children scoring higher, but after training the differences disappeared on both the tests. In general, the performance improved after pictorial exposure and training, and training effects were almost equally stable in both the groups.

Conclusion

The studies discussed here do not directly examine the mental health status of tribal children, but they do suggest ways in which the problems of mental health among these groups could be approached. With regard to the identification of problems, it is necessary that the tests used are culturally appropriate and sensitive to the demands of the cognitive life of children in their sociocultural milieu. Only then an appraisal of the cognitive abilities of these children can be done in meaningful ways. It is important to abandon the practice of intelligence testing, and to emulate Sinha (1969; 1978; 1984a) by showing greater innovativeness in developing new tests for use with these children and examine their criterion validity. There are certain highly valued aspects of behaviour in each tribal community. These are generally nurtured among children through various kinds of role assignments and socialisation practices. For example, there is a great emphasis on achieving independence and autonomy in the process of child socialisation among nomadic Birhors (Sinha, 1979; Mishra, Sinha, & Berry, 1996). This could be used as a resource for designing a programme of intervention in their life. Associated with role performance are a set of abilities which evolve automatically in the course of the child's adaptation to the surrounding environment.

Spatial analysis and perceptual disembedding are two specific abilities which are highly valued among hunting–gathering populations. These abilities have been reported to be associated with an individual's success in a variety of activities (Witkin & Goodenough, 1981). If the educational system is so developed that these abilities are reinforced in the school, the cognitive resources available to children would find an opportunity to flourish without much effort. On the other hand, if the goal is to develop a new set of skills which are not so well placed among children, then perhaps some kind of special education would be required. The third study discussed here indicates that even short-term exposure and training with pictures leads to a significant improvement in children's skills of pictorial perception and interpretation. These effects are not so easily washed away. What is needed is a firm commitment and a kind of missionary zeal for achieving goals that are set forth. All are well aware of the social and political constraints which are generally beyond the control of psychologists. Hence, psychologists have to search for their roles within the existing sociopolitical contexts. A great variety of difficulties, which appear to be problems of mental health, can be handled in this manner by using the resources of the community and the school. For other problems, which are serious and involve behaviour pathology, clinical psychologists need to come forward to address them in the local context of the community.

❧ EIGHT ❧

Being and Becoming — A Child, Youth, Adult, and "Respectably" Aged in India

❧ T.S. Saraswathi ❧

As a child development professional, I am a member of a small tribe of professional child developmentalists that is barely but surely beginning to make its mark on the Indian social science scene. The acceptance and almost reluctant recognition of the members of this small and predominantly female tribe has come to be, not so much because of "muscle" power or path breaking contributions to knowledge, as because it was pushed into the limelight by several contextual factors. These factors include the increasing global consciousness of the state-of-the-world's children during the late twentieth century, political awareness in most nations that children constitute a major resource for the future of these nations, and the spotlight focus on children and their development through the UNESCO's formulation of Rights of Children and the declaration of the International Year of the Child, the Youth and so on.

Despite all this focused attention, however, child development professionals are not taken as seriously as they should be (at least in my unbiased opinion). In my immediate circle, my grandmother, aunts and other female family friends of that generation (most of whom reared no less than six children) viewed my professional development with fond affection yet firmly believed that no scientific knowledge could supersede the grandmother's wisdom on child rearing. On the more public, academic, interdisciplinary and policy forums (uncoloured by personal affection and indulgence), the response to the discipline is as uncertain, even if more varied. On the one hand, there is the reluctant acceptance of the significance of a child development professional when children (youth, women) are the central issues for consideration. On the other hand, it is the near transparent scepticism regarding "what can child development as a discipline contribute to policies regarding children (and their more mature forms) that cannot be handled by economists, medical professionals, nutritionists and others from allied disciplines?". Perhaps one answer to this scepticism is to follow the advice repeated quite often in recent years that the discipline needs to "sell itself more aggressively", that is, let the world know what it has to offer. Modesty, at least in these circumstances, does not seem to be a virtue.

More seriously, there is another dimension to this complex issue that warrants careful consideration. This relates to the need for introspection and soul searching on the part of child development professionals in order to surmount the fairly valid criticism that the knowledge base in child development as it exists today leans heavily on the Western (read American) contribution and hence is neither ecoculturally sensitive nor valid in the Indian setting. While there has been a conscious and active movement during the past decade and a half to break away from the barriers of Western intellectual colonisation in the discipline, a lot of culturally sensitive fertilisation and nurturance is needed before indigenisation takes root and results in a robust species. What is needed is hard core data obtained using valid measures, representative samples, and appropriate (meaningful) analysis.

In the following I have indulged in a kind of free associative speculation regarding the possible areas of search and research within the broad framework of developmental psychology/human development, that could serve to strengthen the thrust of indigenisation of knowledge and in turn enrich Indian contribution to cross-cultural developmental psychology. The topics span across the stages of human development, from infancy to aging.

Infancy and Earlier

At the outset, one could gain much from a systematic investigation and documentation of the implications of the overreaching fertility control, preferred sex, acceptance of individual differences, and child rearing practices. The belief systems associated with the value of children and the mode of socialisation practices no doubt create a *development niche*. Subcultural variations and the commonalities that characterise the "Indian" are pertinent topics of study.

The stage from conception to infancy also provides a fertile ground for testing the *ethnotheories* related to parenting and child rearing. The continued beliefs in the *samskaras* (defined as the rites and ceremonies that mark the developmental stage transitions) and the significance attached to the rituals provide both the social setting and the cultural belief system that lay the foundation for early child development. Significant contributions to cross-cultural developmental psychology could be made by a better understanding of the role of social support during pregnancy and its consequences for successful lactation and reduction in the incidence of post-partum depression.

The rapid pace of social change with its apparent impact on family structure and size, and on gender roles generates a host of researchworthy issues. Some examples are women's employment and alternative child care supports; small family size and heightened aspirations for children; longer life span and fewer care givers in the family; and delayed age at marriage and child bearing. Among the poor, for whom child survival is not as much of a constant threat as earlier, the relevant applied research pertains to ways and means of ensuring better quality child care and development.

Early Childhood

A common anecdotal observation among both specialists and lay persons is the noticeable continuity in the world of children and adults in most Eastern societies, in contrast to the segregation of the child and adult experiences and living space in most Western cultures. This coupled with the attribution of temperamental differences to inherent predispositions (that may even have their antecedents in previous births) call for child rearing experiences that facilitate "growing up" in a social setting rather than being "socialised" or "trained" to become an acceptable member of a society. Ethnographic descriptions could serve a useful purpose in understanding differential consequences of these alternative approaches for child and adult personality development.

Cultural expectations regarding training for independence vs interdependence is another topic that has sustained the interest of cross-cultural psychologists and cultural anthropologists. Even within any one culture, growing up in a joint family or a large family setting, learning to cooperate, share, tolerate, resolve differences, seek emotional support and choose from a wide range of role models to imitate and imbibe values is very different from that of growing up in a child centred nuclear family with only two or three children. Hypothetical deductions regarding the implications of experiential differences for the development of prosocial behaviour, and social and moral values that appear logical need to be empirically verified.

As with infancy, the rapid pace of change in the larger context is bound to affect the life experiences in early childhood also. Prominent among these, especially for the middle class, are the stress of school admission procedures; curriculum load right from entry to school; high teacher–pupil ratio and the consequent lack of individual attention aggravated by the difference between language spoken at home, in the playground and at school—the last being the most alien for a large number of children.

School related problems are compounded by the increasing number of mothers joining the workforce out of choice or economic compulsions and the lack of good quality alternative child care support. Pediatricians and clinical psychologists have increasingly expressed concern about the growing number of psychosomatic problems and the possible stressors responsible for these. All these offer numerous avenues for both basic and applied research.

A major lacuna in one's understanding of how children grow relates to how little one knows about the scars of violence on children's psyche. Violence can take various forms such as desensitising projections on the television and silver screen; domestic violence involving family conflicts; communal riots where friends become foes; and terrorism which has obliterated the memory of peace and normal life in several states.

The Early School Years

In practically all cultures, regardless of the existence of a formal system of education, the school years are considered the period during which children are socialised to become acceptable members of a given society and acquire the basic skills of living. The transmission of culture and cognitive skills through the learning of activity based spontaneous concepts (a la Vygotsky) is initiated from birth. However, the more formal training even in non-school, real life settings is evident during the early school years between the ages of 6 and 12. The process of enculturation is most evident in the skill transmission of artisans such as weavers, basket makers, potters and tailors, and in the performing arts be it folk or classical music, dance, drama, and other arts. Learning, as it should be, is embedded in real life contexts and becomes a way of life. Even when the responsibility for formal education was transferred to a non-family member with expertise in the concerned area of knowledge, the *gurukula* system entrusted the total child to the complete and holistic care of the master, once again resulting in education embedded in the total life setting of the child, during his critical years of training. The disciplined lifestyle, the rigorous training and the open-ended goal of mastery and perfection encompassed the lifestyle of both the teacher and the disciple.

The introduction of the formal Western-type schooling, combined with the belief system of those at the higher echelons of educational policy that unless school children are made to cram the exploding information, India as a nation would be left behind in the rat race of global development, has led to such consequences for children's growth and development that have yet to be understood.

What one sees today is learning without comprehension, a heavy load of curriculum with the focus on information and not knowledge acquisition, long hours of "study" in crowded classrooms followed by tedious homework. Even to a casual observer it is evident that children are disenchanted, learning is no fun, pressure due to parental expectations and competition for the limited choices results in psychosomatic disorders. What is worse is that play time becomes a luxury especially for middle class children. The invasion of cable television has been no boon from the heavens either. For what children seem to receive by their own confession are contradictory messages of fun in easy life, of lax living coloured more by narcissism rather than by interpersonal cooperation, and the rewards of violence in various shades from rape to gun shots. Has any one a full comprehension of what havoc the combined influence of joyless learning in school and the illusion of a blissful life on the small screen in the family living room, is playing on the psyche of young children? I am afraid not. Every one has impressions, beliefs, and opinions, but lacks understanding based on systematic study.

The discussion so far pertaining to formal education reflects essentially the reality of middle class children in India today. On the broader canvas, the situation is even more complex. A large percentage of children from the below poverty line families (which exceeds 40 per cent of the population depending on the cut-off point) child labour is an integral part of the life situation of the labouring poor. Education, even in the primary grades, is not compulsory and despite declared intentions, there is no political will to make it a reality. Other social, political and economic exigencies always take priority making education for all only a distant dream. On the flip side of the coin, there is a catch-22 situation, with concern expressed by many academicians and social workers about the irrelevance of education for the poor, the alienation caused by such an education which makes children maladjusted to their peoples' way of life and the consequent widespread disillusionment. The opportunity cost of child labour and the psychological costs of becoming adults before being children have been only superficially understood. Perhaps, there is a greater understanding, at least socially, of the lives of children under difficult circumstances such as street children, juvenile delinquents, and disabled. The credit for *conscientisation*, however, goes to the social activist and not to the psychologist.

Late Adolescence and Youth

Among school going children, the competition in the numbers game for securing marks and ranks gets intensified in the later school years with the selection for channelising children into the Science, Commerce, and Arts streams following the Grade 10 examination. In tune with the job market demands, the three streams fall into a "natural" hierarchy of prestige with the Science stream (which keeps open the entry into Medicine and Engineering) ranking number one. Seats in good institutions are limited resulting in added pressure on the children to cram, often with the aid of tutors after school hours. Again, the stress is not on learning to learn but only to cram and regurgitate the information without comprehension, the sole goal being to secure the required marks to qualify in the race.

The announcement of the public examination results in the newspapers in summer witnesses a sociological phenomenon unparalleled anywhere else in the world, except in Japan. The reference here is to the high incidence of suicide among adolescents due to failure in public exams, a twentieth century cultural phenomenon, the product of a peculiar educational setting, that has strangely evoked little interest among child development and family studies specialists.

Less extreme, but equally pathological corollaries of the stressors of schooling and examination system are school dropout, drug addiction, anti-social activities and yet another unique cultural phenomenon called "eve-teasing". The last refers to harassment of young girls and women by adolescent boys and youth (referred to in common parlance as roadside Romeos), who hang around literally on the pavements and near roadside cafes or petty shops that sell cigarettes, betel leaves, nuts, and other oral "pacifiers". With cultural constraints on heterosexual relationships during adolescence and whetted by sexually suggestive scenes in films and on television, boys resort to "eve-teasing" as an outlet often leading to verbal harassment and at times physical molestation of the victimised girls.

Discussions with youth in formal and informal settings highlight the infrequency and dearth of role models in educational and public settings, contradictory messages related to moral and social values, and the inability to communicate with those whom they perceive to be equally confused adults, be they parents or teachers. Again, the television is seen to intrude in the family sharing time. The high teacher–pupil ratio in schools and colleges limits adult–youth interaction therein. Especially evident in the university campuses is the decadence in the youth's participation in co-curricular and extra-curricular activities. Even a few decades ago these provided opportunities for interaction of adolescents and youth with their more competent adult mentors who acted as role models while encouraging participation in organised youth programmes such as debates, plays, and fun-fairs. Today, there is a marked preference for the spectator's role and that is also highly coloured by rowdyism and disruptive behaviour not confined to the gender with "Y" chromosomes. Materialism, addictive consumerism, and self-centred goals seem to have successfully replaced the idealism of youth so evident in high schools and college campuses only a few decades ago. The economic, social and political forces that have unleashed this wave of change could be a fertile ground for understanding the development of youth in societies in transition from the traditional to the free market economy. Associated issues that call for investigation and understanding are acquisition of values and prosocial behaviour; identity crises; role models; and the impact of the broader ecocultural changes on child and adolescent development.

Young Adulthood

The two major social issues that confront young adults in India today are related to career options and the selection of a marriage partner. In both cases, the shrinking globe and exposure to alternative lifestyles as well as expanding career options resulting from technological development and the new economic policy make matters more complex and challenging than ever before. Indepth and extensive database on factors that influence career choice and mate selection would be useful in individual counselling as well as school guidance.

For the hundreds of upper middle class youth who graduate from elitist institutions like the institutes of technology and medicine, the career prospects are often bright and clear. The former especially opens the doors of migration to other lands of better opportunities for career development and economic growth. Their training combined with parental support makes them highly eligible for competition in the international educational arena and once they are exposed to good laboratory facilities and a supportive work climate elsewhere they join the pool of "brain drain", a phenomenon much discussed in political and educational forums but little understood in terms of steps that may be taken to reverse the flow.

Migration, whether for higher education and/or new career opportunities, brings with it demands on the young in terms of a different work climate from what they have been used to. These include expectations to act independently and make decisions without constant adult nurturance and dominance; changes in daily life experiences including cooking, mode of living quarters and its maintenance; and in dress. A major upheaval in the process of enculturation is the adaptation to a value system, especially in terms of heterosexual (or even same sex) relations. Those secure in their own cultural roots and who have enjoyed and continue to retain cordial family relations in the home country appear to cope in a balanced manner integrating the strengths of the new culture without losing sight of one's roots. Others pay a heavier price—rejecting either their own cultural values or those of the new land in toto, thereby leading to alienation, loneliness or unstable self-identity. The emotional backlash of this trauma becomes particularly evident in the choice of a marriage partner either impulsively on one's own without due consideration to its long-term implications or the other extreme of letting the "folks back home" choose a bride (rarely is a bridegroom chosen in this fashion) on their own. The green card holders marry during their annual or biannual vacation home and return, often alone, leaving the new bride to cope with the problems of obtaining a visa and adjusting to a new family. These are not isolated instances but are common occurrences in the lives of several thousands of youth every year. The consequences of these life experiences for marital and social–personal adjustments as well as child rearing practices offer a rich area for investigation.

Again, as in the case of schooling, another end of the population spectrum consists of the economically not-so-privileged youth, for whom the problems of young adulthood is one of under- or unemployment, the great divide between what is and what one dreamt it will be, and the glaring disparity in the lifestyles of those more fortunate. The forced economic dependency, the consequent strain on family relations and the resulting feeling of despondency and self-depreciation call for the attention of developmental psychologists.

Adulthood

Work in the area of developmental psychology in India has concentrated mainly on childhood and adolescence. The focus on adult socialisation and development is conspicuous by its absence. In the area of family studies, some aspects of marital adjustment and problems of aging have been investigated. Current interest in women's studies has stimulated work on gender issues especially as related to women's work, child care alternatives, changing family structures and dynamics. A decade review in this area can provide significant leads.

In a cultural setting where marriage is expected, accepted and is predominantly stable, despite a noticeable increase in the divorce rates and the number of women-headed households, compatability of married partners and their conjugal relations offers much scope for theory building and empirical research. The changing social scene, especially among the middle class, of delayed age at marriage, increasing opportunities for higher education for women, women's participation in the workforce, reduction in family size, and the increasing cost of housing in metropolitan cities, is bound to have a telling impact on husband–wife relations. As in the case of the youth, the mass media bombards families with images of the superwoman model on the small screen, always well dressed, competent at work as well as at home, ever smiling and ever-so-loving. Unfortunately, nothing is known about it and how it impacts expectations of the married couple from each other as well as their own self.

In many cases adulthood is accompanied by a phenomenon that is particularly characteristic of developing countries. The reference here is to large-scale migration from rural to urban areas and from one city to another in search of employment and better job opportunities. Among the several consequences of such migration, those of particular interest to human development/developmental psychology are family disruption, crowded living conditions, and loss of familiar social support. Very often only the male breadwinner migrates leaving behind the woman to head the household and to manage the farm and children's education and upbringing. The disruption of family life is particularly evident when men find new sexual partners to cope with their loneliness and women on their part resent their men's intrusion in their decision-making during their periodical visits home. When families do migrate together, the problems are living under insanitary conditions of squatter settlements, children's school admission, and women being uprooted from their familiar way of life.

The changing scene of women's employment and empowerment especially among the educated raises major issues related to child care arrangements and child rearing practices. A related concern is that of parental investment in and expectations from their offspring in terms of achievements both in school and in extra-curricular activities. The diminishing availability of social support from extended family members for child bearing and child rearing is also interrelated with the changing family values regarding care of aged parents. The availability of limited living space, especially in big cities and towns, increasing assertion on the part of women (daughters-in-law) and grandchildren for a right to lead their lives the way they wish to without being encumbered by the traditional age and gender hierarchy makes the experience of the three generation households less harmonious. Aging parents often view themselves as irrelevant and of no value. The situation is particularly poignant in the case of those who had made heavy economic investments in their children's education with no concern for saving for their old age in the expectation that their children would care for them as they cared for their own parents.

In states like Kerala, Punjab, and Gujarat from where there is large-scale migration to the Gulf countries, the USA and the UK, many residential areas, at times even entire villages, are populated by only aging couples. In such cases, children often send a liberal allowance for maintaining their parents' home. However, the fact that money alone cannot solve all problems is evident from the issues concerning the aged discussed in the following.

Aging and the Aged

The stage of life that has perhaps seen the most marked change in the cultural connotation attached to it is that of old age. In India, like in most traditional agrarian cultures, being elderly was associated with status, wisdom, and respect. Whether in the family or the village, one sought the advice of senior members on all matters pertaining to selection of a spouse for one's children, deciding on their educational choices, purchase of land and other assets, settling disputes and so on. The celebration of the 60th and 80th birthdays with great pomp and splendour and the homage paid to those who had achieved these milestones signalled the recognition of both the wisdom of experience and the achievements of a full life well lived. Knowledge came with life's experiences, and if one lived long, one naturally grew wise. In a stable society where the pace of change was slow and knowledge accumulated gradually with experience, the system of age hierarchy functioned fairly smoothly.

However, in a rapidly changing world, with technological advances that have had a dramatic impact on the daily lives of people, the power of knowledge has shifted to the youth who have the technical expertise not possessed by the older generation. The rate of change has been too fast for the older generation to keep pace with and in most cases the aged have quietly withdrawn into their own shell, since there is not much advice they can offer about what they do not understand. This coupled with the separation of the aged from intergenerational family life due to accommodation/space problems in cities and a host of changing sociological conditions, has resulted in loneliness, feelings of uselessness, and even despair. The changing demographic profile of the aged in India and predictions that by the year 2000 more than 12 per cent of the population will be above 60 years, should be a matter of interest and concern to the developmental psychologist interested in what Erickson has called the stage of integration, the last stage of Hindu *ashramadharma* (life stages). Understanding how the individual and society handle the stages of *vanaprastha* and *sanyas*, the last two stages of life according to the Hindu description of the life cycle, is of significance to both basic and applied developmental psychology.

Does the erosion of ethical values in general and religious values in particular in the larger setting result in disillusionment and mental disharmony in the last years? What is the impact of loss of status on the persons' life experiences in contrast to the respect they extended to the previous generation? Is facing death, the ultimate reality, more anxiety provoking for the aged today than it was in the past? How do families and society adapt to the requirements for the care of the aged in the context of changing family obligations coupled with the lack of systematic social welfare services for the care of the aged? These and many more related questions are in search for answers that developmental psychology needs to address.

Concluding Comments

An attempt has been made in this paper to view the field of developmental psychology in India through the lens of the consumer, be it parents, teachers, social workers or policy planners. The aim of the speculative meandering has been to examine the kind of questions that need to be answered, in order to provide knowledge that will be useful to the consumer. Viewed from the perspective of knowledge construction that is both indigenously meaningful and of relevance to cross-cultural developmental psychology, the issues raised call for embedding research in the larger context. Research questions need to emerge from real life, taking into account both the prevailing cultural milieu and the forces of change, and the findings need to be interpreted in terms of what they signify from an ecological perspective. Only then can developmental psychology in India move from its present status of uncertain adolescence to one of robust adulthood. If I have understood him right, this is the kind of development that Professor Durganand Sinha had been advocating for the discipline of psychology as a whole during the past three decades. Realisation of even a part of his dream is the best tribute one can pay to him.

❧ NINE ❧

Multicultural Attitudes and Identities in Canada

❧ John W. Berry ❧

Introduction

Multiculturalism is a matter of both fact and public policy in Canada. It is also the object of attitudes and the subject of debate. This paper briefly establishes the nature of the fact and the policy, and examines how people feel (their attitudes) and how they see themselves (their identities) in relation to the fact and the policy. The paper concludes by examining what these psychological phenomena contribute to one's understanding of the policy, and how they contribute to the debate.

Multiculturalism as a Social Fact

Since the time of the confederation in 1867, when 91 per cent of Canada's population was of French (31 per cent) and British (60 per cent) origin, there has been a constant change in the ethnic composition of the country's population. According to the most recent census (1991), 39 per cent were British, 24 per cent French, and 37 per cent of other than British or French origin. This "other" category has increased steadily in size, but variably in ethnic composition since 1867; initially, large numbers of people of Eastern European origin arrived, followed by those of Southern European origin, and for the past 25 years, by those not of European origin, particularly from East and South Asia. In 1995, 65 per cent of the 200,000 immigrants to Canada were from Asia.

In addition to these demographic facts, two key points need to be made: multiculturalism in Canada does not depend on immigration; nor is it just a matter of the presence of peoples of diverse ethnic origins. In principle, cultural diversity in Canada has a life of its own, and is not solely a function of immigration flow; this is because ethnocultural groups have established themselves and are alive and well, as constituent parts of the Canadian "mosaic". Second, people have cultural identities that link them psychologically to their cultural origin group; that is, the mosiac is more than a statistical (origin) category, it is a matter of active links and activities within the various groups. Both these points illustrate the importance of social and psychological factors in maintaining a culturally plural society.

Multiculturalism as Public Policy

The plural Canadian society largely evolved on its own, without any help from public policy or programmes. Indeed, many observers believe that it evolved *in spite* of the implicit (and sometimes explicit) policy of Angloconformity, or assimilation to British culture. However, by 1956 the Federal Government's view was that assimilation had not worked anywhere in the contemporary world, and that it was impracticable as a general policy. By 1971, the Prime Minister announced a policy of multiculturalism. The key sections were:

A policy of multiculturalism within a bilingual framework commends itself to the Government as the most suitable means of assuring the cultural freedom of Canadians. Such a policy should help to break down discriminatory attitudes and cultural jealousies. National unity, if it means anything in the deeply personal sense, must be founded on confidence in one's own individual identity; out of this can grow respect for that of others and a willingness to share ideas, attitudes and assumptions. A vigorous policy of multiculturalism will help create this initial confidence.
It can form the base of a society which is based on fair play for all. The Government will support and encourage the various cultures and ethnic groups that give structure and vitality to our society. They will be encouraged to share their cultural expression and values with other Canadians and so contribute to a richer life for all.

To advance understanding of the policy, it is important to identify and place four elements of the policy within a framework (see

Figure 9.1) which also shows a number of their interrelationships. First, it is clear that the policy wishes to avoid assimilation by encouraging ethnic groups to maintain and develop themselves as distinctive groups within Canadian society; this element may be termed as "own group maintenance and development". Second, a fundamental purpose of the policy is to increase intergroup harmony and the mutual acceptance of all groups which maintain and develop themselves; this is termed as "other group acceptance and tolerance". Third, the policy argues that group development by itself is not sufficient to lead to group acceptance; "intergroup contact and sharing" is also required. Fourth, full participation by groups cannot be achieved if some common language is not learned; thus the policy promotes the "learning of official languages". In addition to identifying these four elements of the policy, Figure 9.1 also indicates some interrelationships (connecting lines between elements). A few of these are explicit in the policy, others are implicit, and yet

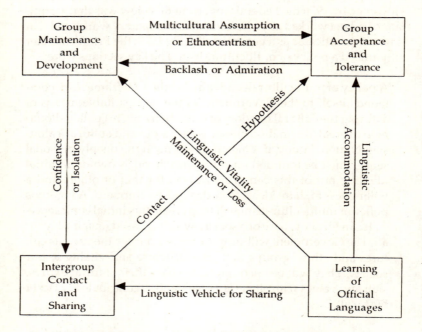

Figure 9.1 Four Components of Canadian Multiculturalism Policy with Sociopsychological Links Among Them

others may be derived from the social–psychological literature on ethnic relations.

A central question is whether the policy intends to encourage the maintenance of numerous and full-scale cultural systems (as implied in the term multiculturalism), or whether it is designed to be supportive of some lesser phenomena (such as various aspects of ethnicity which are derived from a full cultural system). Burnet (1975) argued that "ethnicity" rather than "culture" is the actual and realistic focus of such a policy: most groups lack their own separate social and political institutions, many lack their own (ancestral) language and they are not always large. Thus, the maintenance of shared features which are derived from a heritage culture (i.e., ethnic phenomena) are more likely to be possible than the maintenance of full-scale cultures ("museum cultures" in Burnet's terms).

These demographic facts and public policies constitute the background or context for this discussion. As a social and cross-cultural psychologist, I am aware that all human behaviour is profoundly affected by the cultural context in which it developed, and is manifested. The following information and analyses may or may not generalise to, or even be relevant to India; this is for the reader to decide. However, the purpose of this paper is to illustrate *how* a social psychologist can approach such issues, and *what* may be said about them in order to influence and improve human relations in other plural societies.

Multicultural Attitudes

The ideas and data presented here are based on a long period of study of ethnic attitudes and identities in Canada in collaboration with Rudy Kalin (Berry & Kalin, 1995; Berry, Kalin, & Taylor, 1977; Kalin & Berry, 1995; 1996), and on related projects sponsored by various versions of Multiculturalism Canada (e.g., Berry, 1984; Berry & Laponce, 1994).

How can social psychology contribute to these issues? In social psychology, the focus is typically on *individuals*, who are studied through interviews; but the data are usually aggregated into social and demographic categories. This has allowed the investigation of these phenomena at both the individual and group levels of analysis. The guiding conceptual framework for this work has been *ethnocentrism* theory, which is useful at both these levels of analysis. The concept refers to the universal tendency for *groups* to generally favour themselves (i.e., an "ingroup bias" to have a relative preference for one's own group over others), while allowing for the possibility that some groups will exhibit this relative preference more than others. It also refers to *individuals* who typically manifest an ingroup bias, while allowing for individual differences in the extent of this preference; some individuals may be very ethnocentric, while others may be less so.

The fundamental question being addressed at this point is "Under what conditions can we all live together in a plural society?". Among the many other answers (involving economic, political, and human rights issues), some psychological preconditions may be suggested:

First, there needs to be general support for multiculturalism, including acceptance of various aspects and consequences of the policy, and of cultural diversity as a valuable resource for a society. Second, there should be overall low levels of intolerance or prejudice in the population. Third, there should be generally positive mutual attitudes among the various ethnocultural groups that constitute the society. And fourth, there needs to be a degree of attachment to the larger Canadian society, but without derogation of its constituent ethnocultural groups (Berry & Kalin, 1995, p. 302).

Several of these conditions have been addressed in the two national surveys (1974 and 1991) and a few community and small group studies. This paper is based primarily on the results of the 1991 survey (N 3,325). Since the study dealt with some fairly fundamental psychological characteristics, it is likely that, while more than 10 years old, the basic picture remains valid.

This paper contains three major pieces of information. First are some *general indicators of acceptance of cultural diversity*: do Canadians like to live in a heterogeneous society, do they enjoy intercultural differences and encounters. Second pertains to some *specific intergroup attitudes* based on a single measure of how comfortable people are being around those from various specific ethnic backgrounds. And finally, how people *identify themselves* (in civic or ethnic terms), and to what extent they identify with the nation-state of Canada. In most cases, the information is aggregated by ethnic origin of the respondent

(British, French or other) and region of residence (within or outside Québec).

The two scales of interest are the *Multicultural Ideology* and the *Tolerance-prejudice Scales*. In the national population as a whole, both the acceptance of multiculturalism, and the level of tolerance (essentially the opposite of prejudice) are moderately high, and the long-term trends for both show an increase over the past 15 years. On the 7-point response scale used, the means were 4.59 and 5.37 respectively. When analysed by ethnic origin and region, Figures 9.2 and 9.3 show the resulting pattern (Berry & Kalin, 1995).

While there are some similarities in the distribution of these two general orientations (such as no effect of ethnic origin), there are some important differences. Most evident is the presence of a regional effect for tolerance–prejudice, but an interaction effect for multicultural ideology; this difference indicates that dissimilar explanations are

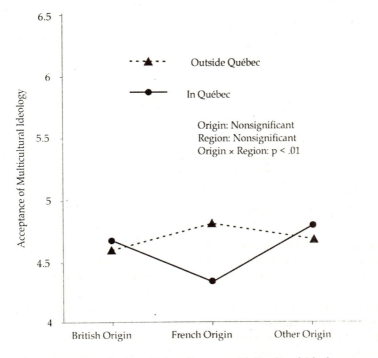

Figure 9.2 Distribution of Mean Scores on Multicultural Ideology by Ethnic Origin and Region of Residence of Respondents

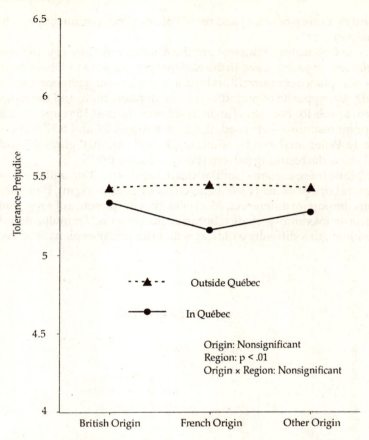

Figure 9.3 Distribution of Mean Scores on Tolerance–Prejudice by Ethnic Origin and Region of Residence of Respondents

needed to account for the two scores. For tolerance–prejudice, it may be that where intergroup relations are contentious (for instance, in Québec) all groups are relatively less tolerant. For multicultural ideology, a type of "self-interest" accounts for the distribution: where people are advantaged by policies and programmes promoting multiculturalism (for example, British and others within Québec; French outside Québec) support is high; but where people may be threatened by pluralist policies (such as French in Québec) support for diversity is lower.

Ethnic Attitudes

Respondents indicated their degree of comfort being around persons from selected ethnic backgrounds. These "comfort levels" according to the ethnic origin of the respondent (in the total sample), and for the three major urban centres (N 500 each) not broken down by ethnicity (Berry & Kalin, 1995) are depicted in Figures 9.4 and 9.5.

The data from the national sample (Figure 9.4) have three important aspects. First, while comfort levels were generally high, not all groups received the same ratings. A hierarchy of acceptance was noted in which British–Canadians through to native Canadians were evaluated more positively than other groups. Second, while there were no differences between British and other origin ratings, those given by French origin respondents were markedly less positive.

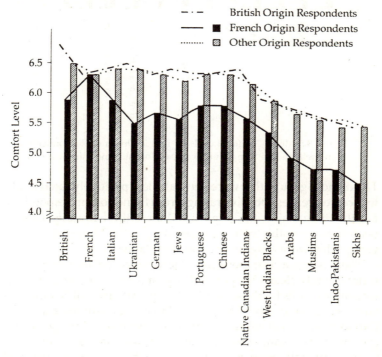

Figure 9.4 Mean Comfort Levels by Ethnic Origin of Respondents in the National Sample

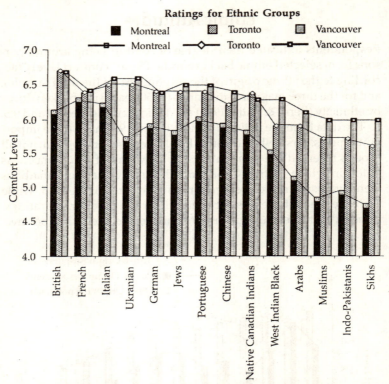

Figure 9.5 Mean Comfort Levels by Ethnic Origin of Respondents in the National Sample in Montreal, Toronto, and Vancouver

Third, those groups that were generally less positively rated tended to receive even less positive ratings from French origin respondents. For the three main cities (Figure 9.5) these three findings were repeated, but possibly with a steeper drop-off in Montréal for those groups that were lower in general acceptance.

There is thus a clear hierarchy of acceptance, but its interpretation is not entirely clear. One possibility is that prejudice (in particular, racism) accounts for these ratings. This possibility will be examined later, but it can be noted here that Chinese–Canadians and native Canadians are as generally highly rated as those of European background; thus, a simple *racism* interpretation is not generally valid. Other explanations include *familiarity* with various groups, with those groups which are less numerous and not as long established

with a slightly higher strength rating for a "provincial" (i.e., "Québécois") identity.

When these identities were related to the two general orientations within the three ethnic origin categories, some variations surfaced (Kalin & Berry, 1995). For respondents of British origin, those with a "provincial" identity were lower than those with other identities on tolerance (but not on multicultural ideology). The reverse was true for respondents of French origin, those with a "provincial" identity were lower than those with other identities on multicultural ideology (but not on tolerance). As expected, among other origin Canadians, those with an "ethnic" identity were most supportive of a multicultural ideology, while those with a "provincial" identity were least tolerant. Most importantly, there was no evidence that those who identify as "Canadian" were less supportive of diversity.

Findings obtained from the Canadianism scale are depicted in Figure 9.8, according to ethnic origin and region of residence.

Unlike the two other scale distributions, scores on Canadianism varied significantly by ethnic origin and region, and in their interaction (Figure 9.8). All three features were evidently due to the lower score on the scale obtained by respondents of French origin living in Québec. When these scale scores were related to the three identity categories, a common and significant pattern appeared in all three ethnic origin groups: those with a "provincial" identity scored lower on Canadianism, and (not surprisingly) those with a "Canadian" identity scored higher. For British and other origin groups, those with an "ethnic" identity did not score lower on the Canadianism scale, indicating that the much maligned "hyphenated identity" did not pose a threat to a person's attachment to Canada.

Implications and Conclusions

What can be said about this pattern of findings, and how can they be of use to psychologists working in other plural societies?

1. Diversity appears to be alive and well in Canada, and there is a broad general acceptance of this social fact.
2. Ethnic attitudes are generally positive.
3. Identity as "Canadian", and attachment to Canada are generally widespread and strong.

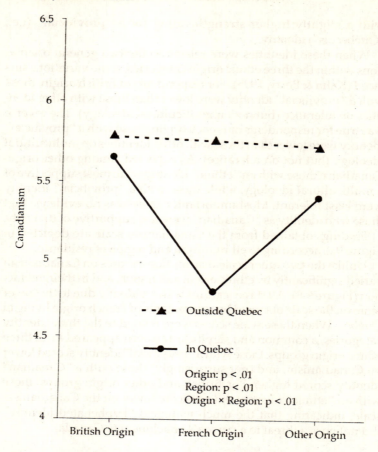

Figure 9.8 Distribution of Mean Scores on Canadianism by Ethnic Origin and Region of Residence of Respondents

Obviously, this general pattern is affected by ethnic origin, region of residence, and the object of the attitude (i.e., which group, which issue). More specifically, compared to other respondents, Québecers (sometimes only Francophone Québecers) expressed a slightly lesser acceptance of diversity (multicultural ideology, tolerance), lesser attachment to Canada (Canadianism), less positive ethnic attitudes (comfort levels), lower frequency of identity as "Canadien" (more frequently as "Québécois"), and a weak identity as "Canadien" (more strongly as "Québécois").

The meaning of these findings is not clear. Some researchers (Richler, 1992; Sniderman et al., 1993) have interpreted them as indicating a pervasive prejudice and ethnocentrism in Québec, particularly among Francophones, and specifically in the form of anti-Semitism. An alternative interpretation is that such a pattern of attitudes reflects a lack of *cultural security* which may be historically rooted, but is neither a necessary nor a permanent quality of intergroup relations within Québec, or between Québec and the rest of Canada (see Berry, Kalin, & Taylor, 1977, for an elaboration of the role of cultural security in attitudes). An implication of these findings is that in order to accommodate such a lack of security, people must stop threatening each other.

Beyond this, the two fundamental principles of *familiarity* and *similarity* in the social psychology of attitudes provide some options for the future.

The "two solitudes" (British and French elements) have clearly remained intact despite policies (for example, Official Bilingualism) and programmes (such as school exchanges) to reduce it. Given that socioeconomic status and educational differences have been virtually eliminated between Québec and the rest of Canada, one precondition for intergroup contact to succeed (that of *equal status* between the groups in contact) is now in place. It is, thus, reasonable to propose a crash programme of bridge building and interaction, using existing institutions (for instance, CBC, NFB), and increased bilingual capacity. For example, within the European Union, the ERASMUS (and similar) programmes encourage a minimum of 10 per cent of each university's students to be from another nation. In broadcasting, Eurovision similarly enhances intergroup familiarity. Enhanced mutual *familiarity* may be a useful vehicle to bring about improved mutual acceptance.

Second, while diversity is here to stay, it is clear that there are substantial *similarities* in the findings (for instance, mutual English and French positive reference group status generally shared high levels of tolerance). It may be timely to emphasise such similarities (as well as others like common values) to enhance awareness of how much people actually have in common. Social psychological research (Tajfel, 1978) has demonstrated clearly that groups will typically focus on small differences, even exaggerate them, to the point where they overshadow fundamental similarities. A refocusing on what is common could serve as another vehicle to achieve increased mutual acceptance.

Are there any general lessons for other plural societies to be derived from this work? Given the "universal" nature of many theories and findings in the social psychology of intergroup relations (Gudykunst & Bond, 1997), and of their thorough study and extension in India (Singh, 1988), I believe that there is a strong possibility that the lessons drawn from this programme of research in Canada can facilitate understanding diversity elsewhere.

First, the three sets of phenomena examined in this paper are almost certainly present whenever ethnicity is salient, including India (Hutnik & Sapru, 1996). General orientations toward diversity, specific attitudes towards one's own and other groups, and one's sense of attachment to cultural and civic entities can be understood by individuals and assessed by social psychologists.

Second, existing cleavages (be they ethnic, regional, linguistic, religious or class/caste) provide a framework for analysing these three sets of phenomena to understand both their origins and their potential for hostility and conflict.

Third (and this may not be universal!) my experience is that politicians and policy makers usually prefer to make informed (rather than uninformed) decisions. Having a valid description and interpretation of the state of group relations in one's society should serve well the public interest. However, it would be naive to believe that decisions will be made on the basis of social psychological findings alone; obviously, other considerations will be taken into account. But the point is that psychologists have a role to play, and a responsibility to play it, even though they may not always be heard.

❧ TEN ❧

Women, Work and Family in Urban India

Towards New Families?

❧ Shalini Bharat ❧

In the context of a changing world order in which women's participation in the economy, mass displacement of populations and families, experimentations with lifestyles, and increasing numbers of alternate family forms are some of the significant social trends, family researchers are concerned with a fresh question: "Are there new families?". More specifically, the question is: Are families disappearing due to singlehood, childlessness and divorce (no families), or, are they becoming more egalitarian as a result of rapid changes in gender roles, women's increasing participation in the paid labour force, and a more balanced division of domestic work (new families)? (Goldscheider & Waite, 1991).

This paper examines the concept of "new families" in the context of urban India on the basis of a review of a select set of Indian researches on women, work, and family. The paper addresses the question: Has the entry of urban based Indian women in the organised labour force resulted in "new families" that are characterised by egalitarian norms of family relationships, equitable distribution of domestic labour, shared decision-making patterns and gender free role perceptions? In other words, are urban based dual earner families in India moving towards the notion of "new families" following women's participation in the workforce? Beginning with a general introduction to the concept of "new families", a summary of empirical linkages between women's work and family found in literature in the West is presented. This is followed by a brief outline of the sociocultural reality of India and Indian women's participation in the labour force to set the framework for subsequent discussion. Finally, some of the available researches on women, work, and family are examined to throw light on the trend towards "new families" in India.

The Concept of "New Families"

The concept of "new families" may be viewed as an extension of the old debate in family research which put forth conflicting viewpoints with regard to the status and future of the "family".

An early viewpoint firmly believed in the importance of family as a basic unit of society, but also predicted its decay and demise in the prevailing turbulent social structure of the 1960s and 1970s (Cooper, 1970; Gorden, 1972). Another viewpoint considered the family as an obsolete, archaic, dying institution unable to fulfil its role under the demands of a modern high-tech society (Bernard, 1972). A third viewpoint, emerging in the 1980s, reposed faith in the capacity of the family to adapt and modify itself according to the needs of changing times, and on its flexibility to change forms and be amenable to experimentations of various kinds. This viewpoint was reflected in researches on non-traditional, alternative or variant family structures (Lamb, 1982; Macklin, 1987; Shamgar-Handelman & Palomba, 1987). The "new families" theme is more akin to the theme of alternative family patterns as it seeks to draw linkages between societal changes and family adaptation and transformation, as opposed to the collapse of a social institution.

Women, Work, and Family: Evidence from the West

Increasingly, work and families are being recognised as closely interacting structures with far-reaching, but non-uniform, implications for individuals in different societies. Findings of some early studies (Epstein, 1971; Poloma, 1972) highlighted the problems of working women such as role overload, role conflict, multiple responsibilities, and role stress and strain. The studies that followed in the early 1980s (Aldous, 1982; Hood, 1983; Huber & Spitze, 1983; Rapoport & Rapoport, 1980) examined family dynamics in relation to women's co-provider role. These studies revealed that women continued to shoulder a major share of household work despite their co-provider status.

Coverman and Sheley (1986) examined changes in men's housework participation between 1965 and 1975 and found no significant change despite women's increased labour force participation. The time-budget analysis used in several studies (Hartmann, 1981; Pleck, 1985) supported these findings. Hartmann (1981) found that the husbands of working women did not contribute any more to housework than did the husbands of non-employed women. Nickols and Metzen (1978) noted that while the wife's work hours were positively related to the husband's housework hours, the impact was quite modest. Baruch and Barnett (1983) did not observe any difference in the extent of help in housework between men whose wives worked and men whose wives did not. Yogev (1981) reported a leisure gap of 30 hours between professional women with children and their husbands. In the groundbreaking study "Second Shift", Hochschild (1989) observed that in only 20 per cent of the dual career families did men share housework equally with their wives. Largely, at the end of a workday, it was the working mother who did the "second shift" at home.

While studies nearly uniformly demonstrate that there is no change in household duties and roles of women despite their involvement in economic activities, some changes are now beginning to be noticed in the attitudes of working couples in the West. For example, researchers have begun to question the notion of men as the sole breadwinners of the family regardless of the ratio of their contribution to the household income (Bernard, 1981; Slocum & Nye, 1976). Recent studies have documented changes in the perception and performance of gender roles. Egalitarian values and norms and the wife's co-provider role are being more seriously acknowledged in Western societies (Bernard, 1981; Hood, 1986; Pleck, 1985). Goldscheider and Waite (1991) observed that due to an increasing number of women workers in the US, family relationships and work patterns were slowly changing in the egalitarian direction. They reported that both the husband's and children's share of domestic work increased when the wife/mother was employed outside the home, and their contribution became greater as the woman's earnings increased. However, data revealed that women continued to do more than the amount of work done by their husbands and children together. A critical review of research in this area reveals that "while time availability based on employment status may influence the division of home labour, it does not result in an equitable distribution of home labour" (Hardesty & Bokemeier, 1989, p. 255). For example, men usually perform light, mechanised and sporadic tasks like lawn mowing, leaving the tedious, time consuming and routine jobs like cooking and child care for women. In other words, equitable distribution of domestic work is yet to be achieved.

It is argued that non-egalitarian family patterns exist because women's greater involvement at home is a part of the family strategy to maximise economic gains through the husband's greater involvement at work and less or nil at home. Since men are considered the chief breadwinners, they are required to focus on work and women to take care of the home. This purely economic approach (Becker, 1976), it is argued, overlooks the cultural patterns of sex stratification (Huber & Spitze, 1983). Men do less work at home not only for economic reasons, but also because of the strong cultural belief that household work is not their job rather it is women's responsibility.

In non-Western cultures, the linkages between women's employment status and their personal and family status, as well as egalitarian family patterns, are not as direct and conclusive (Stichter & Parpart, 1990). Thus, the presumption that women's paid employment will lead to a rise in women's status both within and outside the family remains a controversial issue and the presumption that it will lead to a decrease in fertility remains inconclusive for want of more evidence (Stichter & Parpart, 1990). In non-Western cultures, the traditional family structures, norms of patriarchy, class position, and economic security of the husband are identified as some of the factors that influence the relationship between women's employment status and patterns of family roles and relationships (Safilios-Rothschild, 1982; 1990).

Women, Work, and Family: The Indian Context

To understand the linkages between women's employment and changes in family roles and relationships, it is important to understand Indian society, the nature of family structure, and the position of women in the family and in society. The following description is based on the works of Gore (1968) and Ross (1961).

Indian society is highly structured and hierarchical in nature. The hierarchies within the family (of age, gender, and kinship relationships) are reflected in a set of traditional values, beliefs, customs, and practices. These norms and practices determine how, and with whom, one may maintain social relations and enter into kinship bonds. Both societal and family relationships in India are marked by deference to superiors and authority, and an unquestioning attitude to perform one's duties as they are passed down the line. In such a hierarchical structure, the concepts of equality and personal freedom are alien. Indian society is governed by norms of patriarchy whereby women are placed in an inferior position to men and subjected to a relationship of dependency throughout their lives.

The family provides an important context within which norms and practices find expression through early socialisation practices. The Indian family is first and foremost characterised by a definite system of role relationships and sentiments that bind members together. Members share feelings of family solidarity or familism and strive to uphold family dignity and status in society. A high premium is placed on family unity and cohesiveness which are perceived as the essential prerequisites for family stability and survival. Behaviour that threatens the cooperative spirit and unity is discouraged from being manifest. Sharing and mutual dependence are encouraged in the Indian family, and members are made to feel secure and safe within the family fold. Elaborate family practices and rituals foster a feeling of belongingness and convey the message that family bonds are immutable, life long and dependable.

The family operates in terms of a well-defined hierarchical system based on the principles of age and sex seniority. Age seniority determines both ritual and authority status within the family. A great deal of value is attached to age seniority and due respect is shown to older members which extends to the world outside the family as well. Deference shown to age is a basic and consistent theme found in the Indian family system. Male supremacy is another characteristic feature of Indian families. Male members occupy a position of greater power and authority while females are placed in a secondary position in all spheres of life be it status, power, food allocation, health or education. Within each group the principle of age seniority operates to determine relative status. The division of family tasks and responsibilities is strictly along gender lines and on the basis of age and generational status. Thus, men are responsible for the more valued outdoor tasks and women for the less valued domestic work; the aged have primarily the directive, decision-making responsibilities, and adults have the responsibility for active, physical work; children have to perform either light jobs or no major tasks.

The position of the woman in Indian society presents a contradiction of sorts. In Hindu ideology she is identified with nature and extolled as the creator and protector of her children. At the same time, she is to be shunned as an evil and destructive force (Wadley, 1988). On the one hand, the woman is worshipped as goddess, or *devi*, and revered as a mother, on the other hand, she is denied personal freedom and treated more as an object of sexual pleasure. In terms of demographic indicators too, women present a somewhat paradoxical picture. Indian women have a weak position in terms of sex ratio (929 women to 1,000 men),[1] literacy rate (39.42 per cent compared to 63.86 per cent for men),[2] average age at marriage (20 years compared to 25 years for men),[3] and work participation rate (22.73 per cent compared to 51.56 per cent for men).[4] Yet, Indian women compare quite favourably with their Western counterparts in terms of their representation in professions: they account for 7.1 per cent of doctors, 1.2 per cent of lawyers, and 10.9 per cent of scientists (Wadley, 1988). They are also making their entry into male dominated professions like the police and the armed forces; a beginning yet to be made in many developed nations. Indian women enjoy equal rights to work and wages and are protected under progressive legislations for property rights, divorce, medical termination of pregnancy, and are termed as "partners in development" in government plans (Chitnis, 1988). Chitnis (1988) even stated, "If a cross-cultural or multinational analysis of legal provisions for women is made, India is likely to emerge as one of the top most most progressive countries" (p. 88).

However, social reality does not conform to this happy progressive picture and women in Indian society continue to be a disadvantaged group. Several reasons have been identified for this, these include

---

[1] Census of India, 1991 — Series 1, Paper 1 of 1991 — Provisional Population Totals. Registrar General and Census Commissioner, India.
[2] *ibid*.
[3] National Family Health Survey (MCH and Family Planning) India, 1992–93. Bombay: International Institute for Population Sciences.
[4] Census of India, 1991 — Series 1, Paper 3 of 1991 — Workers and Their Distribution. Registrar General and Census Commissioner, India.

low awareness and poor use of existing legal and political rights and privileges; unequal socioeconomic structures whereby the poor and needy have little or no access to educational, legal and employment benefits; a bureaucratic set-up that is slow to deliver the goods; and above all an orthodox value system that is shaped by norms of patriarchy and male-oriented culture (Chitnis, 1988; Ramu, 1989). Indian values and ethos place a premium on women as homemakers or *grihani* and on their role as a good mother, wife, and daughter. Devotion to husband is regarded as their supreme duty which is idealised in the concept of *pativrata* (one who is vowed to her husband) and motherhood is viewed as the ultimate aim in life as it confers upon them a purpose and identity that nothing else in their culture can (Kakar, 1978). In short, the Indian woman does not stand alone; her identity is defined by her relationships to others as daughter, wife, and mother. Unlike in the West, the Indian woman's identity, after marriage, is not rooted in the conjugal relationship, but in the family as a whole into which she is wedded and in which her "self" gets lost in the complex web of gender and age prescribed roles, relationships, and expectations.

Women's Participation in the Indian Labour Force

Estimating women's work participation in India is marred by problems of satisfactorily defining what constitutes women's economic activity. There is both ambiguity and non-uniformity in definitions of women's work across decennial censuses except in 1981 and 1991. In the Indian context definitional problems have serious consequences, for minor alterations in the definition result in the inclusion, or exclusion from the labour force, of a few million women workers (Anker, 1983; Anker & Khan, 1988). Besides, repeated changes in definitions render comparison across censuses difficult and meaningless.

There are two major sources of data on labour participation: the decennial censuses and the National Sample Surveys (NSS). Since the census definition of work is ambiguous, non-uniform and as the census is a one-point enquiry of employment, NSS data are sometimes preferred over census data (Acharya, 1996).

The overall picture, whether based on census or on NSS data, is that Indian women's participation in the labour force is low compared to most other parts of Asia. Also, there exists a gap between the work participation rates of men and women in India. A comparison of 1981 and 1991 Census data reveals a slight increase in women's participation rates (from 19.67 per cent in 1981 to 22.73 per cent in 1991). For urban India, the overall work participation of women during the same period rose only marginally from 8.31 to 9.74 per cent (Deshpande & Deshpande, 1992). The size of the organised economic sector is small in the country and the participation of women in this sector is low and largely restricted to the urban areas. NSS data indicate only a marginal increase in urban women's work participation from 14.5 to 16.2 per cent between 1972–73 and 1987–88 (Acharya, 1996).

Despite a not too rosy national picture, there is a small yet numerically noticeable segment of educated, middle and upper middle class women from the metropolitan centres in the organised labour force. Acharya (1996) reported a significant increase in the number of women among professionals, administrators, and clerical staff between 1977–78 and 1987–88. This was partially facilitated by the overall sociopolitical changes, rising cost of living, feminist challenges to patriarchy, and comparatively better educational opportunities for girls than ever before. Some trends also point to a very small but growing number of women opting for non-traditional professions like engineering, commerce, management and marketing, hitherto considered male domains (Narsimha Reddy, 1979).

Towards New Families?

In the subsequent sections existing researches on women, work, and family are reviewed to examine the influence of women's work on family roles, relationships, and work distribution patterns. The major objective is to obtain evidence for "new families" that are more egalitarian and liberal in conjugal relationships, distribution of domestic responsibilities, and norms of gender role perceptions. The review of literature is restricted to a perusal of the following aspects of employed women's family life: (*a*) family decision-making patterns; (*b*) perception of sex roles; and (*c*) distribution of household responsibilities.

Women's Work and Family Decision-making

It was expected that wives' employment and consequent wage earn-ing capacity would be translated into increased decision-making power for them within the family. Traditionally, decision-making power rests with the eldest male or males in the Indian family and women may have very little say, especially on important matters related to finance, children's marriage, and future planning. Not many studies have analysed the patterns of decision-making in dual earner Indian families. Khanna and Verghese (1978) reported that working women's role in family decision-making did not differ ap-preciably from that of non-working women. Devi (1987), on the other hand, observed that the husband's decision-making power in dual earner homes was significantly lower than his counterpart's in single earner homes. In other words, husbands in dual earner families shared power with their wives thereby lowering their own position on the decision-making scale. Similar findings have been reported by R. Sinha and Prabhu (1988) among working women in Bihar. Some of the recent studies are more explicit on this aspect. Shukla (1987) compared single and dual earner couples in a city in north India on a decision-making scale that included items of both routine and specialised nature. She found that employed women played a greater role in decision-making in nearly all matters. She concluded, "When wives are employed, wives have more power, husbands have less, and marriages are more egalitarian than when wives are not employed" (p. 628). She interpreted these findings on the basis of Rodman's (1972) resource theory according to which employment, income, and education are treated as resources by husbands to bar-gain for greater power than their wives. In a more recent study Bharat (1992) also found that career women and their spouses shared decision-making power more than non-career women and their spouses. Thus, as expected, career women used their higher profes-sional status, income, and educational status as resources to bargain for more power. However, power sharing tended to be restricted to routine and seemingly less significant areas like choice of menu, inviting guests to parties, choice of movies, and recreation. In areas that were more important and crucial from a financial point of view like savings, property investments, and purchase of a vehicle or consumer goods (durables), the power balance tilted towards hus-band dominance. Thus, as reported by Scanzoni and Polonka (1980), although employed wives had power, they still enjoyed less power than their husbands especially in areas that entailed greater financial control.

Taken together, these findings indicated that for urban Indian women at least employment was helpful in increasing their role in the decision-making process. But as revealed by Bharat's (1992) study, it may not be uniform across all spheres of decision-making. In financial matters, husbands may still wield more power. It is, of course, not clear whether this is because wives are not given more power or because wives are conditioned to trust a male, be it their father or their husband, on such matters.

These results are not entirely surprising. Ramu (1989) observed that although conjugal sharing decision-making power is against the traditional orientations that shape sex roles in India, they may simply be continuations of what prevailed in joint family patterns where women shared power which few researchers are ready to acknowledge. According to him, in traditional societies women develop strategies to exercise power informally and are able to influence outcomes of critical domestic decisions. In nuclear families, on the other hand, women are already in a position to bargain and negotiate with their husbands in the absence of extended kin. In short, it is argued that greater egalitarian decision-making may not be explained solely by the wife's employment status.

Ursula Sharma's (1990) observations support this contention. According to her, it is difficult to trace a direct causal link between women's wage work and their personal autonomy and decision-making power as there are many factors influencing these. One such factor pointed out by Safilios-Rothschild (1982) is the extent to which men feel comfortable and confident in their breadwinner role. In Kenya, Greece, and Honduras she found that middle class men shared power with their wives because they had demonstrated their capacity to earn. Another factor identified by Standing (1991) in her study of working women in Calcutta is the meaning attached to marriage by the couple. In households where power is shared the ideology is often that of a "modern" marriage, in which women are considered as having equal rights to be earners and decision makers. Thus, in the Indian context greater sharing of power among dual earner couples may be because either the husbands do not feel threatened or they hold modern views or, as Ramu put it, Indian women have always managed to share power in family decision-making through their own unique strategies.

Perception of Gender Roles

While the family is recognised as a source of solidarity and support to individual members, it is also identified as a source of gender inequality. Male and female roles are segregated within the family, underpinned by an ideology of conjugal co-operation which favours men more than women.

In Indian society gender roles are rigid and strongly influence marital life. Husbands are accorded a superior status and wives are expected to treat them as their lord and master. Husbands are expected to earn for the family and take care of family needs while wives are supposed to "build" a home, fulfil their responsibilities as dutiful wives and nurturant mothers. Rao and Rao (1988), Sripat (1989), and Bharat (1994) reported that Indian women were primarily perceived in their traditional, that is, domestic, homemaking, and marital roles, while men were more often seen in their provider role.

Standing (1991) observed that the concept of men as supporters and women as economic dependents was deeply entrenched even in the case where wives shared earning responsibilities. For instance, while the women in her sample were willing to accept the idea of earning higher wages compared to their husbands, they were aware of its potential for conjugal conflict and admitted to feeling embarrassed at the idea, even if it was hypothetically stated. Men on their part not only felt threatened by their wife earning higher wages, but were also clearly sceptical of the possibility of their wife earning more.

Ramu (1989) and Bharat (1995) examined sex role perceptions among working couples. Both the studies used a similar procedure which involved ranking of nine role attributes, separately for men and women, from "most important" to "least important". These role attributes were grouped into four broad roles: domestic, provider, familial, and marital. Both these investigators found that despite their work status, working women were conservative in their perception of sex roles. They perceived their husband in the breadwinner role and themselves mainly in the homemaker role. Their husbands also held such conversative perceptions. In other words, both working women and their spouses continued to regard breadwinning as essentially a man's job and home management as a woman's. Employed women in Ramu's sample were the most conservative in their perceptions.

Bharat's study differed from Ramu's study in that it compared career women with non-career women. Their spouses, too, were compared. An interesting finding was that career women and their spouses appreciated the companionship role of each other which was at variance with the Indian ethos, but in their perception of the provider role and domestic role they were as traditional as the respondents in the non-career group.

These findings suggest that women's employment status has not been instrumental in altering the traditionally held gender role perceptions. Men continue to be perceived as providers and women as homemakers. Even career women, holding high profile jobs, fail to perceive themselves as earners and providers alongside their spouses.

Division of Household Labour

The division of domestic work is considered the litmus or acid test of couples' attitudes towards gender equality. Culturally, the Indian woman's place is her home and the label of "queen of the house" is meant to bind her to the interests of her husband and children. In Indian society a high premium is placed on a woman's capability to successfully manage her house and keep her husband and children happy. She is entrusted with all domestic responsibilities that are tiring, monotonous as well as burdensome.

There are a fair number of Indian studies on this aspect (for example, see Bharat, 1992; Chakraborty, 1978; Devi, 1987; Khanna & Verghese, 1978; Ramu, 1989; Rani 1976; Savara, 1986; Standing, 1991; Wadhera, 1976). The findings of these studies are fairly uniform indicating that women bear the major burden of household responsibilities regardless of their employment status. Women reported performing all the major household tasks along with their jobs outside the home resulting in a "double day", multiple roles and strains. Ramu's (1989) extensive study of domestic chores of working families revealed extremely traditional beliefs and practices. In terms of attitudes, the single earner couples were the most conservative as they believed that housework was essentially a woman's duty and that she had no right to claim her husband's help in it. The woman's earner status only partially influenced such traditional attitudes for, although dual earner couples largely agreed that housework should be shared between spouses, there were a few (40 per cent wives and 60 per cent husbands) who did not support this contention.

In behavioural terms, working women have failed to take any mileage out of their earner status for demanding a fair distribution of domestic responsibilities. Regardless of their job status, women continue to perform routine and burdensome household tasks without much support from their spouse or other family members. Ramu (1989) reported that working wives performed certain tasks just as much and for as long as non-working wives, excluding commuting time. Although a few husbands in dual earner families were conscious of their wives' double role burden, they did little to help out because they believed that domesticity was a part of a woman's social obligation to her family that gave her a meaning and purpose in life. Further, it was observed that not only did husbands not extend any help, but also women did not demand help for they believed that it was right for men not to help in housework. In short, despite the woman's role as earner, working couples continued to adhere to their traditional attitudes and behaviour regarding gender based housework.

Standing (1991) reported that the household division of labour was one between female members or between female members and domestic servants, but not between female and male members of the house. Consequently, employed mothers shouldered the heaviest burden of household work. Husbands and sons were largely of no help except in casual and sporadic ways. Although most of the women respondents strongly felt that men should share housework, their explanations for men's nonparticipation revealed that men's time was valued differently from women's time by both women and men. Even when they themselves were hard-pressed for time, women stated that their husbands had no "time" to contribute to household work.

Bharat (1992) obtained similar findings for career and non-career women. The former were expected to be better able to negotiate sharing of domestic chores on account of their higher educational, income, and job status which are resources men use to bargain for more power. However, among all working couples domestic duties were unevenly distributed with routine, burdensome and time consuming tasks like cooking falling within the wives' domain. Husbands "shared" certain outdoor tasks that were either infrequent like repairs or not as burdensome like operating bank accounts.

Conclusion

The findings reported here do not provide any definite evidence of the emergence of "new families" as a result of urban Indian women's participation in the workforce. Though decision-making patterns are more egalitarian in dual earner homes compared to single earner homes, it is clear that decision-making may still be dominated by husbands in crucial matters concerning money investments and long-term financial planning. Women's employment status has failed to help couples change their gender role perceptions in nontraditional ways. Both employed wives and their husbands continued to perceive women mainly in domestic roles and men mainly in provider roles. Thus, despite having a "co-provider" status, women prefer to perceive themselves in their traditional roles of homemaker, mother, and wife and accord the provider status to their husbands. The husbands of employed women, too, perceive their "earner" wives in conservative terms as they attach greater importance to their domestic roles than to their provider role. Above all, women's employment status has not led to an equal and fair distribution of domestic responsibilities, the most crucial indicator of couples' liberal attitude towards gender equality. Regardless of wives' employed status, domestic responsibilities continue to be shouldered by women and perceived as their primary duty in life.

Several factors help explain why women's work status in India has not changed family roles and relationships in the direction of egalitarian norms and values. These factors are firmly embedded in the sociocultural reality of Indian society which is hierarchically arranged and in the complex network of family bonds and obligations in which women's position is governed by a set of traditional values and patriarchal norms. Ramu (1989) identified some structural conditions which perpetuate contradictory values leading to personal dilemmas for women and societal ambiguity towards their changing roles. These conditions are contradictory values and norms regarding women's status, poor implementation of social and legal reforms designed to benefit women, and women's low literacy rate. The findings have to be interpreted in the light of the overpowering influence of traditional beliefs and expectations about sex roles and marital patterns in contemporary Indian society. While social, legal, and economic reforms have helped women in a small measure to join the workforce, the continuing influence of normative attitudes and values have prevented them from altering society's and their own perceptions of sex roles and demand an equal distribution of domestic responsibilities. In other words, working couples have to give up these conservative attitudes and norms of gender roles and acknowledge the significance of wives' earner role. Until then the emergence of "new families" based on egalitarian norms may seem a distant reality.

❦ ELEVEN ❦

Leadership Research

Basic Assumptions, Modal Orientations and Future Directions

❦ R.N. Kanungo ❦ J.A. Conger ❦

Introduction

The study of leadership as a group and organisational phenomenon has been the focus of both theoretical and empirical analysis for over half a century (Bass, 1990a; Bennis & Nanus, 1985; Burns, 1978; Hollander, 1978). Literally thousands of articles, papers, and books on the topic have examined and probed the leadership phenomenon from every conceivable angle and have revealed its complexity. As in the case of any complex social psychological phenomenon, in spite of decades of research, understanding of this topic remains incomplete. Commenting on the state of knowledge in 1959, Bennis (1959) wrote,

> of all the hazy and confounding areas in social psychology, leadership theory undoubtedly contends for top nomination. And, ironically, probably more has been written and less known about leadership than about any other topic in the behavioral sciences. Always, it seems the concept of leadership eludes us or turns up in another form to taunt us again with its slipperiness and complexity... (pp. 259–260).

After more than three decades following Bennis' assessment, the situation has not changed much. Commenting on the "leadership mystique", Kets de Vries (1994) observed,

> As far as leadership studies go, it seems that more and more has been studied about less and less, to end up ironically with a

group of researchers studying everything about nothing. It prompted one wit to say recently that reading the current world literature is rather like going through the Parisian telephone directory while trying to read it in Chinese! (p. 73).

Social scientists of many persuasions such as political scientists (Burns, 1978; Wilner, 1984), sociologists (Bradley, 1987; Roberts, 1985), organisation theorists (Nadler & Tushman, 1990; Pfeffer, 1977), psychoanalysts (Kets de Vries, 1994; Zaleznik, 1990), and psychologists (Bass, 1990a; Hollander & Offermann, 1990) have contributed to the enigmatic nature of the leadership phenomenon by proposing various analytical frameworks and focusing on different content and process aspects of leadership in a range of contexts. Very often, these multidisciplinary approaches have spoken different languages specific to their own disciplines and have presented varying levels of analyses (micro and macro, individual and interactional, process and structure, etc.) while explaining the constructs and processes related to the phenomenon. The resulting diverse analytical treatments (see Bryman, 1986; Hunt, Baliga, Dachler, & Schriesheim, 1988; Yukl, 1989) and empirical attempts have provided conflicting evidence on the role of leadership in organisational and group performance and as a result have clouded one's understanding of the phenomenon. One is reminded of a certain Sufi story where several blind individuals were asked to describe an elephant. The problem was that the elephant was covered by a large drape. Finding openings in the drape, they touched the different parts and described the elephant in terms of the part they were able to touch. Some said that it was a firm, round cylinder (the leg), or a flexible, hairy wand (the tail), or a large, soft flap (the ear). None of them was able to comprehend the elephant in its entirety.

Given this situation, at a conceptual level, researchers have faced great difficulty in developing integrative and comprehensive frameworks for an understanding of the leadership phenomenon. At the empirical level, the ambiguity of research findings has led some to even question the usefulness of research endeavours in the leadership area. Researchers in the areas of both psychology and management (Fiedler & Chemers, 1984; House, 1988; Kerr & Jermier, 1978; Pfeffer, 1977), have debated the issue of what are the critical properties and processes of the leadership phenomenon. They have tried to establish the empirical validity of the leadership construct by asking whether or not leadership makes a difference in explaining and predicting organisational and group success or failure. Such attempts have neither produced a unifying and comprehensive theoretical framework (Bryman, 1986), nor have they succeeded unequivocally in linking leadership to organisational and group performance at an empirical level (A.B. Thomas, 1988). Hence, there exist several splinter theories of leadership and numerous empirical studies within each camp. Many have described this state of affairs as a "crisis in leadership research" (Hunt, Baliga, Dachler, & Schriesheim, 1988, p. 243).

From this discussion, it should not be inferred that previous research on the leadership phenomenon has been totally fruitless. Likewise, it would be wrong to infer that research pursuits in the area should be abandoned because of the existing "crisis" or because of the complex and enigmatic nature of the phenomenon. Rather, the phenomenal complexity and the elusive character of the leadership construct should be seen as enhancing one's knowledge. In essence, it is a challenge for the social scientist whose major task is to describe and unravel the mysteries underlying such a social phenomenon. This is particularly true for social and organisational psychologists whose objective is to study behavioural processes in groups and organisations of which the leadership process forms an essential part.

The purpose here is not to get embroiled in the controversy of whether one should study the leadership phenomenon at all because of its elusive nature. It is our contention that "the romance of leadership" in groups and organisations and among both researchers and management practitioners is too strong to deny its legitimate status as a behavioural phenomenon to be studied scientifically (Hogan, Curphy, & Hogan, 1994; House, 1988; Meindl, Ehrlich, & Dukerich, 1985). We also agree with House's (1988) assertion that critics of leadership research often "misinterpret the current state of leadership knowledge" and "underestimate the amount of knowledge produced to date" (p. 248). Accepting the importance of the existing knowledge and continuing scientific research on leadership for a better understanding of the phenomenon, it is not the intention here to provide an exhaustive review of the vast psychological literature on the topic. Such reviews exist elsewhere (Bass, 1990a; Yukl, 1989). Rather, the aim of this paper is to enhance one's understanding of the leadership phenomenon by seeking answers to questions such as what has one learned from the earlier leadership debates in psychological literature, on what issues do most researchers agree, and what directions should leadership research in psychology follow in the future. Though leadership research has encompassed many disciplines such as anthropology, sociology, and political science, the focus here will be on the social and organisational psychology perspective. Thus, the objective is fourfold: first, to identify some basic assumptions underlying leadership theory and research; second, to indicate the modal orientations in leadership paradigms reflected in the writings of social and organisational psychologists; third, to assess the limitations of the existing leadership paradigms; and fourth, to suggest a shift of focus from the study of the conventional leadership parameters to the study of parameters largely ignored so far by psychologists.

Basic Assumptions

All volitional acts in response to an environment are guided by one's assumptions about the nature of that environment. Research activities are no exception. While exploring a behavioural phenomenon, researchers' theoretical and investigative strategies are to a large extent directed by their assumptions about the nature of the phenomenon. Often controversies and misunderstandings among researchers stem from a lack of realisation of their differences with respect to these implicit assumptions. To avoid a possible misunderstanding while attempting to identify the modal orientations in leadership research, the paper begins by explicitly stating a set of commonly held assumptions about the leadership phenomenon among psychologists.

First, researchers in social and organisational psychology have come to accept leadership as an organisational or equal group phenomenon. The phenomenon is observed as a set of role behaviours on the part of an individual (called the "leader") in a group or organisation when there is a need for influencing and coordinating the activities of group members to achieve a common goal. Thus, instead of studying leadership as a cluster of stable personality traits in isolation from their context (as attempted by early trait studies, see Cowley, 1928), leadership is today viewed as a set of role behaviours by individuals in the context of the group or organisation to which they belong. Thus, as Cartwright and Zander (1968) pointed out, "leadership consists of such actions by group members as those which aid in setting group goals, moving the group toward its goals, improving the quality of interactions among the members, building cohesiveness of the group, and making resources available to the group" (p. 304).

From this description of leadership as a set of role behaviours in a group context follows the assumption that leadership is both relational and an attributional phenomenon. The existence of a leader depends upon the existence of one or more followers and the kind of status or power relationship that develops between them. However, it is the followers' perception of a leader's behaviour, their acceptance of his or her influence attempts, and the subsequent attribution of leadership status to the individual that give rise to the identification of the leadership phenomenon. Without followers' perceptions, acceptance and attributions, the phenomenon would simply cease to exist.

Third, it is commonly assumed that while studying the phenomenon, one can reveal both its contents (i.e., what behaviours leadership roles represent, what attributes leaders, followers and situational contexts possess when the phenomenon is observed), and its processes (what kinds of social influence processes are in operation, what psychological dynamics underlie such processes). Thus, leadership implies exercising influence over others by utilising various bases of social power, reinforcers, tacts, etc., in order to elicit the compliance and commitment of group members to achieve group objectives. Leadership also involves manifestation of properties of individual leaders, followers, and situations. Often these properties refer to sets of role behaviours of leaders that serve to achieve the group's objectives by influencing the attitudes and behaviours of other group members. The properties of followers and situations (task, social climate, etc.) that facilitate or hinder the manifestation of the leadership phenomenon can also be identified.

This distinction of content and process in leadership research leads to a further assumption that in order to understand the leadership phenomenon, one must analyse properties of the three basic elements — the leader, the followers, and the situational context — and the three major relational processes — the leader–follower influence process, the leader–follower relational process, and the context–follower relational process (see Conger & Kanungo, 1988c, for this type of analysis of charismatic leadership).

This leads to the final assumption. The role behaviours of a leader are intended to directly influence the followers' attitudes and behaviour within the group or organisational context. Thus, leadership effectiveness should be measured in terms of the degree to which a leader promotes (*a*) instrumental attitudes and behaviours for the achievement of group objectives, (*b*) followers' satisfaction with the task and context within which they operate, and (*c*) acceptance of the leader's influence which is often manifested through the followers' emotional bond with the leader, attributions of favourable qualities to the leader, and compliance behaviour. Instead, more often leadership effectiveness is measured in terms of group or organisational productivity. As Yukl (1989, p. 6) pointed out,

> the most commonly used measure of leader effectiveness is the extent to which the leader's group or organization performs its task successfully and attains its goals. In some cases, objective measures of performance or goal attainment are available, such as profit growth, profit margin, sales increase, market share, sales relative to targeted sales, return on investment, productivity, cost per unit or output, costs in relation to budgeted expenditures, and so on.

Since these objective indices of group or organisation level productivity depend not only on the followers' instrumental behaviour, but also on the available environmental resources, technology, market conditions, etc., over which the leader has little control, these are not appropriate measures of a leader's influence.

Modal Orientations

The modal orientation of previous leadership research in both social and organisational psychology attempted to address three specific issues related to ways of viewing leadership and leadership effectiveness constructs. First, concern for understanding the "leadership" construct led to the research issue identifying *leader role behaviours* in group contexts. A similar concern for understanding the nature of leadership effectiveness led to the second and third issues. Specifically, the second research issue dealt with the task of identifying the *contingencies for leadership effectiveness* through the study of the interactions between the leader, the follower, and the situational context. The third issue focused on understanding the nature of leadership effectiveness by analysing the underlying mechanisms of the *leader–follower process* itself. Each of these three modal trends will be briefly discussed in the following.

LEADER ROLE BEHAVIOUR Early research studies aimed at identifying leadership role behaviours by examining small formal and informal groups in both laboratory and field settings. These investigations (Bales & Slater, 1955; Cartwright & Zander, 1968; Fleishman, Harris, & Burtt, 1955; Halpin & Winer, 1952) converged on the thesis that leadership role behaviours are functionally related to two broad objectives: group maintenance and group task achievement. A group member in an informal group or an appointed leader in a formal group is perceived to be acting as a leader when he or she engages in group maintenance and/or task goal achievement-type activities. Following this lead, later studies of supervision and leadership in organisations (Yukl, 1989) identified two major leadership roles: a consideration or people orientation (social role), and an initiating structure or task orientation (task role). The first consideration orientation reflects social–emotional leadership: "the degree to which the leader's behavior towards group members is characterized by mutual trust, development of good relations, sensitivity to the feelings of group members, and openness to their suggestions" (Andriessen & Drenth, 1984, p. 489). The second initiating structure reflects task-oriented leadership: "the degree to which a leader is bent on defining and structuring the various tasks and roles of group members in order to attain group results" (Andreissen & Drenth, 1984, p. 489). The two dimensional approach greatly influenced management practice as evidenced by the popularity of leadership training programmes such as the management grid (Blake & Mouton, 1964).

CONTINGENCIES OF LEADERSHIP EFFECTIVENESS The second research issue, identification of conditions or contingencies of leadership effectiveness, has also been studied in small groups in both laboratory and field settings. Expanding upon the earlier constructs of leader role behaviours, Fiedler (1967) put forward the notion that a particular leader attribute (such as initiating structure versus consideration or Fiedler's operational measures of low and high LPC) was contingent upon the situational context for its effectiveness. In certain situations with certain types of tasks and follower attitudes, initiating structure would be more effective than consideration and vice versa. In a related approach, Kerr and Jermier (1978) identified two kinds of situational factors referred to as substitutes or neutralisers of leadership influence on subordinates. Their "substitutes for leadership" specify a set of characteristics of followers, tasks, and organisational contexts that reduce or nullify the effects of relationship and task-oriented leadership roles.

Building upon the classic studies of autocratic and democratic leadership by Lewin and his associates (Lewin, Lippitt, & White, 1939; Lippitt & White, 1947), another stream of contingency theorists emerged. These researchers explored the effects of autocratic, consultative, and participative leadership behaviour on the effectiveness of a leader in achieving group objectives, be they people or task related. Their findings published in both social psychological and organisational behaviour literature (Coch & French, 1948; Likert, 1961; McGregor, 1960; Tannenbaum & Schmidt, 1958; Vroom & Yetton, 1973) revealed that the extent to which a leader involved followers in the decision-making process was a critical factor in leadership effectiveness. Using a continuum of styles from autocratic to consultative to participative, they identified their appropriateness depending upon the situational characteristics involving both tasks and followers.

LEADER – FOLLOWER INFLUENCE PROCESS The third research issue delved into the question of how leaders become effective in their influence attempts or what are the psychological mechanisms that account for the linkage between leaders' role behaviour and the elicitation of followers' compliance and commitment to achieving group or organisational objectives. These questions were explored from three different theoretical perspectives: (*a*) the bases of social power (Dahl, 1957; French & Raven, 1959), (*b*) the nature of social change (Blau, 1974; Hollander, 1979), and (*c*) motivational dynamics (Evans, 1970; House, 1971; Luthans & Kreitner, 1975).

Exploring the reasons for leadership power and influence, Cartwright (1965) stated that leadership effectiveness stems from followers' perception that leaders possess and control resources valued by followers. Control over such resources forms the bases of power (Dahl, 1957) of leaders. Most studies of leadership effectiveness that have adopted this perspective (Kanungo, 1977; Student, 1968), however, have utilised French and Raven's (1959) formulation of five kinds of resources that form the bases of social power such as reward, coercive, legal, expert, and referent power bases. The first three bases of social power are often assumed to stem from one's formal authority position within a group or an organisation. Hence, they are referred to as position power bases. The last two, expert and referent power bases, are considered as inherent in the leader's idiosyncratic ways of influencing followers. Hence, they are called personal or idiosyncratic power bases.

The second theoretical perspective which seeks to explain leadership influence makes use of social exchange theory (Blau, 1974) in human interactions. Leaders gain status and influence over group members in return for demonstrating task competence and loyalty to the group. Hollander and Offermann (1990) termed this type of explanation as "a process-oriented transactional approach to leadership.... It emphasizes the implicit social exchange or transaction over time that exists between the leaders and followers, including reciprocal influence and interpersonal perception" (p. 181). Using this approach, Hollander (1958; 1986) advanced the "idiosyncratic credit" model of leadership that explains why the innovative ideas of leaders gain acceptance among followers. According to this model, leaders earn such credits from followers' perceptions of their leaders' competence and loyalty. A leader can then utilise such credits (or trust on the part of followers) to influence followers' compliance and commitment to innovative goals.

Finally, leaders' influence on followers has also been explained by analysing the motivational processes governing follower satisfaction and performance. A path-goal theory of leadership was first proposed by Evans (1970) and later advanced by House (1971) using the expectancy theory of motivation to account for leadership effectiveness. According to House and his associates (House & Dessler, 1974; House & Mitchell, 1974), each of the four types of leadership role behaviour such as directive, achievement-oriented, supportive, and participative, influences followers by increasing the personal payoffs to them for group accomplishments and "making the path to these payoffs easier to travel by clarifying it, reducing roadblocks and pitfalls, and increasing the opportunities for personal satisfaction en route" (House, 1971, p. 324). Similar motivational explanations for the effectiveness of various leadership activities have been offered by Oldham (1976), when he observed that leadership activities such as rewarding, setting goals, and designing job and feedback systems heighten followers' motivation. Other researchers (Podsakoff, Todor, & Skov, 1982; Sims, 1977) have explained leadership effectiveness in terms of the behaviour modification principles of contingent reinforcement. Maintaining influence over followers through the use of contingent reinforcement has also been interpreted as a form of transactional leadership (Avolio & Bass, 1988).

To summarise, these modal trends have led to a focus on three major leadership role dimensions: people concern (relationship orientation, consideration, supportive, etc.), task concern (work facilitation, initiating structure, goal emphasis, achievement orientation, etc.), and concern for making and implementing decisions (interaction facilitation, consultative, directive, autocratic, democratic, etc.). These specific role dimensions have been studied in the situational context involving varied characteristics of three distinct elements: tasks, followers, groups or organisations. Most contingency theories of leadership consider these three elements as possible contingencies for understanding leadership effectiveness. Finally, the nature of the leader–follower influence process is also understood in terms of the three theoretical perspectives: control over valued resources, social exchange processes, and motivational dynamics. During the last quarter of a century, leadership contingency models dealing with the three behaviour dimensions, the three situational elements, and the three classes of explanations have dominated scientific literature both in the East (Misumi, 1988; J.B.P. Sinha, 1980) and the West (Fiedler, 1967; Heller, 1971; House, 1971; Vroom & Yetton, 1973).

Limitations of Modal Orientations

Recently, however, these leadership models have been viewed as too narrow and sterile (Hunt, 1984). There has been disappointment about their failure to move beyond the simple social versus task dimensions, or autocratic versus participative dimension which underpinned the work of early theorists (Bryman, 1986). Of greater significance, they ignore certain core aspects of leadership role behaviour, such as a leader's articulation of a future vision, or the formulation of goals for followers, or the building of trust and credibility in the minds of followers which develops commitment to future goals beyond day-to-day routine compliance.

The narrowness of the existing theories and research on leadership is also reflected in the inadequate attention to the study of followers' behaviour, their perceptions and motivations in following their leaders. As Hollander and Offermann (1990) noted, "Although the study of leadership has always presumed the existence of followers, their roles were viewed as essentially passive" (p. 182). Thus, there is a need for follower centred approaches to the study of leadership.

Such narrowness of the existing models stems from the research strategies employed to understand the phenomenon. Three sources are principally responsible. First, these models are chiefly based on small groups. When leadership is studied in small groups whether in a laboratory or in organisations, certain elements of leadership as observed in large corporations or in religious, social, and political organisations (such as the formulation of a mission or a strategic vision) are omitted. Second, studies of supervision in organisations have always treated follower attitudes and behaviours as dependent variables, rather than as antecedents or explanations for the leadership phenomenon. Consequently, follower centred approaches to the understanding of the leadership phenomenon were neglected.

Third, most leadership studies in the organisational context have been in actuality studies of supervision or day-to-day routine maintenance rather than true leadership as observed in society. The core element of supervision or managership is the effective maintenance of the status quo, whereas a core element of leadership is effectively bringing about improvements, changes and transformations in the existing system and in its members.

In organisational behaviour literature, several scholars (Jago, 1982; Mintzberg, 1982; Zaleznik, 1977) have acknowledged the distinction between "leadership" and "managership", and yet the distinction has neither been seriously considered by researchers nor been sharply delineated for developing future research agendas. If it is to be taken seriously, it is imperative that the focus of leadership research shifts from the current preoccupation with supervisory or managerial styles (task, people, participative orientations) to the study of other behaviour dimensions such as visioning, articulating a vision, and developing strategies to achieve the vision which are observed in leaders who bring about profound changes in their organisations and in their members (Bass, 1990b; Conger & Kanungo, 1988a). Likewise, follower centred approaches with an emphasis on followers' perceptions and attributions in the leader–follower dynamics be paid greater attention (Hollander & Offermann, 1990). This type of paradigm shift (Hunt, 1984) has already begun as reflected in the recent emergence of interest in charismatic and transformational leadership (Bass, 1985; Burns, 1978; Conger, 1989; Conger & Kanungo, 1987; House, 1977), and followers' attributions and the empowerment process (Conger & Kanungo, 1988c; Hollander & Offermann, 1990; Thomas & Velthouse, 1990).

Emerging Frontiers in Leadership Research

To examine the new frontiers of leadership research, we will draw upon the three categories we employed to explore earlier research efforts: (*a*) leader role behaviour dimensions, (*b*) contingencies for leadership effectiveness, and (*c*) leadership influence processes.

LEADER ROLE BEHAVIOUR Beginning with the leader role dimension, there is a need to move beyond the task, social, and participative roles to those identified in the recent work on charismatic and transformational leadership (Bass, 1985; Bennis & Nanus, 1985; Conger, 1989; Conger & Kanungo, 1988d; House, 1977; House, Splangler, & Woycke, 1991; Shamir, House, & Arthur, 1989). Specifically, earlier research had underemphasised the complexity of two of the important dimensions of the leadership process as defined by Cartwright and Zander, "setting group goals, moving the group toward its goals" (1968, p. 304). Research on charismatic/transformational leadership has focused particular attention on these areas in terms of role behaviours. For example, recent investigations of strategic vision in management literature have directed attention to the leader's role in setting group goals at the organisational level. While there is agreement on the significance of this role behaviour (Bass, 1985; Bennis & Nanus, 1985; Conger & Kanungo, 1988a; House, 1977; Sashkin, 1988; Shamir, House, & Arthur, 1989; Westley & Mintzberg, 1988), the actual process of strategic visioning as a behavioural process is poorly understood. Two polar positions are generally prevalent. One argues that the process is deliberate, rational, and therefore trainable (Sashkin, 1988). The other considers visioning by the leader as a more complex, emergent process (Conger, 1989; Westley & Mintzberg, 1988). These distinct positions raise several interesting research questions: (*a*) whether strategic visioning is indeed deliberate or emergent or both, (b) whether it may be possible for both deliberate and emergent visioning processes to occur simultaneously, and (c) whether under certain contextual conditions one process is more appropriate and feasible than the other. Unfortunately, not much is known about this critical aspect of leader role behaviour and it calls for more sustained and encompassing research attention.

The second area for exploration in terms of leader role behaviour involves "moving the group toward its goals". The literature on charismatic/transformational leadership reveals that there is a consensus on the leader behaviour characteristics that appear to be helpful: (a) emotional expressiveness, (b) articulation skills, (c) high activity level, and (d) exemplary modelling behaviour (Conger & Kanungo, 1988b; House, 1977). These behavioural attributes facilitate trust, provide direction, and stimulate motivation in followers to achieve the vision for the group. There is also some degree of agreement on the unconventional behaviour and risk taking activities of leaders affecting followers' acceptance and attribution of leadership (Conger & Kanungo, 1988b). In general, however, there is scant knowledge of the exact nature of these leadership dynamics or how and when these leader behaviours influence followers' attitudes and behaviours and it calls for greater research attention.

CONTINGENCIES OF LEADERSHIP EFFECTIVENESS Within this context of charismatic/transformational leadership roles, one can also examine the contingencies of leadership effectiveness when effectiveness is measured in terms of transformational (as opposed to transactional) influence on followers. At least three categories of contingencies need to be explored in future research: the task context, the follower characteristics, and the social–cultural environment within which the leader operates. The task context within which a leader sets group goals or formulates a vision as a future target for the group to achieve can act as an important contingency for leadership effectiveness. There may be certain contextual conditions that are more ideal, or at least, more helpful in facilitating the charismatic/ transformational leadership process. For instance, a context in crisis or one with important shortcomings may heighten the leader's attractiveness and influence. Some scholars believe that the leader may play an active, if not primary, role in creating a belief among followers that a contextual crisis exists in order to achieve leadership effectiveness. For example, Conger and Kanungo (1988a) argued that charismatic leaders, because of their intolerance of the status quo, tend to quickly identify and exaggerate existing deficiencies in the environment and articulate these to their subordinates. Such leaders are sensitive to shortcomings and are able to discern how environmental constraints frustrate followers' needs. Thus, the identification of a crisis in the task context is partly due to deficiencies in the status quo and partly determined by the way in which charismatic leaders relate to their context. In other words, a crisis situation is exploited by the leader, and to some extent, the situation is the result of the leader's own actions and behaviour. Further research on the dynamics of how the task context acts as a contingency is needed. Both theoretical development and empirical verification of how, why, and when leaders identify and articulate crises and deficiencies in their environment need to be part of the future research agenda.

Besides "crisis" in the task context, leadership effectiveness can also be influenced by the leader's perception of unexplored positive opportunities in the larger environment. As already mentioned, a leader's transformational influence may be enhanced when the leader identifies or articulates a crisis in the status quo, but at the same time he or she may also identify a potential opportunity in the environment and articulate an inspiring future vision that plays upon that opportunity. Depending on the emphasis the leader places while relating to the context (either on the status quo or on the vision), his or her influence could be characterised as a crisis or ideological influence. More work is needed to examine the extent to which crises and opportunities in the context are used by leaders to foster their influence.

From the viewpoint of follower characteristics as possible contingencies, there are two important issues that require immediate attention — first, the process of leadership attribution by followers, and second, the dispositional characteristics of the followers themselves. Starting with the first issue, it is obvious that in order to be effective as a leader one must first be recognised as such. This recognition or attribution of leadership status is an important measure of leadership effectiveness. Given its importance in understanding the leadership process, it is ironic that so little is known about it. As Calder (1977) argued, leadership is a label which followers attribute to leaders performing certain behaviours. The followers' "belief that a certain leadership quality produces a certain behavior (which) is transformed into the expectation that an instance of the behavior implies the existence of quality" (1977, p. 198). Calder (1977), and Meindl, Ehrlich, and Dukerich (1985) stimulated thinking on the mechanics of this leadership attribution process itself. The implications for future research are that there is a need to examine the factors that followers consider when attributing outcomes to leadership and specifically to a particular form of leadership such as charismatic or transformational. Bryman (1986), however, argued that experimental and quantitative approaches to the study of this issue may be premature. More suitable are qualitative approaches at this stage as they may more fully capture the range of criteria that followers take into account when accepting and attributing leadership status to the leader. There is, however, limited understanding of the circumstances and the processes by which "leadership" is invoked as an explanation in followers' minds.

The second issue of follower characteristics that calls for further research is the possibility that certain dispositional attributes may enhance the receptivity and commitment of followers to a leader and as such leadership effectiveness. For example, various studies in charismatic/transformational literature have indicated that certain follower predispositions may in part be responsible for behavioural outcomes such as a high level of emotional commitment to the leader, heightened motivation, willing obedience to the leader, greater group cohesion, and a sense of empowerment (Conger & Kanungo, 1988b). They have hypothesised that charismatic leaders have followers who tend to be submissive and dependent (Downtown, 1973). Low self-esteem and strong feelings of uncertainty are believed to characterise these individuals and in turn foster a receptiveness to the self-confident and directive charismatic leader (Galanter, 1982; Lodahl, 1982). Directly related to the issue of dispositions are the psychological and behavioural outcomes of charismatic leadership on followers. Research has indicated that charismatic leadership can induce in followers trust and obedience to the leader, a willingness to accept, and an enthusiastic commitment to the leader's mission. Some of these may have negative outcomes as evidenced by Conger's (1990) discussion of the liabilities of followership. Both of these issues require further empirical investigation.

A consideration of the followers' perceptions of the context as possible contingencies of charismatic/transformational leadership effectiveness suggests that when followers experience psychological distress, transformational influence is facilitated. In other words, when the context evokes feelings of high uncertainty (Conger, 1985), helplessness, powerlessness, and alienation (Kanungo, 1982) among followers, conditions become ripe for a leader's influence within the organisation. Followers become "charisma hungry" when they experience a loss of control over their environment, or when their needs and expectations are frustrated because of perceived environmental barriers and threats, or when they see an uncertain future, or when they experience an identity crisis because of a state of anomie (decline of old values and rituals). Iacocca's charismatic influence on Chrysler's employees can be partly explained by the way that Chrysler employees perceived their context. They perceived significant future uncertainty (fear of company bankruptcy and loss of job) which led to psychological distress and consequently made them more susceptible to Iacocca's influence.

Both Bass (1985) and Kets de Vries (1988) discussed perceived anomie, upheaval, and crisis in the environment leading to a sense of helplessness and regressive forms of follower behaviour, such as unquestioning and blind trust in the leader. However, the psychological processes underlying helplessness (Garber & Seligman, 1980) and alienation (Kanungo, 1982), and the identification of specific organisational conditions (Martinko & Gardner, 1982) that promote such psychological states among followers have received little attention. Future studies should explore this issue in greater depth.

Finally, in the literature on leadership effectiveness, there has been little emphasis on culture as a contingency variable with few exceptions (J.B.P. Sinha, 1980). There are innumerable cultural dynamics that influence the leadership process (Kanungo & Conger, 1989). For example, followers are more likely to attribute leadership to an individual when they perceive his or her leadership behaviour to be culturally appropriate and in congruence with their own cultural values. Thus, in a traditional organisational or national culture that subscribes to conservative modes of behaviour among its members and the use of conventional means to achieve organisational objectives, leaders who engage in excessive unconventional behaviour may be viewed more as deviants than charismatic or transformational leaders. Further, individuals in leadership positions whose visions do not incorporate important values and lack relevance for the organisational culture are unlikely to be attributed leadership status. Certain behavioural components may be more critical and effective sources for attributions of leadership in some organisational or cultural contexts than in others. The relative importance and specific characteristics of a particular behaviour category will most probably differ from one cultural context to the other. For example, different cultures will have distinct modes of articulation, vision formulation, and impression management. Explorations of these variations are critical for identifying leadership effectiveness in different cultures.

LEADERSHIP INFLUENCE PROCESSES With respect to the third issue of leadership influence mechanisms, we find that transactional or social exchange approaches to leadership have been extensively explored (Hollander, 1964; 1978; Hollander & Offermann, 1990). What needs to be understood at this point are the mechanisms of the transformational effects of leadership on followers as there is limited understanding of these influence dynamics.

Explanations for why and how leaders exert transformational influence on followers who in turn develop and maintain their emotional involvement with a leader principally come from two sources: social psychological theories of influence processes (French & Raven, 1959; Kelman, 1958) and Freudian theories of ego defense mechanisms (Freud, 1946). For example, Conger and Kanungo (1988a) proposed that the charismatic leader–follower relationship is one of referent power (French & Raven, 1959) where followers accept the leader's influence primarily because they like the leader and identify with him or her. Howell (1988) explained the relationship in terms of both identification and internationalisation using Kelman's (1958) theory of social influence. Shamir, House, and Arthur (1989) postulated that transformational leaders influence through implicating the self-concept of followers. They increase the intrinsic value of efforts and goals by linking them to important aspects of the followers' self-concepts. From the Freudian perspective, a psychological process involving unconscious tendencies has been elaborated by Kets de Vries (1988). Followers try to resolve the conflict between who they are and what they wish to become by projecting their ego ideals on to the leader, and thereby make the leader their own conscience. The leader thus gains influence by being a model of what followers consciously or unconsciously wish for themselves (Downton, 1973). These explanations, however, remain at a speculative level and require empirical validation in future research.

Another area of significant debate centres on the leader's power orientation and its impact on influence tactics. House (1977) proposed that charismatic leaders possess a high need for power which in turn motivates them to assume the leader role. Drawing upon McClelland's (1975) work on socialised and personalised power, some researchers have argued that charismatic/transformational leaders who are high in self-serving activity inhibition become "socialised leaders" expressing their need for power through socially constructive behaviour and that it is only through this behaviour that the transformational influence process is able to take effect. While other leaders low in activity inhibition become "personalised leaders" who express and satisfy their need for power through personally dominant and authoritarian behaviour negating the transformational influence process (Howell, 1988). This position (Conger & Kanungo, 1988b), however, has been challenged. We believe that this conceptualisation of charismatic leadership in terms of power orientations calls for further exploration before any definite conclusions can be drawn.

A second area of the influence dimension that deserves further study is the process of empowerment. In the discussion of modal orientations, three mechanisms for explaining leadership influence were identified, all of which explain the transactional nature of the leadership influence process. There is a need to go beyond these to explain the charismatic/transformational influence process. Empowerment is one important area for explaining such influence. Traditionally, empowerment has been viewed more as a transactional process of sharing power and resources. Several researchers (Conger & Kanungo, 1988c; Thomas & Velthouse, 1990), however, have argued that the empowerment process be viewed as a process of enabling followers through the enhancement of their personal self-efficacy beliefs and intrinsic task motivation. Viewed in this way, leadership influence is a process of transforming followers' self-concepts and attitudes toward the task and goal set for the group. Thomas and Velthouse's (1990) model of empowerment defined around increased intrinsic task motivation suggests that critical to the process of empowerment is an understanding of workers' interpretive styles and global beliefs. However, their hypothesis has yet to be verified. Likewise, the nature and mechanisms underlying the empowerment process as suggested by the self-efficacy model proposed by Conger and Kanungo (1988c) need to be empirically validated.

Finally, the transformational influence process that results in follower empowerment is largely influenced by the leader's altruistic motives and ethical conduct (Kanungo & Conger, 1993; Kanungo & Mendonca, 1994) in the organisational context. Future research should explore the roles of altruism and morality as the basis of transformational leadership influences.

Conclusion

In conclusion, the general field of leadership research needs to be studied along both content and process dimensions. In the area of content dimensions, there is a need for a shift in focus from supervisory/managerial behaviour (e.g., consideration, task, participation) to leadership behaviour (e.g., visioning, goal setting, empowering). As well, there needs to be an additional shift in research focus from followers' need satisfaction to attributional, dispositional, and perceptual dynamics. Third, research attention needs to be redirected from the exclusive preoccupation with specific task characteristics in small groups to the study of the larger context within which tasks are accomplished. This should also include a study of cultural variables as possible contingencies. Along process dimensions, earlier research had emphasised largely the transactional influence processes. Future research must be directed towards exploring the basis of transformational influence. A significant challenge awaits leadership research.

❧ TWELVE ❧

East and West in Harmony

A Glimpse of Managerial Practices Among Chinese Corporations in Hong Kong

❧ Henry S.R. Kao ❧ Ng Sek Hong ❧

Introduction

The purpose of this paper is to argue that the celebrated traditions of the Chinese "mandarins" and their scholarly flair have been an important legacy shaping the managerial philosophy and practices adopted and propounded by corporate leaders in Chinese societies such as Hong Kong. However, it is also suggested that such a benevolent imagery and paternalistic culture often associated with the heritage of Confucian classics and ethics in Chinese enterprises have been heavily compounded by the influences of Western business and work values to which highly industrialised Asian cities like Hong Kong are exposed. The result has been a seemingly integrated mix of cultural values derived from both Oriental as well as Western sources in a hybrid fashion which is espoused by the corporate leadership in many business or even public organisations. This has in turn affected the corporate philosophy, the style of management or even work and organisational behaviour of the lower level staff members in these organisations. The intention of this paper is hence twofold: first to ascertain how authentic Chinese cultural values, especially the classic scholarly prescriptions, are being conserved in these enterprises, and second, to what extent these managerial practices and ideologies have been amenable to reshaping and modification under the impact of Western influences. Where appropriate, illustrations and evidence are drawn from the empirical findings which a number of case studies of Hong Kong business have elucidated.

The Chinese Ideology about "Mandarin" Administration: The Aspirants of Corporate Statesmanship

What is noticeable in these case studies is a common yearning, either articulate or implicit, among these established Chinese corporate leaders in the "managerial echelon" to demonstrate a cult of enshrined capability which is beyond the realm of business "entrepreneurship" and managerial proficiency. Such desired qualities to which they aspire, especially if there is a tendency to sanctify the "cherished" practices as a built-in or well assimilated aspect of the corporate culture, can be tentatively described by the notion of "corporate statesmanship". The notion of "corporate statesmanship" was discussed by Kao and Hong (1995b) in an Asian, non-Western context:

> Rather, it is here argued that a key to effective government in corporations — especially in achieving a corporate-wide *esprit de corp*...has to reside upon the governing ability of the corporate leaders beyond the ordinary horizon of either "management" or "entrepreneurship". Such an aptitude is suggested in the qualities and vigor of "corporate statesmen" in their governorship, which are hard to be emulated simply within the boardroom under collectivised decision-making. In other words, the thesis of "corporate statesmanship" also offers an alternative perspective to the "mainstream" orientation of western theoretical prognosis which utilises basically an institutional mode of treatment, in approaching the corporate agenda of internal "government". Other than invoking notions like the governing board (of directors), celebrated "agency" and pluralistic "stockholder" theories, it is here proposed that the reign of man — with a flair of "statesmanship" — can be equally, if not more, efficacious in welding together the human enterprise collective and advancing it to a higher realm of responsible "governance" (pp. 5–6)

There is, moreover, an associated and important assumption about the possibility to perpetuate such a style of governance, in spite of the personalised qualities that are obviously necessary to sustain the "charisma" of the "corporate statesmen". The notion appears to apply, in this connection, to certain cherished norms in dealing with the thorny issue of top management succession in corporations. The characteristic allusion held by the sample of Hong Kong corporate leaders of Chinese ethnicity is noteworthy for two features they betray about this question. First, these corporate leaders believe that, understandably, if they are able to govern well their organisations, the ingredients of such a benevolent governing "regime" — in particular its moral and logic—should be readily translated into the organisation's "corporate culture". What is hence buttressed purportedly in a "corporate culture" of such a solidaristic nature is a "normative consensus", which suggests and exalts for both its present and future membership of unison of purpose, a bond of mutual trust and identity, as well as faith that the employer–employee relationship will not be a dehumanising, exploitative and unethical one. In other words, the nexus is to upgrade and strengthen the legitimacy of "corporate statesmanship" (of such a normative approach) by creating and assimilating a series of "psychological contracts" which transcend both the "divide" between manager and the managed, the governor and the governed — by virtue of a "corporate culture" which espouses such a spirit and an identity.

The second property of corporate statesmanship, in order to sustain its claim to resilience, is associated with its subtle ability to perpetuate its "reign" through managerial succession. Characteristically, the traditional Chinese approach relies upon the hereditary inheritance norm of tracing through and passing down the "lineage" along an "in-house" path of descent. However, such an approach, in nurturing an essentially "patrimonial dynasty in business" is abhorred for what is described as its self-perpetuating "inclusivity" — let alone its insensitivity to the problems of inefficiency and incapacity bred due to, say, the designated heir's incompetence. However, if such patronage can be practised in a technocratic style so that the heir groomed for the future helmship can be sought, without discrimination or favouritism, from either consanguine posterity or a network of entrusted and capable deputies or associates (that is, the sponsored protegé), it can be argued that "corporate statesmanship" can be cherished in its "realm" where these "succession" processes are institutionalised by a threefold design of (*a*) inculcating the "sponsored" legitimacy of the heir's designate; (*b*) the technocratic development of the latter's leadership qualities; and (*c*) enhancing the organisation's bureaucratic continuity. In other words, what has been celebrated as the classic three type spectrum of ruling authority in the Western Weberian tradition (differentiated into charismatic, traditional, and bureaucratic authority) can be fused together, to be nurtured in a hybrid fashion to sponsor the accomplishment of statesmanship in the next generation of corporate leaders. The common prescription given by the incumbent leaders in the Chinese enterprises, as the study has elucidated, is to achieve these arrangements using the mandarin style. Specifically, the Confucian teaching about the ethics of loyalty, sincerity, trust, fidelity and reciprocity is cherished widely as the core values, to be advanced and inculcated in the mandarin leader's "corporate culture" which is to help perpetuate the elite's governing mandate as it is transmitted between the successive generations of corporate leaders.

Sustaining the moral nexus of such a mandarin system of governing the Chinese enterprise and making possible its continuity beyond the present leadership is the institution employed by many of these corporations. It involves a spontaneous "normative consensus", the basic assumptions of which are shared typically across the entire work hierarchy between the top echelon and the lower level members. In a sense, the imagery of Chinese mandarin, cherished also in this parallel benevolent and altruistic business administration, exalts that a man of letters should behave like a scholar–official and a gentleman with appropriate etiquette. When applied to the logic in administering the state Chinese enterprises, such a mandarin protocol seems to engender an implicit assumption that the subordinates' deferential consent is better elicited by a humble, modest and self-effacing helmsman than a self-seeking, aggrandising and ambitious leader (Kao & Hong, 1995a). Attesting to the qualities of statesmanship in the business domain are, therefore, the humble and noble deeds of the corporate leader to deflate psychologically his ego and his readiness to indulge in self-sacrifice for the benefit of his significant "related" others. For these corporate leaders in the Chinese enterprises, such an orientation is a key mental imperative which explains the moral discipline of the aristocratic "self" (that is, the leader) and his interrelatedness with his important others in his contact networks. The latter are embraced, both socially and industrially, within his networks of work, business and other contacts and associations. Kao and Hong (1988) discussed its ramifications:

> ...it gave rise to an affective concern for their welfare as well as a desire (or motive) to maintain harmony and a stable web of reciprocity vis-à-vis them. Rather than representing a collectivist spirit *per se*, the cognisance was about the need and position of

the individual — yet not in isolation but vis-à-vis his related others. It was somewhat paradoxical, because of the individual's search for self-harmony that he developed an altruistic affect and sentiments for others within his "social" set (p. 256).

In essence, this is an abbreviation of the minimal self thesis, which offers a tenable perspective for appreciating and interpreting the low key and quiescent appearance of many Asian business leaders who have won conspicuous admiration and support from their subordinates because of and in spite of their self-efficacing posture. On most occasions, such a sentiment of mutual identification across the employer–employed divide seems to have made possible the claim that defensive industrial combinations like the workers' unions are irrelevant or obsolete. While negating the otherwise "we–they" industrial dichotomy and abhorring the "union" notion for propagating the distinctiveness of the employee's interests (let alone the idea that labour's organised power is an alternative or even opposite to the corporation's), such a leadership ethos, by emphasising the captain's integration with the related others in the hierarchy, contributes to his governing mandate based upon an imperative of trust — which helps cement together both the manager and the managed by instilling in them a union of purpose, a positive attitude, and commitment towards work. Purportedly, such a harmonistic and integrated workforce, inspired spiritually by an altruistic nexus upheld by the corporate leaders at the helm, is likely to excel as a well motivated human enterprise able to perform with high morale and productivity.

An interesting case study which was illustrative of the Chinese mandarin style in corporate leadership was furnished by a leading large mechanical engineering plant in Hong Kong which produces both fully assembled machinery as well as parts catering to the East Asian markets and other Third World economies. Set up as a petty machine shop, it was housed in a poorly equipped temporary building in the early 1950s, shortly after the 1949 liberation of China. Its success and rapid development in the 1960s and 1970s, reaching its massive scale of operations by the mid-1980s, betrayed a typical case of those industrial dramas which featured the legend of the destitute yet self-efficacing entrepreneurs who arrived in inland capital as refugees due to sociopolitical upheavals of the mid-century Chinese mainland.

The meteoric rise of this enterprise was largely due to a patient gestational process orchestrated by its patron–founder. This owner–manager had hitherto viewed his headship more as an enlightened regime of benevolent governance than one of technocratic (if not bureaucratic) management. However, what was espoused in the corporate philosophy of this engineering plant, as it was later consolidated into its present scale of business, was its prudent rather than idealistic nature. Basically, it cherished a grass-roots type of mentality which appealed to the importance of austerity. Such a work spirit was vaguely reminiscent of both the rationalism of scientific management as well as the non-materialistic belief in human relations ethos as the combined dictum of a holistic orientation towards people in the workplace. It was typical of the celebrated Chinese paradox mixing both the soft and hard properties, that is, the "yin–yang" dualism, made possible because of the Chinese "plastic" temperament which tolerates non-specificity and implies subtlety. When translated into action plans, such a philosophy purportedly gave rise to a business strategy which prescribed a set of ambitious yet interesting operational goals for this plant. Specifically, it sought to produce at costs as low as in mainland China (the low cost areas) and at the same time at quality levels comparable to the Japanese (who were high quality producers). In order to inculcate both productivity and excellence in quality, this enterprise subscribed to a corporate belief, as designed by its owner–manager, that it would pay off to (a) commit to industrious, dedicated, vigorous and disciplined performance, which was able to win the customers/buyers' approval and compliment; and (b) invest in human resource upgrading, by way of training, education in technical know-how, including self-learning, institutional instruction as well as on-the-job osmosis, in order to enhance the individual's capabilities for better performance.

It was reminiscent of the Confucian principle of governance that there was a relatively clear hierarchical ordering of the different classes of beneficiaries which were able to claim the attention and allegiance of the enterprise, as they were ranked in terms of importance as primary, secondary and tertiary stakeholders. At the core of the corporate mission was the stake of the shareholders, whose interests as owners were viewed as paramount. Second to these were the interests of the workforce which symbolised the paternalistic and benevolent concern of the enterprise for the altruistic wellbeing of its appointed membership as a "commonwealth". Third and at the periphery, were the tertiary and indirect interests of such outside but associated parties like vendors, buyers or competitors. The moral dictum followed in dealing with the tertiary class of the peripheral stakeholders was to abide by the rules of the game and not to abuse, exploit or to act injuriously to harm those others. Such a quasi-parochial corporate philosophy seemed to be a micro manifestation of the Chinese logic of prudent governance: to reign and perpetuate a state of decent prosperity, rather than to strive for the visionary utopia of attaining a global realm of communist and egalitarian commonwealth, which was viewed by these workers and their corporate leader as more ideological than practical. Apparently, pragmatism dictates and prevails in saying the corporate philosophy of this machine building industrial works (Kao & Hong, 1988).

In this case study, the owner–founder demonstrated his "statesmanship" by betraying a mix of both his entrepreneurial insights, business alertness and imagination as well as governing wisdom. These qualities were reflected in a series of structural and technological innovations he introduced in the 1980s in order to modernise the plant and rationalise its operations. He was particularly keen to update and advance the technical competence of his staff members by strengthening their knowledge nexus in performance and for this reason, corporate sponsorship for staff training and development was common, as noted earlier. Moreover, what gave a humanised image to this technocratic concern to enhance the man–machine capabilities of his machinery plant was his insistence to "move around the shopfloor" as an ordinary member of the workforce in the rank-and-file. By talking and dining regularly with his staff members and by involving himself effectively in the activities and interactions of such a personalised and solidaristic nature, this owner–manager prided himself in having transcended the status distance in work and the workplace hierarchy. Such a personal touch earned him profound and widespread approval and respect from the shopfloor, where he was enshrined as the "enlightened old guard" with a strong charismatic appeal, and backing by the rank-and-file workmen and staff.

Ironically, such a mandarin style of noble and popular qualities which the corporate patron–leader consolidated impeded the long-term resilience of his corporation by complicating his strategy about planning managerial succession after his "reign". His original plan was to groom his daughter, who held a doctoral degree in engineering from an American university to succeed him. However, what is always crucial in most attempts to perpetuate an administrative

regime of personalised "governorship" is the transfer, often problematic, of the old leaders' personalised charisma, which has served
strategically in buttressing their regime or "statesmanship", to the
next generation of corporate leaders. Almost invariably, a highly
popular regime of charismatic leadership cemented by an earlier
administration has been paradoxical in implication, inasmuch as such
popularity tends to work to the detriment of the succeeding incumbent's
charismatic basis, especially if the patron and his heir(s) belong to
the same family and are linked by hereditary bonds to the patron.

The strategy adopted by this owner–patron in order to conserve
his corporate estate yielded a relatively unconventional formula by
"socialising" the ownership of his company, in spite of the Chinese-
ness of his management style. This was institutionalised by setting
up a trust foundation for furthering education development within
China. Such a decision of donating to a social cause attested seemingly to a selfless flair of statesmanship. In addition to detaching his
enterprise and its assets from the holding of his family, he listed the
company on the open stock and share market by reconstituting and
incorporating it as a public limited company. His intention was to
depersonalise and deprivatise the ownership and control of the plant
so as to institutionalise a collective governance arrangement in place
of his oneman leadership with the appointment of a board of directors. Such a subtle manoeuvre to transform the system of corporate
governance from a personal mandarin style into an institutional
and structured (and also impersonal) mechanism was not entirely
free of problems.

There were several problems. The first was the owner–patron's
ambivalence and indecision about the actual configuration of his
succession plan. His "statesmanly" vision of not perpetuating an
in-house family dynasty of control was noble yet vague. The actual
process of transforming it into a quasi-public estate devoted to a
public cause proved to be staggering and obviously circumscribed
because of other associated factors. Hence, a second constraint in
this connection was the mandarin assumption, also implicit in the
dilemma which this case study betrayed, that the destiny of a well
governed domain (which could be the nation-state, the business
enterprise or the family) depended critically upon the personal cali-
bre of the leaders who were governing. The elitist and mandarin
self-image of the owner was also evident in this case as he articulated, in his interview with the researchers, a belief that he remained
the most resourceful member in the enterprise to pilot and steer its

development, after, and in spite of, his nominal retirement from the chief executive portfolio. Making the situation more fluid was the third factor, "tribal" expectation, rooted in the Chinese patrimonial tradition of inheritance norms which was harboured by his family, that he owed his relatives and close kin a native duty of sponsoring those capable young members of his family for key positions of responsibility in his enterprise.

In summary, such normative inconsistencies and contradictions are likely to make the entire issue of corporate succession a blurred, obscure and oscillating one. Such an issue is not unique to this machine building and engineering plant. Instead, other successful Chinese enterprises have faced similar dilemmas as the first generation leadership began to age.

The next case study makes reference to how such a transitional issue has been successfully accommodated in a Hong Kong Chinese bank which is now managed by a younger governing elite of the second generation leaders. This is the Wing Lung Bank, a leading bank of Chinese capital in Hong Kong, where the legacies of the mandarin governorship of an earlier generation of corporate helmship are still evident in the present administration, constituted of a mix of both hereditary and appointed successors who are selected and retained because they are technocratically competent in managing a bank.

The bank has a history of almost 60 years; it has always prided itself in having established an image of hospitality and trustworthiness which appeals to Chinese families. It has cherished a time-honoured tradition of its prudent, conservative policy and personalised, sincere service. In the bank, conservatism refers to basically a rational business strategy, as claimed in its annual reports, that it would persist "in retaining the fine traditions of a local Chinese bank" and "spare no effort in providing more diversified and sophisticated services to customers", thus hoping to contribute to the prosperity of the territory (Wing Lung Bank Limited, 1993).

The bank is a benchmark case of those Chinese family enterprises which have modernised and expanded significantly in scale, yet are now conspicuous in having consolidated a Confucian-dominated organisational culture. Such a mandarin style corporate culture was sponsored, in the beginning, under the zealous and almost doctrinal patronage of the founder–patron of the business. The enterprise and its culture has now been inherited by the second generation. However, this younger echelon of family-based lieutenants needed to legitimise their ascendancy to the realm of power by demonstrating that they were qualified not merely by the ascriptive criterion of consanguine bonds with the owner–patron and his family but also their own proven abilities and competence. In order to neutralise the stigma associated with network hiring, there was even a heavier premium attached to their ability to perform, that is, to vindicate the case that they were technocratically proficient in their inherited managerial capacities, in spite of the practice that such inheritance norms are enmeshed in particularistic nets of kinship ties.

All these expectations and cross-cutting pressures emanating from the business and industrial norms of the past and present, when combined together, have been conducive to the emergence of a second generation managerial mentality — a psychological orientation of these modern and Western educated heirs to the first generation patrons and captains of industry which was, while still committed to conserving the mandarin character of their governance, unavoidably, self-effacing and ambivalent in certain aspects of the interface between tradition and modern technocratic dictates. It appears that these younger corporate leaders have endeavoured to build and deliver an agenda of corporate governance which is efficacious in cementing the perpetuation of the hereditary control of the family and, at the same time, reconciling between the progressive introduction of Western inspired innovations (which included hardware as well as managerial methods) on the one hand and on the other, such sustained strengths as (*a*) the retention of the old loyal staff, and (*b*) the conservation of the pioneering corporate spirit of austerity, fidelity, dedication and propriety which enshrines the founding of the bank (Wing Lung Bank Limited, 1993).

Inasmuch as this bank could be represented within the milieu of a "cultural embrace", its culture was apparently a melange of both Chinese paternalism and rationalistic welfare-corporation. Not surprisingly, it was characterised by a Chinese mandarin style bureaucratism, which was perhaps not unusual among the large-scale workplaces in the modern context of advances in both market and technology like banks. However, its corporate culture was both conservative and altruistic in essence, emphasising the primacy of collective security and placing the organic wellbeing of the firm and its staff members above its accelerated growth. Even its hallmark of corporate development and growth was heavily reminiscent of the owner–founder's preference for the wellbeing of the corporate family.

The self-imagery of the bank was that of a community of "common-wealth" to excel collectively, and not in motivating unreservedly the self-seeking spirit of competition among individuals (Stewart, Hong, & Ting, 1993).

Such a Confucian inspired corporate culture, distinctive of emphasising the nexus between stability and commitment, in turn helped fashion various aspects of the bank's human resource and management strategies — which again reflected an overall theme of concern of the patron–founder in his mandarin approach to institute and sustain a Confucian realm of paternalistic stewardship in managing his workforce. In this connection, the bank emulated the civil service in offering its staff members a stable and bureaucratic type of permanent employment and steady career advancement within its hierarchical structure.

In addition, following a practice strongly reminiscent of the Japanese "welfare corporation" approach (Dove, 1993), the bank sought not only to groom and retain its staff members for a lifetime career under a steady process of stepped promotion, but also catered to the employees' welfare. An instance of this was its time-honoured custom of allocating an entire floor's space (at its headquarters which was located in the high rental banking centre, the Central District on the Hong Kong Island), as well as similar facilities elsewhere for its branch offices, to serve as staff canteens catering to its 1,000 strong workforce. The provision of free or subsidised meals was reminiscent of an old employment norm which was widely adopted by traditional Chinese employers to symbolise the sharing of the same destination between the employer and the employed under the "same roof". While such a tradition was steadily eroded in Hong Kong as it became industrially more affluent, the bank and its management were apparently proud in having conserved such a solidaristic norm intact.

When responding to the question about the most effective way to achieve productivity improvements in the bank, the most preferred method adopted by the bank was to "reward the staff with appropriate salary increase". The other alternative was to introduce a corporate culture so as to enhance job commitment of the employees. Another option was to organise training and skill upgrading. The least preferred option was the idea of rewarding the staff by incentives such as a higher (lump sum) year-end bonus.

Several reasons help explain the bank's reserved attitude to the efficacy of an "incentive" arrangement of adjustable year-end bonus payment, in spite of its appeal in terms of flexibility and efforts. The first was the conservatism of the bank, whose management still perceived themselves as having the moral responsibility of ensuring the stability and security of their employees' jobs and incomes. Second, the bank articulated a belief that it was acting morally in the interests of the staff, as the latter looked for longer term security and more stable rewards such as regular advances in salary as well as promotions. Inasmuch as the effective instruments in committing the staff's loyalty and motivating their performance were attributed by management to these processes of periodic staff reviews, the role of bonus payment as an incentive arrangement was marginalised. Being fixed at the level of one month's salary equivalent (normally reckoned in law as the 13th month pay common to every employee), such bonus seemed to epitomise nominal incentive effects at best.

The mandarin style of the second generation management was mirrored in the bank's attempts to decommercialise its human resource and staff relations approach by way of the above and other associated policies. In this connection, the design of the employee performance appraisal system, by building the linkage between appraisal and rewards into the exercise itself, involved a simple arrangement which made visible the mutuality between the individual's performance and his/her advances in salary and on the corporate ladder. The declared objective of the bank in its staff motivation strategy was, as far as possible, to incorporate any substantive improvements in conditions into its normal and basic salary structure.

Given the premium attached by the bank to such a system of regular staff reviews of performance, salary and appointments, any defaults in its appraisal system were liable to subvert seriously the objectivity, fairness and staff's consent to such a review-cum-reward system. A critical issue which could have beset management in this connection was whether the appraisers (who were normally the work supervisors of the appraised) were sufficiently sensitive, objective and fair as to make such a mechanism work in order to motivate effectively and reward justifiably the workforce. Over the years of the bank's history, it appeared to have consolidated a refined and mature system of evaluating staff performance, in spite of its apparent simplicity and conservative nature. The appraisal system was reported to have worked satisfactorily in sustaining consistently the stable commitment of the bank's staff. Moreover, the dedication and consistency of its management in pursuing these policy norms helped secure, in turn, an intrinsic bond of mutual trust between the manager and the managed, the employer and the employed, in other words, in helping to cement the "psychological contract" in the workplace.

The mix of staff benefits provided by the bank was designed in its entirety to enhancing the security of the workforce, rather than spurring individuals to strive to seek short-term inflation of efforts and rewards. The logic of staff management was primarily a concern to stabilise a loyal and trustworthy workforce by applying with care and discretion the incentive notion. For this reason, management's response was "lukewarm" to suggestions to introduce "participative arrangements like a profit-sharing scheme" or to institute an explicit incentive system like a variable wage component pegged to the individual's measured performance or productivity. Even the year-end bonus, as noted earlier, was invariable as it was fixed at the uniform rate of one month's additional pay for everyone.

The bank's approach to the linkage between incentive and performance was low key. It was implied naturally, as in harmony with the bank's Confucian doctrine of mandarin governance, that the employees would be better looked after, inasmuch as the bank was able to prosper, enlarge its profit margins, extend its business scope, and enhance its quality of service. Any productivity gains stemming from the higher efficiency of the workforce — or similarly, of the hardware and software equipment — were interpreted by management within a normative system which suggested that such yields from improved productivity would enable the enterprise to pay its staff higher basic salary by strengthening "its ability to pay".

The Challenge of Western Managerial Assumptions and Work Values and the Dilemma of Second Generation Corporate Leaders

The Confucian doctrine of mandarin governance of a Chinese enterprise seems to have worked to vindicate the efficacy of paternalistic management where the business is headed by the first generation patron–founder. Typically, a corporate reign of what is reminiscent of the "statemanship" ideal has been bettered because of normative consensus which the mandarin and benevolent helmsman is able to nurture by virtue of (a) his own charismatic qualities, often attested by his story of outstanding success in having steered the enterprise to its "estate of the realm"; and (b) his assiduous appeal to the corporate and altruistic virtues of observing the ethical prescriptions of classic Confucian teaching, hence, in enshrining his mandarin image, and his claim on the subordinate's deference, loyalty, and commitment.

However, the legitimacy of such a governance style is inherently volatile and fragile, as the highly individualised nexus of "charisma" is hardly sustainable when there is a "changeover" in personality within the leadership echelon. An earlier study had canvassed the apparent logic of hereditary succession as a prudent practice which Chinese family businesses have instituted as the norm of passing on the rein of "corporate helmanship". It was suggested that the relative "closeness" of the Chinese system of inheritance, itself rooted in the kinship networks, and the supposed "trustworthiness" of "blood" relationships, were conducive to the conservation of the family's control and power over the business, where it is extended from one generation to the next (Kao & Hong, 1995a).

Apparently, such a Chinese approach represents distinctive strategic advantages vis-à-vis the Western bureaucratic conventions.

Industrial syndrome of such a nature is perhaps not an uncommon organizational dilemma besetting Western enterprises on the issue of succession....

By contrast, the relatively "tribal" approach of the Chinese business provides an alternative perspective on the organization's treatment of managerial succession which may yet help avert similar pathos otherwise endemic to Western-style bureaucratization. Typically, Chinese family business great faith... on the "particularistic" considerations of the appointee's "loyalty", "allegiance" and "subordination", are often at the expense of such impersonal criteria as technical competence and credentials of formal qualifications. In this connection, succession of the "organisational reign", always coincides with the norm of property inheritance, perpetuated in-house and restricted to transfer of mandate between the successive generations of the "father" and "son".... The practice of such an inheritance norm is able to sustain, amongst its ramifications for the Chinese family enterprise, (*a*) the solidarity and unison of a collective enterprise, made up of a core of the "loyalists" and dedicated staff; and (*b*) the continuity and solidarity in style, philosophy, and inner logic between the old and new leadership, in spite of the power transition (Kao & Hong, 1995a, p. 184).

However, it is argued that on the basis of more penetrative evidence uncovered in subsequent inquiries on Chinese corporate leadership and its succession, that the efficacy of such a prescription by the celebrated inheritance norm can be doubted, where the second generation corporate heirs tend to drift into adopting Western bureaucratic and impersonal methods of organising the authority hierarchy and motivating the workforce. Such a dilemma is implicit in the succession syndrome which has been documented in the case study of the machinery plant. The owner–founder began to institutionalise his mode of governance by creating an education trust as the beneficiary while vesting greater administrative control of the enterprise in a board of directors as a result of growing diffidence and doubts about the abilities of his daughter, the apparent heir designate, in commanding the continued allegiance and faith of the old-timers, who were his faithful and key lieutenants in the present establishment.

Regarding the case study of the bank, although the second generation is at the helm, yet it has made clear its corporate tradition of disapproving any excessive reliance upon Western style incentives like performance bonus. It has conceded to the competitive imperative of making the bank an attractive employer — when labour shortage was almost phenomenal in Hong Kong in the late 1980s — by adopting an *ad hoc*, yet industrywide practice of offering its "teller" staff a special incentive bonus for retention and recruitment purposes. There is an additional prospect that the bank would review and overhaul its salary structure in order to enhance its sensitivity in motivating individual staff members to improve their performance. Such adjustments in personnel policy (possibly by instituting a more flexible form of performance-oriented incentive bonus) were deemed essential by management to help rationalise its human resource strategy in order to upgrade its quality of customer service and to remain competitive in the banking industry which attached increasing importance to excellence in such services. Although the second generation management members emerged as loyal heirs to the corporate leadership

which founded the bank, and were anxious to maintain its mandarin style (showing disdain for "commercialising" its human relations, especially staff relations between the employer and the employed), they had to recognise the shifting parameters of business in
the banking industry and to respond proactively to an environment
of change and intensifying competition with a readiness to innovate. Coming from a background of Western education, it is likely
that they would look to the mainstream literature of Western management ideas and theories for prescriptions and inspirations as
the "recipe" for reforming the business, modernising its human resource policies, and rationalising its work organisation.

These tendencies of the Chinese enterprises to assimilate a greater
number of Western ideas in managing business and the workplace
are perhaps not uncommon as they evolve from the domain of the
first generation patron–founders to that of the second generation
successors. Characteristically, the latter are more technocratic managers than charismatic entrepreneurs like their predecessors and
are, hence, less prone to be indulged in such visionary self-images
as a mandarin style corporate statesman. The pragmatic dictates of
adopting selected Western fashioned solutions to their motivational
and other organisational problems often constitute a rational, and
technocratically justifiable, policy option for these Western educated
hereditary managers when they are faced with the challenge of restructuring their inherited business in order to cope with a changing business environment of enlarged and intensified competition.

Such a syndrome is demonstrated by another case study. The
enterprise investigated was a local Chinese family business. It began as a small operation in 1940 (employing 30 workers) and grew
into a large enterprise with over 400 staff members on its payroll. It
was being managed by a corporate leadership of the second generation, the Western educated chief executive was the son of the dairy's
entrepreneur–founder.

The incumbent chief executive and his key staff believed in the
virtues of classic Chinese business and work ethics as prescribed by
Confucian teaching but they were sceptical about a mandarin, almost doctrinal, way of seeking merely to conserve the *status quo* in a
traditional fashion, without drawing reference from the Western
perspective for new insights and inspirations in order to innovate
and upgrade the efficiency and performance of the enterprise. Advances in managerial practices and methods were deemed to be the

key leverage to enhancing the capability of this dairy plant to compete in a market which had become increasingly diversified and amenable to the entry of imported dairy products from overseas. As a result of the internal reforms and rationalisation measures adopted since the late 1970s, the dairy was able to modernise its image and improve steadily its performance: it captured almost 30 per cent of Hong Kong's market in supply of fresh milk and dairy products. This was a remarkable achievement considering the fact that the local market was earlier almost dominated by the other dairy farms financed by Western (British) capital. Its share in the market stabilised at 50 per cent.

The management system practised and its underlying philosophy revealed a "hybrid" which included elements of both the instrumental nexus of the Western instructed rational management approach as well as the moralistic ideals of mandarin style governance of business in the classic Chinese tradition. What was exemplary of the solidaristic importance attached by the chief executive to the propriety of Confucian norms and assumptions was his adherence to the normative imperative of "trust" and its implicit significance as a "bond" of mutual allegiance and dedication which, in turn, made him marginalise the salience of the written and formal contract. There was a consistent tendency to de-emphasise the instrument of the labour contract and other related norms, such as those embodied otherwise by a highly structured body of in-house rules and regulations. Where trust was conserved and prevailed in the workplace, this dairy took pride in having been able to retain a group of long-serving, loyal and committed "core" staff. The bulk of its members had been in its employ for at least 5 to 10 years and some of the "old-timers" had worked for 20 years or more.

Such apparent informality of workplace practice by virtue of the weight of Confucian inspired trust was, however, balanced by the application of Western management techniques which appeared to feature, conversely, a higher instrumental degree of work motivation and control than the case of the bank. Specifically, there was an explicit effort at institutionalising a system of measuring individuals' contribution and performance and linking the appraisal directly to a bonus-like incentive arrangement. The following narrative is an abbreviated profile of how such a motivational mechanism based upon merits and result assessment worked, as outlined by the chief executive himself in his interview:

We have a profit sharing scheme, applied basically to the shopfloor supervisors and above. If we are able to earn a profit, we shall allocate a certain amount of the surplus gained to be shared among our staff members. Of course, the structure of distribution has to be rational and graded to allow for a higher rate for the managers in the upper tier than the floor supervisors. In spite of the hierarchy which differentiates the payment level, such a "bonus" system has worked well and it represents a form of care to the "core" staff.

Pay raise depends upon the staff's contribution to the company. We have an annual increment system. If the staff member has worked for a long time and made a contribution, we may adjust his salary by 20 per cent. That really depends upon one and other high-level managers' recommendations. If he performs well, we will have special adjustments in recognising his performance suitably. We will promote him or offer him more increments, plus a letter of appreciation. The logic is to make him feel proud and satisfied with his work (Yee, Hong, & Chung, 1995, p. 59).

Hong Kong as a Meeting Point between the East and West

What has significantly compounded the authentic practice of mandarin style management of Chinese enterprises in Hong Kong, especially when the reign of corporate leadership passes from the first generation entrepreneur–founders to the second generation successors, is the hybrid nature of the Hong Kong environment and its multicultural background. Hong Kong has always served as a meeting point for Eastern and Western cultures by virtue of its highly urbanised and cosmopolitan character. The workplace practices in Hong Kong are significantly influenced by its history of sociocultural affinities with China and Britain. Custom and practices relating to Chinese traditional mores and British legal and professional practices have been a key factor in shaping the emergent features of the work and employment system in this industrial city.

In addition to the mandarin vision of corporate governance which relies heavily on the Confucian code of etiquette and moral standards, as illustrated by the case studies discussed here, the Chinese approach to workplace management in many Hong Kong firms is conspicuous for two themes. These are (*a*) the paternalistic assumption of the employers or owner–managers in providing their employees with a net of security and welfare benefits, yet at the employers' discretion rather than being regulated by clearly prescribed rules specifying these provisions as contractual obligations; and (*b*) the preference of employers for non-detailed and informal arrangements, so that activities and decisions are always relatively fluid and un-structured. It is not clear as to whether the option of keeping relation-ships and activities informal, non-express, subtle and personalised is intrinsically a Chinese cultural trait or not (the "particularisa-tion" of socioeconomic relations as such practices would have im-plied is not uncommon in Third World economies, or even in the highly industrialised nations prior to industrialisation — hence, a preindustrial syndrome of "traditionalism"). However, in the Hong Kong milieu, it has become normative to associate such an attitude with the Chinese ethics of upholding trust. It has, today, from the modern or postmodern perspective of managing a "lean" enterprise, a still trendy appeal of affording a business with the advantages of adaptability and flexibility to cope with various types of uncertain-ties beyond corporate anticipation in the market.

For pay and benefit administration, the combined effects of these two factors have led to a myriad of supplementary incomes and benefits whose nature is not always exactly specified because they are sustained by the employers' paternalistic goodwill and trust. The subtlety of such a mix was illustrated by England (1989):

.... An essential part of this process is that employers retain a very large degree of discretion over the size...which pay increases may be granted.... Bonuses can be paid for Chinese New Year, attendance, night-shift working, as long-service incentives.... The key point, however, is that the manipulation of payment systems and fringe benefits, combined with the imposition or withdrawal of over-time, provides individual employers with the necessary flexibil-ity to maintain profit margins (p. 155).

However, it appears that these local Chinese employers have be-come increasingly concerned about attempts to rationalise and regularise such a diversity of wage supplements by consolidating them into a coherent and systematically defined structure of incentives. Largely inspired by Western management theories and as the corporate leadership passed from the first generation to the second generation echelon, wage and benefit reforms have been widespread among many large-scale Chinese enterprises as they modernise. An obvious example is revamping of the retirement and fringe systems recently introduced by a number of family controlled and officially franchised businesses in the public transport sector, such as the Kowloon Motor Bus (KMB), the China Motor Bus (CMB), and the Yaumati Hong Kong Ferry Service. Behind these corporate reforms, there is also the underpinning pressure from the government which acts as the public agency monitoring the performance of these public utility organisations.

What emanates from the hybrid situation in Hong Kong, where Chinese–Western arrangements combine to produce a variety of mixed practices and prescriptions, is the paradoxical co-existence of a managerial ethos exalting the flexibility of the work organisation on the one hand and an inevitable concern for legalism on the other hand, as identifiable and shared among both employers and the employed in deciding such employment benefits as annual leave, rest days, sickness, allowance, maternity leave, and severance pay (Hong, 1982). As a result, in spite of the virtues of flexibility and freedom of individual discretion and choice in market attributed to Hong Kong for having "operated" successfully as a free enterprise economy, there is ironically a competition-induced tendency towards homogeneity of these substantive terms and conditions of employment within the rank of the territory's salaried and wage earning labour force, "thanks to the harmonising effects of these protective labour statutes" (Hong, 1982).

A Postscript

It can be said that in spite of the mandarin style of paternalistic and benevolent governance of many Chinese enterprises by their first generation patron–founders in Hong Kong, these businesses are largely headed by the second generation which, although comprising predominantly the offspring of the mandarin entrepreneurs, are anxious to buttress their new (and perhaps dubious) legitimacy by rationalising the management structure with an evident shift towards a technocratic (if not bureaucratic) style which leans, at least in part, upon the instructions and prescriptions drawn from the mainstream body of modern management theories and practices developed in the industrially advanced Western world. An example is the increasing reliance on the integrative and linking function provided by the performance appraisal instrument in human resource management by most of these Chinese enterprises in the process of their modernisation and renewal exercises. Given the increasing diversification of their trades, business, product lines and markets, it is evident that the variability and plurality of these enterprises' activities make it essential for a common conversion rod, as in the form of a centrally designed performance appraisal instrument, to be applied across all offices/sections within the firm for discriminating individual staff member's achievements in productivity and performance. Moreover, a system of performance appraisal, linked systematically and fairly to merit pay increments and career advances, has afforded these enterprises with an integrated mechanism to recognise and regulate, on an organisationwide basis, staff efforts, contribution, and (output) performance.

In spite of the scientific and technocratic appearance of these imported (Western) tools of managing human incentive, staff motivation and discipline by measured appraisal, it seems that most of these Hong Kong enterprises of Chinese capital are able to administer a reward and incentive mechanism which is simple to understand and appreciated by the entire workforce. Simplicity of design helps explain why arrangements like these have worked well in soliciting effective, dedicated effort from the staff. By contrast, a highly sophisticated yet complex structure of pay and incentives often arouses little awareness and interest among the employees, simply because its sensitivity is blunted unwittingly by its cumbersome nature.

In many of these enterprises of local Chinese origin, the importance attached by management to efficiency and excellence in staff performance is also indicative of the labour intensive nature of business and industry in Hong Kong. In spite of the introduction of large-scale automation and computerisation, these firms have continued to rely upon a skilful, experienced and adaptive workforce for the sustenance of a high quality level of service to their clientele. Such versatility of the labour they employ, in turn, reflects the typical pressure of a highly competitive industry, which induces enterprises to enhance and improve the provision and effectiveness measures for purposes of staff motivation.

It is surmised that the normative and spiritual properties of the society and culture of Hong Kong, as identified earlier, have important implications in enabling local enterprises to consolidate such practices. For example, the apparent efficacy of the organisational pay and promotion system geared to annual staff appraisals is in part buttressed by the mutual trust stemming from the psychological contracts firms have with their workforce. The nature of the main incentive and reward instruments in these firms, which are largely "mixed bag" packages of promotions and merit salary raises, is such that they are intrinsically deferred kinds of payment and gratifications. The fact that such deferred payment systems have worked attests, at least indirectly, to the resilience of trust in these situations. As in accord with the Confucian norms exalting reciprocity and one's "altruistic conscience", most of the Chinese employees are ready to sacrifice immediate personal interests and convenience because they are confident that this diffuse goodwill would be reciprocated in due course. It follows that in these enterprises, the appropriate prescription would be to provide the staff with commensurate wage and salary adjustments as well as promotion awards in line with their efforts as measured by the performance appraisal system.

At the root of these practices and arrangements lies the moral force of trust associated with the cultural context of Hong Kong enterprises and their workforce. In spite of its cosmopolitan nature, Hong Kong is a new industrial society with an Asian cultural heritage, having conserved vestiges of the Confucian tradition in its value systems which continue to impact the industrial and work values of the employers and the employed. Moreover, the various case studies discussed here reveal that many of the firms owed much of the structural and manpower flexibilities they enjoyed to the widely documented parochial character of this territory, that is, its "native" respect for the natural logic of the market and free enterprise, and by implication, its "doctrinal" tradition of institutional permissiveness toward private sector activities and voluntary practices. There are numerous examples of these structural freedoms from official prescriptions and other institutional regulations, including the absence of any legal provisions on a territorywide minimum wage, or of any statutory controls on standard work hours (except for women and young persons employed in factory industrial work), the weakness of union representation in the workplace, and the feeble practice of collective bargaining or joint consultation in the private sector. While the rationale and morality underlying such a state of normative openness at the macro level have always remained contentious in public policy debates, this feature of an institutional and official reluctance to intervene has no doubt contributed to managerial flexibilities and resources in most private sector enterprises, while allowing the employed individual a great measure of self-discretion in his/her freedom to work or otherwise.

In spite of the apparent harmony that has been achieved by these Chinese enterprises in combining Chinese traditions with Western modern prescriptions in the management of their business and work organisation, their versatility and reformist spirit in transcending the cultural divide of "Easternisation versus Westernisation" are not entirely free from potential tensions and disharmony due to contradictions stemming from various conflicting sources. An illustration of such a reservation is the hybrid nature of the body of business, industrial and work values in Hong Kong, which is itself a distinctive mix of both Confucian altruistic prescriptions and a classic free market preference for flexibility, adaptiveness, and contractual individualism and impersonality. While the former attributes are legacies from the territory's Chinese cultural background and heritage, the latter are evidently the manifestation of recent experiences of this young Asian society. Most of its people were or are the offspring of insecure, defensive-minded immigrants and refugees in the 1950s and 1960s. The Hong Kong syndrome, in having cradled a mixed culture that will probably remain amorphous because of and in spite of changes (a patent illustration of which is 1997), may serve as a modest benchmark for understanding the work values and attitudes in other new and rejuvenated economies in Asia. It is likely that their social and industrial experiences will become more comparable to those of Hong Kong in the wake of international movements of labour and capital across national boundaries in Asia which are now on the rise.

❧ THIRTEEN ❧

School-based Social Services as a Strategy for Community Empowerment and Human Development

❧ Wayne H. Holtzman[1] ❧

A major international conference on the impact of psychology on Third World development was held in Edinburgh, Scotland, in 1982 in association with the XXth International Congress of Applied Psychology. Durganand Sinha and Holtzman had organised the conference under the aegis of the International Union of Psychological Science and with the financial support of UNESCO. The 15 papers presented at the workshop by distinguished psychologists from all over the world, especially developing countries, were fairly timely and significant to merit publication as a special issue of the *International Journal of Psychology* in 1984. Twelve years later at the XVth International Congress of Applied Psychology in Madrid, a similar symposium was held subsequently and the papers published under the editorship of John Adair and Cigdem Kagitcibasi as another special issue of the *International Journal of Psychology* (1995). The emergence of major social trends affecting psychology and its impact on national development were evident in 1982. These trends are now accelerating into global movements.

The optimistic view of the 1960s that the social and behavioural sciences, especially psychology, could contribute in major ways to

[1] Hoff Professor of Psychology and Education and former President, Hogg Foundation for Mental Health, The University of Texas at Austin. The author wishes to thank his research associates, especially Scott Keir, Louise Iscoe, Susan Millea, and Lyndee Knox, for their assistance in providing much of the information on which this chapter is based and for their constructive criticisms of the final manuscript for which the author bears sole responsibility.

the resolution of increasing social problems throughout the world was shattered by the Vietnam War, the energy crisis, cynicism of the young, spreading conflict, migration, refugees, family disruption, uncontrolled population growth, environment pollution, and the pervasive realisation that life for many was getting worse rather than better. Previously muted criticism of Western psychology by some psychologists as being irrelevant to the many national and regional problems confronting them was voiced more forcefully in the early 1980s.

At the Edinburgh conference in 1982, Durganand Sinha eloquently argued, "unlike other social sciences, the discipline (of psychology) as such has remained for too long outside the orbit of social change and development" (1984b, p. 17). At the same conference, Hiroshi Azuma pointed out that the drastic ecological change sweeping across most developing countries in their attempt to transform their societies in a span of a few years had resulted in the violent destruction of a people's traditional ways of living and thinking. For him, psychology had an important role to play in helping people master the necessary changes and cope with the shock brought about by such changes while preserving psychocultural continuity. Although not disagreeing with this point of view, many other Third World psychologists at the 1982 conference chose to present more traditional Western-oriented ideas of psychology or merely to describe the present state of psychology in their countries.

At the Madrid symposium in 1994, criticism of traditional Western scientific psychology was voiced more strenuously, leading to a consensus among all participants for the development of indigenous psychologies, especially in applied social areas. Illustrative of this emerging consensus is the essay by Kim (1995) who conducted a cross-cultural analysis of national psychologies by pointing out the major differences between Euro–American cultural values and those of East Asia and other developing societies. The modern development, entrenchment, and proliferation of psychology is seen largely as a creation of American society even though its roots may be traceable to Europe.

Euro–American cultural values stress rational, liberal, individualistic, and abstract ideals that are embedded in predominant psychological theories and methods. As Hofstede (1980) pointed out, such individualistic societies emphasise autonomy, emotional independence, individual initiative, the right to privacy, pleasure seeking, financial security, the need for specific friendships, and universalism. By contrast, the more collectivistic societies such as those in Asia stress collective identity, emotional dependence, group solidarity, sharing duties and obligations, the need for stable and predetermined friendships, group decisions, and particularism. J.B.P. Sinha (1995) carried this argument for indigenous psychologies a step further by stating that even Western psychology itself is often a victim of logical positivism and operationalism, professing to be value-free, context-free, and therefore universal when in fact it is usually the opposite.

This challenging wake up call is being heard with increasing attentiveness by Western psychologists, particularly in the United States. In the wake of the economic shocks, political upheavals, and disillusionment of the 1980s, many American psychologists have seriously considered this plea to re-examine their value orientations, methods and theories as they pertain, in particular, to major changes in American society and accompanying social issues. At the national level, both the American Psychological Association and the American Psychological Society have stressed the need for psychologists to address difficult social problems dealing with health, education, welfare, and human development. It is already apparent that greatly increased global communication with its accompanying diffusion of ideas, coupled with changing national priorities, will accelerate the rearrangement of psychology's priorities in the highly industrialised countries as well as in the developing nations. At the same time that psychologists of Asia, Africa, and Latin America are debating how to incorporate the best of Western psychology without betraying their cultural values and national identities, American and European psychologists are also looking at ways to improve their science by adopting ideas from non-Western societies.

A closer look at the events during the past several decades in American society, and the challenges as well as opportunities this social change presents psychologists will set the stage for a more detailed illustration in the form of a specific project in which Holtzman has been deeply involved for 6 years — a project that has more relevance to human development in other countries than may be apparent at first glance.

The majority national consensus in the United States — politically, socially, and economically — was largely guided by individualistic values in the first two-thirds of the twentieth century. The counterculture youth revolution of the 1960s, the awakening of ethnic identity and the accompanying demands for social equity, the accelerated immigration of Asians and Latin Americans rather Europeans, and the massive internal migration from rural to urban, from affluent urban to suburban, and of poor Southern blacks to Northern cities or to California dramatically changed the nature of society, especially in large urban areas where accompanying social problems are most evident. With the recent explosion of mass communication through television and computers, even many residents of remote rural areas live in virtual cities, psychologically speaking. Quite clearly, as reflected in the current political turmoil and social debate, the United States can no longer be considered one monolithic, individualistic society, if it ever was one.

Probably most representative of this new look in psychology within the United States is the somewhat diffuse field of community psychology that is rooted in the group and organisational dynamics and decision-making processes of Kurt Lewin and other social psychologists. First recognised as a new approach in the mid-1960s, community psychology is based on systems and ecological thinking that integrates into one strategy health, human resources, education, social interventions, citizen empowerment, and cultural values, focusing in particular on well-defined communities. This integration recognises the mutual adaptation and interdependence of individuals and social structures so that both individual and collective needs are met (Holtzman, Evans, Kennedy, & Iscoe, 1987), thereby combining key aspects of both individualistic and collectivistic value orientations. A contemporary example of this community approach to social problems confronting the United States and many other countries is the experimental School of the Future programme developed in four Texas cities, with consultation and financial support from the Hogg Foundation for Mental Health (Holtzman, 1992).

Community Psychology in the School of the Future

The social changes discussed earlier have created a major crisis in American cities. National statistics paint a grim outlook for many children and their families. If a child is born to a single mother, chances are better than ever that she or he will live in poverty. Among teenage parents, 7 out of 10 live in poverty. As many as 12 million American children have no assured health care, and many live with the threat of violence on a daily basis. Many observers now firmly believe that major reform in public education, perhaps even radical changes that would scarcely have been voiced a generation ago, will be the driving force to ameliorate these social problems.

Particularly promising are projects demonstrating ways in which traditional education can be integrated with a wide array of health and human services, both treatment and prevention, for which the school is becoming the locus of delivery. This larger vision of the school, not only as a place for academic learning but also as the primary neighbourhood institution for promoting child and family development, has profound implications for community renewal, family support, and the nature of delivery systems for mental health, health, education, and other human services.

Full-service schools as described by Dryfoos (1994) do represent a revolution in the way health and social services are provided for children, youth, and families. The most common social service programme which forms the core of more extensive services is the school-based health clinic, which provides essential care for children from disadvantaged social environments. A model full-service school would provide services ranging from family crisis intervention to social skills training, including specialised services for children and families requiring extra help. In many ways the model would resemble a familiar settlement house but within a school rather than a separate social services agency. The most important feature of this model is its focus on the local community, including the participation of parents and teachers in decision-making and a full array of services offered in one setting. In this respect it differs markedly from the current customary situation where a person seeking help must go to different agencies scattered in distant places. Since each agency deals with only one segment of a complex problem and as most individuals seeking help often become very discouraged by the time and expense involved in contacting more than one agency for help, the traditional plan is very inefficient, and many clients drop out before getting the help they need.

A decade ago there were very few examples of this model in the country. The prevailing views were that the sole purpose of schools was to educate children, leaving health, human services and other support activities to independent agencies located elsewhere. While this simplified view of schooling may have worked fairly well for the earlier generations, it is no longer suitable for most schools in the United States because of the changed nature of families, society, and child behaviour, especially in many inner city neighbourhoods. One of the first behavioural scientists to address these issues seriously was James Comer, a psychiatrist at the Yale Child Study Center who was deeply concerned about the deteriorating neighbourhoods and schools of New Haven in Connecticut. His School Development Program, launched in 1968, did not become firmly established until 7 years later. The programme places a heavy emphasis upon a mental health approach for dealing with problems at the elementary school level. Four major components provide the main thrust of the programme — a government and management team, a mental health team, a parent participation programme, and a programme for curriculum and staff development. Parents play an active role not only in decision-making, but also in classroom activities as assistants, tutors, or aides. Some of the deeply involved parents also participate in school government.

The performance of children, the morale of teachers, the school climate, and the extent of community involvement in the school improved dramatically after several years. Initially, pupils in these primarily African–American schools were among the lowest in academic achievement compared to the other 29 elementary schools in New Haven. By 1975, Grade 4 students in the experimental school who initially ranked at or near the bottom in reading and mathematics, moved ahead of students of all other inner city schools (Comer, 1980). By 1987, 92 per cent of parents visited the school 10 times more (Comer, 1988). The empowerment of parents through the school's involvement in Comer's model invariably led to other school reforms as well as to social change throughout the community.

One of the most critical periods of human development is the first five years prior to school entry. Infancy and early child development have been primarily the domain of the family, especially the mother, in most societies. However, with the increase in the number of families where both parents are employed, where only a single parent may be present, or where the parents have little knowledge of child rearing or lack social support, early childhood intervention and special parental training may be essential. Many of the social experiments of the 1960s and 1970s that were conducted in early child development research centres and within Head Start, have demonstrated that inexpensive, cost-effective programmes are critical. Many schools, therefore, have encouraged the development of preschool readiness programmes. Zigler (1989) proposed a unified system of child care and family support using the public schools as the locus of services.

When these different approaches to providing family support services promoting child development within schools attracted national attention, it became apparent to the staff of the Hogg Foundation for Mental Health and its advisors that a large-scale demonstration of this emerging new model for full-service school would be an important contribution to solving a major national problem. After many rounds of preliminary discussions with community leaders, school administrators, and others, the concept of the School of the Future was developed by the Hogg Foundation as its most ambitious initiative in the 50 years of its existence. As an integral part of the University of Texas, the Hogg Foundation interacts closely with faculty and graduate students in a number of departments, calling upon them to participate in projects that it supports from funds drawn from its private endowment.

Most of the initial planning for the School of the Future project took place in four Texas cities — Austin, San Antonio, Houston, and Dallas. In consultation with school authorities, local government leaders, health, mental health, and social service providers, the Foundation selected one or two elementary and one middle school in each of the four cities as the sites for the new, experimental programme. Initial grants from the Foundation of $50,000 per year for 5 years — a total of $1,000,000 — were committed in the spring of 1990, making it possible for each of the communities to appoint a full-time project coordinator. An equal sum of money was allocated to provide each site with technical assistance and evaluation support. Many community agencies and private corporations were encouraged to join the Foundation and the school systems as partners in support of each experimental School of the Future.

Five essential features characterise each of the four demonstration sites: (*a*) the integration of a broad spectrum of health and human services in public schools; (*b*) the involvement of parents and teachers in the programme activities; (*c*) the involvement of many organisations, both public and private, as partners; (*d*) a strong commitment to the project by superintendents, principals, and other school administrators; and (*e*) a willingness to participate in the evaluation of the project.

The overarching goal of the School of the Future project was to enrich and enhance the lives of children in each of the four communities. Education, physical health, and mental health were all expected to be positively impacted by the project over time. Long-term collaborations were established between local human service agencies, public school systems, and communities of teachers and parents who took an active part in defining the initial goals and objectives for their particular site. It took many months to win over the trust and enthusiastic support of parents in these communities, many of whom were young, relatively uneducated, and alienated from the school because of their own unhappy past experiences.

The key to the success of each programme was the coordinator, typically a highly motivated, professionally trained social worker who was part of the local culture. The coordinator's role being a new one, the positions, requirements, and methodologies were largely unspecified, and the tasks and activities undefined. Each site hired its own coordinator whose primary task was to bring together, in a school setting, an array of appropriate prevention and intervention programmes in the areas of mental health, physical health, and personal enrichment. To accomplish these goals, the coordinator spent months trying to win over the trust of key parents in the neighbourhood, as well as the principal and teachers of the school. While crucial to the project, the coordinators did not work alone. Other key players at each site included principals, school district administrators, community leaders, parents, programme partners, and service providers.

At the preschool level, programmes were designed to include Head Start, primary health care, and some form of parent education and child care. In the elementary and middle schools, efforts concentrated on mental health problems, such as substance abuse, school dropouts, teen pregnancy, and suicide, as well as on programmes designed to promote self-esteem, conflict resolution, gang prevention, and other effective interpersonal relations. While the focus and emphasis differed from one site to another, the fundamental principles, overarching goals, and key stakeholders in the project were essentially the same.

Even under the best of circumstances, planned interventions of this magnitude and the accompanying social change do not occur overnight. Almost a year was spent trying to secure parental involvement, the cooperation of teachers, persuading other external sponsors and human service providers to become involved, and dealing with misperceptions, occasional initial hostility, and un-founded rumours. With technical assistance from outside consultants, each site conducted its own needs assessment and a series of com-munity-oriented discussion groups to reach a consensus on areas of greatest need for children and families within the neighbourhood.

Concurrent with the formative organisation at each site, profes-sional staff from the Hogg Foundation and the several cooperating universities developed a detailed plan for both qualitative and quan-titative evaluation of the ongoing evolutionary progress of each School of the Future, as well as long-term outcome after the antici-pated 5 years. Community psychologists, educational specialists, sociologists, and statisticians played a key role in the development of both short and long term research strategies. A major task in the first year of the project was to develop an appropriate set of assess-ment instruments that could be used for collecting data from thou-sands of children as well as their teachers in schools where the experimental School of the Future programme was being launched. Special emphasis was placed upon instruments that would be appropriate for assessing the mental health of children, their self-attitudes and their perception of the school and the neighbourhood in which they lived.

Quantitative data collected annually from children included Achenbach's (1991a) Youth Self-Report Survey for middle school students, and Achenbach's (1991b) Teacher Report Form for ele-mentary school children to assess changes in their mental health; the National Education Longitudinal Study of 1988 to evaluate the school climate as perceived by the students and teachers at the sites; and Rosenberg's (1965) Self-Esteem Survey as a measure of the stu-dents' general feelings about themselves. In addition, six items from Phinney's Multigroup Ethnic Identity Measure and two items deal-ing with parents' language at home and child's language on the playground were included in the annual child survey to ascertain how familiar the respondent was with his or her own race or cul-ture. These eight questions on the use of language in the home, ethnic pride, and participation in cultural holidays and events, provided a basis for analysing data for bicultural and traditional student re-spondents. Information on each child concerning school grades, standardised test scores, attendance and discipline reports was also obtained from all participating schools.

The Youth Self-Report Survey and the Teacher Report Form were developed by Achenbach and his associates and have been translated and standardised in a number of other languages for use in both clinical practice and research in different cultures. The final draft comprises a total of 102 items which are used for scoring the following syndromes — somatic complaints, anxious/depressed, social problems, delinquent behaviour, and aggressive behaviour. Parallel items for self-report for use by teachers and for informed adults, who know the children, make the instrument particularly attractive for assessing a child from different perspectives. Psychometric studies of large samples in the School of the Future project largely confirm Achenbach's research. Four major factors — anxious/depressed, somatic complaints, delinquent behaviour, and impulsiveness — accounted for most of the common variance in the item intercorrelations of the 102 items. Reliability coefficients of factor scores ranged from .77 to .88, sufficiently high for most purposes (Wilkinson & Diamond, in press).

Qualitative data consisted of repeated key informant interviews, case materials available in the records of human service agencies as well as from counsellors and others participating in the project as partners, periodic observations by research associates and other key participants, and intensive structured interviews with the parents of nearly 300 children in their homes after the 5-year experimental programme was completed. Only a few generalisations drawn on the basis of the data obtained from the numerous studies completed and underway can be presented here. However, before drawing any general conclusions, it is important to understand the essential characteristics of these four communities as well as the key programmes and services that were provided under the School of the Future programme at each site.

Austin

Located in the far southeast part of Austin, the School of the Future served a neighbourhood comprising mainly low income, minority families. Slightly more than half of the population was Hispanic, including an increasing number of Central American immigrants; 27 per cent were African–Americans; and the majority of the others were White. Nearly two-thirds of the families were headed by young single parents in this relatively new and isolated community that had virtually no community amenities or services when the project was started in 1990. Widen Elementary with 1,050 children and Méndez Middle School with 1,200 children, located across the street from each other, provided the focal points for the community.

By the third year, community activities initially organised by the coordinator resulted in the leasing of a vacant building near the schools to serve as an interim multipurpose centre. More than 35 agencies provided services to families throughout the community. While most efforts were devoted to organising and needs assessment in the first year, the School of the Future was able to facilitate direct service to 66 teachers, 33 parents, and 244 children during this period (Millea & Coleman, 1992). A communitywide spring event called the "Family Fair", held at the end of the first year, received such enthusiastic initial response that it became an annual spring event attended by hundreds of parents who obtained information about a wide variety of community resources and health and human services. More than 40 organisations participated in the Family Fair, which included attractions like entertainment, ethnic dancing, and a variety of games in addition to information about support services (Iscoe, 1995a). The growth and importance of this annual event further substantiated the growing solidarity, self-awareness, and empowerment of the community.

Over a period of 3 years, the neighbourhood was transformed from an isolated, fragmented, and economically distraught one to a well organised, invigorated community with effective indigenous leaders and marked by a "can do" spirit with respect to improving the lives of its children and families. An obvious change at the end of 5 years of development, in which the School of the Future played a central role, was the feeling of community pride and self-empowerment expressed by many parents and their success in campaigning for greater public and private support from other parts of the city.

Various award winning programmes were established in the neighbourhood as a result of community empowerment and parental involvement in the schools. At the early childhood, preschool level, pregnant women and first-time parents were provided special, linguistically appropriate services from the Healthy and Fair Start programme, which offered both home- and centre-based services. Home visits included developmental assessments and information on parenting. Children who exhibited developmental delays were attended to by psychologists and other specialists as part of the agency's early childhood intervention strategy. Activities at the centre included parenting classes, parent support groups and a toy lending library for neighbourhood families, and child care providers as well as programme participants. Many volunteers, including teenagers, participated in the programme, and became increasingly aware of the importance of giving a healthy fair start in life to every infant and young child.

At the elementary school level, psychology interns from the University of Texas worked closely with parents, teachers, and children in need of special assistance. A health centre, established at the elementary school, provided services of a nurse, a social worker, a dentist, and specialised medical consultation as and when needed. For the older elementary and middle school children, roving leaders channelled the energies of these youth to constructive neighbourhood activities thereby reducing the incidence of violence and vandalism in the neighbourhood. A local attorney devoted his free time both before and after school to develop a successful peer mediation programme that taught young children how to settle disputes amicably rather than through violent conflict.

As a result of these many successful initiatives, the Dove Springs Collaboration Project was established in 1994 by eight social agencies funded primarily by the City of Austin to offer a variety of additional services for children from birth to the age of 18. Although each programme targeted a different population group, and had a specific focus, all were committed to the same goal, namely, to help produce healthy, non-abusive families who would be capable of helping their children avoid the serious problems that often occur during adolescence and to succeed in school. What was particularly remarkable was that no single service or group tried to take over the project. Rather, this collaboration between schools, independent agencies, and concerned residents is a documented example that people can, with motivation and effort, work together in the best interests of the community.

Houston

The largest metropolitan area in Texas, Houston has grown into an international city over the past 25 years. Many recent immigrants and refugees from all over the world have moved to Houston, often settling in poor, disorganised neighbourhoods. Public schools have been transformed by these massive population movements, creating an urgent need for new solutions to social problems. The School of the Future site chosen by the local planners is located in "the Heights", an area adjacent to downtown that is predominantly Hispanic. The neighbourhood surrounding the two elementary schools and one middle school was characterised by poor housing, large families, high rate of drug use, poor health, violence, and crime. To operate the School of the Future, the Houston Family Service Center, a large social service agency located in the vicinity, formed a partnership with the Houston Independent School District and served as the primary organisation for hiring the site coordinator and receiving grants from other partners to support new programmes.

A full-time bilingual counsellor along with the site coordinator made efforts to elicit parental involvement in planning and decision-making and visited homes throughout the neighbourhood. An interdisciplinary social service support team provided substance abuse prevention and intervention services and educational support in each of the three schools. Training in creative performing arts was organised at the middle school by a new organisation comprising musicians, artists, and actors; the aim was to build confidence and self-esteem. Children in need of mental health services were referred to therapists from the Family Service Center. Other programmes included a parent volunteer programme, parent volunteer classes for Hispanic families, and mentoring programmes by volunteers. In the fifth year, a new programme was launched in the elementary schools for hundreds of young mothers and their preschool children. Everyday the mothers were given training in literacy, basic skills, and child rearing while their young children attended a special Montessori school in adjacent classrooms using educational materials and technical assistance donated by a private organisation.

One of the most pressing needs in "the Heights" was the provision of physical health services in addition to mental health, social service, and education. A high rate of absenteeism at the middle school was due to acute or chronic health problems which received scant medical attention. An opportunity arose in the third year of the project to secure low cost, high quality health services from Community Partners, a private non-profit agency. The school principal mobilised parents in the neighbourhood to advocate for a health clinic.

The school provided the space, the Family Service Center arranged funds for equipment, and Community Partners took over the management. Preliminary evaluations revealed that absenteeism dropped, school performance improved, and teenagers led healthier, happier lives than before the clinic was established (Iscoe, 1995b).

The programmes discussed here represent only a sampling of new activities at the School of the Future in Houston. The number and variety of partners multiplied to over 36, dealing with a wide spectrum of diverse needs at the preschool, elementary, middle school, and community levels. Total financial support for programmes within "the Heights" increased to more than $4 million of new funds in 5 years.

Dallas

The Metroplex consisting of Dallas, Fort Worth and the many suburbs that have mushroomed around them has undergone a major transformation due to massive immigration. By 1990, the Dallas Independent School District was ready to experiment with new ways of delivering social and health services to students and their families. A unique opportunity arose to use what was once a large shopping centre in South Dallas as a site for the School of the Future. Two elementary schools had been set up in this shopping mall, serving nearly 600 students, a large majority of whom were African–American. Most of the students were from poor families which were struggling to survive under difficult circumstances. The shopping mall had a large amount of undedicated space in which the School of the Future could be housed. A coalition comprising many social agencies was formed which realised the tremendous opportunity to provide school-based services for the neighbourhood. A key player in bringing together the various groups was the project coordinator, who was familiar with the neighbourhood and was successful in eliciting strong support from parent leaders.

The first year was spent primarily in planning for the allocation of space on an equitable basis and the remodelling necessary to make it suitable for use by the coalition partners. A community survey was undertaken by the neighbourhood teenagers who were given special training in conducting interviews with parents in the neighbourhood to determine school and family concerns. Child care, jobs, health services, recreation, and other wellness activities were identified as the highest priority long-term needs of the children and their families.

The one-stop, supermarket concept of health and human services offered in the same complex as public education proved to be very attractive to the neighbourhood. Initial indifference and outright hostility were overcome once large numbers of families began to realise the new opportunities for self-help and improvement that were offered by the School of the Future. Many areas within the supermarket were used by more than one occupant since sharing facilities and resources is an essential feature of this multipurpose centre. Located on the first floor were the central offices, recreation, health, and fitness. More specialised services, such as prevention, intervention, and treatment, as well as information and referral, were provided on level two. The third floor housed special education and training, additional social services, and health screening and evaluation (Iscoe, 1995c).

At the end of each day, the rooms from where these services were provided were occupied by other providers in the evening and weekends who offered family therapy, parenting education, and group counselling to older children and adults. By coordinating the sharing of space, the School of the Future was able to bring twice as many services on site as it would if each agency had the sole use of its rooms.

The smoothly operating, synergistic effect of this health and human services supermarket as it functions today took years to accomplish and several major barriers had to be surmounted. These challenges are common to innovative social service programmes, especially those that require extensive collaboration. People are initially suspicious and slow to accept such a project for fear that it would only mean more work for them. Others are initially unenthusiastic or even hostile to the idea of additional social services being offered within the school set up. Innumerable details must be attended to by the coordinator and other staff members. Policies and procedures differ from one agency to another, resulting in different eligibility requirements for clients. Finally, agencies often seek to protect their own turf rather than to see ways in which they may collaborate with others to achieve long-term goals. It cannot be overemphasised how important the coordinator is as the key person to build trust and to coax and cajole potential partners in such an effort. The coordinator must be effective in encouraging parents to organise, to participate in planning and decision-making, and to advocate as a community for better resources. After the programme had been operating for several years, both teachers and parents enthusiastically identified with it, and campaigned for its expansion, and defended it against external criticism.

San Antonio

The fourth School of the Future was situated in the heart of the third largest metropolitan area in Texas. In many ways similar to the poor neighbourhoods of Latin American cities, the poverty stricken area in the near West Side of San Antonio had an overwhelmingly Mexican culture and tradition. The average income of a family of four being less than one-sixth that of the average American family. Less than 20 per cent of the population in the neighbourhood had a high school education. The two elementary schools and one middle school constituting the School of the Future project were in sharp contrast to the surrounding overcrowded, dilapidated area. The flagship of the programme was a large elementary school completely rebuilt in 1978, in the centre of the oldest federal housing project in the nation. Many residents of San Antonio avoided the near West Side area – an area known for prostitution, drugs, gang violence, and early death (Lein, Radle, & Radle, 1992).

The three schools and their earlier forms have long been viewed as safe havens within the community. In spite of the widespread poverty, rundown housing, and a host of social problems of the neighbourhood, the principals were eager to develop the School of the Future concept. The coordinator had lived in the area with his family for 15 years prior to the project and had been actively involved in community development during that time. A social worker by training, he was well equipped to work closely with school administrators, teachers, parents, and graduate students in social work or family counselling from the two local universities.

In the first year of the project, the coordinator and the elementary school principal worked closely together in designing a strategy to involve parents, both as volunteers and as decision makers, in developing new programmes for children and their families. The coordinator was able to quickly design a programme of family counselling and crisis intervention in the elementary school. The inclusion of parenting education set the stage for securing parental trust under the leadership of the project coordinator and his wife, who was also a professional teacher and community worker.

The child and family therapy programme was located within the elementary school and began with five student interns working under supervision in the first year. By the second year, this number had doubled to 10, and by the fourth year, 21 interns and graduate student volunteers were working in the therapy programme. These interns provided therapy to students, their families, and other community members. A mental health team comprising psychologists, social workers, and student interns was set up to discuss individual cases. Consultation was also provided to teachers on how to deal with students' problems in the classroom. Assessment was available for individual children, and families were referred to social services whenever needed. The number of individuals counselled grew from 136 in the first year to 606 by the fifth year. Each client was seen for an average 6 hours spread over several weeks or months.

In spite of the scarcity of resources available in the immediate area surrounding the schools, the coordinator was successful in developing partnerships with 16 other organisations and agencies, both public and private, throughout the city of San Antonio. During the 5-year period, 29 different programmes or services were initiated in the three schools in the four major areas of student and teacher support, mental health and social services, parent education and support, and violence reduction (Iscoe, 1995d).

Preliminary Findings from the School of the Future Project

While much of the massive amount of data collected has yet to be analysed, several outcomes are clear and may be effectively utilised for designing a strategy for community empowerment and human development that uses the school as a locus for developing more effective social support systems. Although each of these four sites is located in a large city, they differ greatly in their ethnic composition, in their organisation of human services, and in their school administration. All four have relative disadvantaged neighbourhoods but differ markedly in whether they are old or new communities, whether they are on the periphery of the city or in the centre of it, and the extent to which potential resources, both public and private, are available. Of the four sites, the economically impoverished, Mexican neighbourhood in the heart of San Antonio closely approximates situations one is likely to encounter in the growing cities of developing countries in Latin America, Africa, and Asia.

In spite of the many differences, implementation of the School of the Future model was highly successful in all four communities. In accordance with the original strategy, the Hogg Foundation's financial support at each site was withdrawn at the end of the 5-year period. The network of supporting partners was sufficiently strong, the four coordinators were so deeply committed, and members of the communities were so forceful in their advocacy of the programme that the transition from external funding to indigenous continuation proceeded smoothly. These changes did not occur overnight, it took several years in each case to reach the point where strong support was forthcoming from teachers, service providers, sponsors, and key members of the surrounding community.

Each of the sites found a way to extend the programme to other parts of the city. In Austin, the programme spread to other elementary schools and the high school within the larger community. Two elementary schools in other parts of the city, together with their surrounding communities, embarked upon a replication of the programme. The planning process was in place during 1995 and full-scale operations were to begin in the fall of 1996. In Houston, efforts were made to encompass 11 new elementary schools, another middle school and a high school, covering a total of over 10,000 children. The coordinator extended his influence to the other schools by employing six new family outreach workers. In Dallas, plans were made for school-based programmes in 14 other schools providing health and social services to low income students and their families. The most impoverished school district, San Antonio, allocated a major share of funds from its limited budget to more than double the number of schools and surrounding neighbourhoods that were to be provided school-based services. Clearly, the general concept of school-based services for neighbourhood children and their families is a very attractive one, and its efficacy has been amply demonstrated.

The success of the School of the Future project in these four sites is due to the close adherence to the time-tested principles of community development and programme evaluation. Among the more important of these, which together constitute a strategy for community empowerment and development, are the following:

COMMUNITY INVOLVEMENT FROM THE BEGINNING Of fundamental importance is the inclusion of community members on the planning teams from the very beginning. Most communities in need of help are understandably suspicious of well-meaning professionals who offer a ready-made plan that has been designed without local involvement. It is important to locate the most respected community members who are either already recognised leaders or have the potential to be spokesmen for recognised segments of the community who have a stake in the project's outcome. There are individuals with whom one must negotiate, involving them from the very beginning in any planning or decision-making process.

STAKEHOLDER INCLUSION The initiators (representatives of the Hogg Foundation for Mental Health in the School of the Future, for example) should formulate a *brief* description of the proposed project and several criteria, clearly and simply stated, that must be agreed upon by all parties concerned before the project can proceed successfully. Considerable time and energy may have to be devoted to preliminary conferences with each of the key stakeholders — school administrators, teacher representatives, human service providers, government officials, and other potential partners who would be clearly impacted by the project's success or failure. While some degree of opposition may be inevitable, it is important to have a strong consensus before proceeding further.

NEEDS ASSESSMENT Every community requires help in order to improve the quality of life of its members. Some needs are far greater than others, some are well recognised while others are latent, and some clearly fall outside the range of any capability of amelioration by any initiative associated with the proposed project. While technical assistance may be necessary to conduct a sound assessment, it is equally important to involve community members in the planning, decision-making, and execution of the assessment itself so that they are committed to the emerging results and understand the relationship between the outcome with respect to priorities and the limited resources that may be available through the project initiative.

ASSET INVENTORY Every community has indigenous resources and potential leaders but often such assets are not self-evident. A realistic inventory of resources and assets is an important complement to needs assessment and should be carried out by the community itself with technical assistance.

EVOLUTIONARY DEVELOPMENT Under a comprehensive approach, specifying too many details or too much structure early in the process may produce unnecessary conflict, misunderstanding, and confusion. As long as the overarching objective and initial commitments are clearly stated and adhered to throughout the process, the unfolding of the project details should follow an evolutionary course with step-by-step discussion and decision-making involving all the key stakeholders. Though often painfully slow, such a process is essential to the eventual understanding and commitment of the involved parties. Such an evolutionary process may lead to different priorities and specific initiatives for each community, while at the same time adhering to the overarching goals and fundamental criteria spelt out initially.

THE COORDINATOR Given adherence to these principles, the most important person in the project is the coordinator who must serve as the project promoter at the local level, eliciting support from the community, the sponsorship of other partners, and the involvement of key stakeholders. Such a person should have appropriate previous experience and training, he or she should not only be strongly endorsed by the key stakeholders, but should also be able to work harmoniously with the predominant cultures of the community. All four coordinators in the School of the Future project fulfilled these criteria and made an initial commitment to stay with the project for 5 years. Of interest is the fact that all four were associated with the project even after the 5-year period because of their enthusiasm and deep commitment to the basic concept as well as to the neighbourhoods in which they worked.

PROGRAMME EVALUATION While evaluation should be under the direction of an experienced, well qualified expert who does not have a personal stake in the project outcome, the community and other stakeholders should be made aware from the beginning of what kind of evaluation would be undertaken and how the findings would be publicised. All parties should agree to their participation in the evaluation. School staff should be involved in decisions about the kinds of data that would be collected and what is expected of them in the process. Teachers, human service providers, and other professionals are busy people who have their own priorities and, therefore, do not have the time to assist except in incidental ways. Where assistance is required for evaluation, the use of incentives for participants may be essential. All relevant research findings should be shared with the key stakeholders at different phases in the evolution of the project and especially after its completion. Commitment to evaluation for the length of the project on the part of key participants is essential. Some kind of evaluation is desirable not only to gain insight into both the evolutionary process and the final outcomes of the project, but also to create awareness among the participants that their project is sufficiently special and important to justify the expense and efforts of systematic evaluation. The continuous nature of evaluation coupled with appropriate feedback to the stakeholders may facilitate midstream corrections and inculcate a sense of pride in the participants.

Strategies for Psychologists in Developing Countries

Psychology varies from one country to another to the extent to which resources are available for linking social support systems to neighbourhood schools. In most cases, traditional public schools are managed by central government bureaucracies which are reluctant to cede control to local initiatives. Existing agencies within health and human services are not only understaffed and poorly funded but also often under government control. Each agency jealously guards what little area it may have, being suspicious of any restructuring of control and influence that may reduce its limited power. Consequently, the most interesting developments to date have usually been introduced by local initiatives — churches, community cooperatives, and small collectives — rather than by central governments. Often encouraged by outside private organisations, these local, non-governmental initiatives have grown in number and variety at an explosive rate in the past few years.

Two examples from the many international, private organisations promoting local initiatives at the neighbourhood and village level illustrate how this focus on activating local community self-help has spread. The Bernard van Leer Foundation headquartered in the Netherlands has been active since 1950 in small communities and neighbourhoods throughout the world. Its efforts are concentrated on the development of low cost, community-based initiatives in early child care and education for socially and culturally disadvantaged children from birth to the age of 8. In 1995, the Foundation provided financial support and technical assistance to over 100 major projects in some 40 developing and industrialised countries. It operates on the principle that participatory learning is an empowering process for self-help that spreads to the whole community. Basically, participatory learning means including people in their learning so that they become both the authors and subjects of their own development (Bernard van Leer Foundation, 1995).

World Neighbors is an example of a grass-roots development organisation that works directly with local communities in promoting Participatory Rural Appraisal (World Neighbors, 1995). Founded in 1951 in the tradition of neighbour helping neighbour, World Neighbors is a self-help movement that does not accept government funding, being supported entirely by private donations, most of which are small. In its view, participation by everyone in the community is the key to a development process in which villages themselves set priorities and work toward their own goals. Community members from the beginning are involved in generating, analysing, and owning information about their situation. Several tools have been developed over the years for enabling local people, often illiterate, to present their knowledge of life and conditions in their communities and to help them develop a plan of action. In 1995, World Neighbors reached over 1 million people through 87 programmes in 21 countries of Asia, Africa, and Latin America on a budget of only $3 million.

Psychologists in developing countries would do well to take note of these new developments and the energy that they unlock for community initiatives. While the two examples cited here do not directly involve school-based health and human services, the similarities in strategy to those of the School of the Future are obvious. At present, the leaders who are involved in the worldwide growth of NGOs and who are devoted to local initiatives are drawn from other fields. As Sanchez (1995) pointed out in his call for psychologists to define a

234 WAYNE H. HOLTZMAN

new methodology for the study of citizen participation, psychology can hardly afford to ignore them.

Joining forces in partnership with others dedicated to human development at the grass-roots level would greatly enhance the likelihood that psychology in general, and community psychology in particular, would be revitalised in a more universal form that is relevant to the human condition in diverse cultures and countries. Such refocusing of theory and practice would only benefit psychology and its contributions to the solution of pressing social problems in the developing nations of Africa, Asia, and Latin America as well as in the more advanced, relatively wealthy countries of the Western world.

FOURTEEN

Culture as a Factor in Community Interventions

❧ R.C. Tripathi ❧

Life is pain, joy, beauty, ugliness, love, and when we understand it as a whole, at every level, that understanding creates its own techniques. But the contrary is not true, technique can never bring about creative understanding.

In over emphasizing technique we destroy man. To cultivate capacity and efficiency without understanding life, without having a comprehensive perception of the ways of thought and desire will only make us increasingly ruthless, which is to engender wars and jeopardize our physical security (Krishnamurthy, 1992, p. 18).

In my lifetime, psychology has undergone a sea change. When I began my training in psychology in the early 1960s, it was earnestly believed that the business of psychology was to discover causal relationships in order to enable the scientist to make correct predictions. This understanding of the cause–effect relationship helped the scientist to control behavioural outcomes and eventually shape the behaviour of individuals in desirable directions. Scientists were absolutely certain about what they needed to change and why. Innumerable systematic approaches and techniques to bring about changes and modification in the behaviour of individuals, groups and organisations were discovered and applied, sometimes with success, but often with little or limited success. Such applications only helped in making scientists realise the fragility of their models and techniques. Meanwhile, the debate on "freedom and dignity" and achieving of personhood got sharpened. As a result, "empowerment" became the byword of all change efforts. With the postmodernistic approaches making inroads in psychology, the dominant paradigm of psychology, although still alive and kicking, is trying to figure out its response to "multiple truths". If truth is not one, how does one plan, intervene or shape systems? Does one need to intervene at all? On the other hand, if truth is not one, does this foreclose all possibilities of action? Perhaps not. Both aesthetic sense and inclinations do not tolerate disorder in any form. A natural response, therefore, is to intervene to improve conditions of any system. For psychologists, the focus seems to have shifted from behaviour to acts of meaning. There are persistent attempts to "rethink" psychology. However, there does not appear to be any possibility of psychologists giving up their attempts to build a better world or putting checks on their visualising possible utopias. The effort is to understand the meaning and value of psychological interventions against this background. Although psychology is primarily a human science, its possibilities as a policy science have been recognised (J.B.P. Sinha, 1990).

Psychology has meaning to the extent it can contribute to enhancing quality of life of people in developing systems and organisations which would protect persons from losing their personhoods. There is much to learn how this is to be achieved.

Meaning of Social Change and Development

Psychological and social interventions aim to achieve an ideal state. All interveners or change agents have a vision and they seek to bring about changes in systems to move closer to their vision. It is, therefore, important to understand the cultural differences in these visions and to explore the possibility of developing a shared vision. It is in this context that there is a need to understand the meaning of the notions of change and development in social systems.

All human and social systems are dynamic, internally as well as externally. Yet, a system's inner dynamics is static in as much as its significant parameters vary within a given and predictable range. This gives the system its degree of order. But in the process of meeting its internal and external demands it also grows. It adds new functions. It forms new relationships. Sometimes it even adds new elements to its structure. Such changes in structure and functions, processes and relationships of human and social systems have come to be denoted by various terms such as social change, development, acculturation, growth, and modernity.

Reviewing the usage and meaning of these terms in various social science disciplines such as anthropology, economics, political science, and sociology, Berry (1980c) concluded that they were confusing. There appear to be at least two sources of confusion. Some terms like social change, development, and modernisation are used interchangeably. Terms like modernisation and development mean different things to social scientists because of their value positions. Specifically, the value attached to the term development is far more than other terms. It is, therefore, important to understand the meaning of the term development because all interventions are aimed to enhance development, whether at the individual level (personal development) or at the group (group and organisational development) or societal levels (human and social development).

There is little doubt that the existing development paradigm which is largely Western, equates development with modernisation. Here, attitudes, beliefs, and ideas are viewed as traditional if they are not in consonance with the notions of economic and scientific rationality which form the core of development of industrialised Western societies. Tradition has no place in this development paradigm. In fact, tradition is perceived as the opposite of development. Various developmental agencies such as the World Bank, the IMF, and the UNDP consider the economic facets of development of primary significance. The new concept of Human Development Index (HDI) developed by the UNDP recently incorporates certain other indicators as literacy, life expectancy, and gender discrimination, as facets of development. The new approaches to the study of development accept the right of developing societies to organise around their own values and objectives and support endogenous development (Alechina, 1982; Belshaw, 1972).

This, however, is done somewhat grudgingly and mere lip service is paid to the rights of people in developing societies and cultures. This was fairly evident in the way the recent negotiations on the formation of the WTO and on similar other matters were carried out. Traditional non-Western societies either do not have the courage to raise their voices or where they have been raised, they have not been heard. The forces of globalisation in a unipolar world have had no time to pause and consider the intrinsic relationship between culture and development. On the other hand, the proponents of endogenous development have not been able to put together their vision of another world and how they propose to use their existing cultural apparatuses to alleviate human suffering in their societies.

Tripathi (1988b) examined the problems associated with the notions of social change and development and attempted to fuse the local with the universal. He distinguished change from development primarily in terms of two criteria: openness and embeddedness which have to be simultaneously satisfied. Change in a condition which removes blocks restricting the growth of a system at one or more levels and consequently makes it more open contribute to development but only if the condition does not disembed the system from its moorings. On the other hand, it should also lead to a greater degree of embeddedness. Embeddedness is reflected in members showing greater emotional investment and involvement, increased sense of personal worth in belonging to the system, and in exerting greater effort in achieving group/organisational objectives. To enhance the degree of embeddedness of its members into a system, new structural or other arrangements need to be evolved to make change more enduring and to transform it into development. A change agent or an interventionist's main task would be to creatively develop and install structures which make the system both open and embedded. A large number of intervention attempts either do not succeed or have limited success because they are not able to remove the blocks impeding development and growth of a system and, therefore, help it in becoming more open, or they threaten its identity and integrity by introducing cultural elements which are inimical to its core values.

Nature and Type of Psychological and Social Interventions

The history of psychological interventions is perhaps as old as psychology itself. The first set of interventions was made at the level of the individual where target variables were school achievement, personal adjustment, work performance, etc. Following the two World Wars, and as social psychology matured as a discipline, there was a shift in the direction of group interventions. It was considered legitimate for psychologists to make interventions in the micro contexts of societies in the 1950s. McClelland and Winter's (1969) work on "motivating economic achievement" is considered one such pioneering effort in this direction. Prior to this, both in analysis and intervention, psychologists had remained at the individual or group level. Psychological applications at the macro level have addressed problems of poverty alleviation, educational development, agricultural and community development, population and health, entrepreneurial development, empowerment of marginalised groups such as minorities, tribal groups and women, etc. As the outcomes of such interventions are by and large temporary, Khandwalla (1988) argued for developing strategic organisations which would bring about social development.

A variety of techniques has been developed for making interventions in communities. They draw largely upon the lessons derived from applications made in organised settings. Some of these tools are used both for diagnostic and intervention purposes such as action research and survey feedback. However, there are other techniques like training for entrepreneurship, achievement motivation, creativity, conflict resolution, conscientisation, participative decision-making, and assertiveness training, which seek to equip individuals in groups, communities and organisations with special skills and competence to achieve their planned objectives. Kiggundu, Jorgensen, and Hafsi (1983); and Reddy (1984) reviewed the applicability of such techniques in developing countries and raised doubts about their applicability as they came into conflict with the cultural, economic and political contexts of these countries. These techniques have their empirical and theoretical bases in psychology as well as in other social sciences. There are, however, organised and planned efforts whose theoretical bases are often unclear. Such interventions are made by agencies, such as governmental organisations, NGOs, voluntary organisations, and special advocacy groups to bring about change. A large number of such interventions in micro contexts are made more often by these agencies and less often by psychologists and other social science professionals.

The nature of interventions can be broadly understood and differentiated in terms of a number of issues like who plans, for whom, for what outcomes, and using what techniques. These need to be elaborated upon.

Definition of the Problem

There are considerable differences in the way a problem is defined and diagnosed by various interveners. For example, governmental agencies are likely to be swayed more by political opinions and ideologies in defining problems requiring interventions and less by expert or public opinion unless they have political implications. Similarly, the agency funding the project is another factor in defining the problem. For example, an NGO which survives on grants from governmental and other sources is more likely to follow the instructions of its funding agencies in comparison to voluntary organisations which have their own sources of funding. Also, the involvement of people in defining the issues is minimal in the case of government initiatives and maximum in the case of community-based organisations.

Who Plans the Intervention

The strategies for intervention and the decision about the technique(s) are planned in a top-down or bottom-up manner. Governmental programmes are announced and sometimes nodal agencies are created for their implementation. The approach, however, remains bureaucratic with minimum opportunity given to people for planning interventions. People are not considered as knowledgeable enough and, therefore, incapable of planning. Other agencies seek to involve people in the intervention being made to varying degrees and for different reasons. An advocacy group may involve people to make them politically efficacious to add credibility to their own voice. While a community organisation may see it as an integral part of the process of empowerment of the focused group of people.

Objectives and Intentions

The nature of interventions by the intervening agencies may also differ with respect to their objectives and intentions. In general, the objectives of governmental agencies are the political programmes of the ruling party. They may or may not implement programmes which the people really need. Generally, programmes which have greater visibility and offer greater "political" mileage are given preference over other programmes by both the government and NGOs. Although political intentions cannot be denied in the case of voluntary and community-based organisations, one expects that interest in solving genuine problems of the people will be higher. Leaders of NGOs, VOs, and COs are also likely to be attracted by prospects of *yash* or good name.

Level of Intervention

The levels of intervention in the case of governmental agencies are macro compared to other intervening agencies. In the case of the latter, they may involve small communities, groups or individuals.

Expected Outcomes

The expected outcomes of interventions made by all agencies are positive changes in the overall quality of life of the people. Some GOs and NGOs may also have a hidden agenda like acquiring legitimacy, so as to become more powerful in cornering scarce resources and in exercising greater influence over people and organisations. People-oriented agencies may seek empowerment of the weak constituents through restructuring of the system itself. In addition to this, such agencies expect that systems will become more cohesive, integrated, and efficient through their interventions.

Technique of Intervention

Governmental interventions focus on bringing about change either through legislation or funding of programmes to raise the living standards of the people. NGOs, however, may seek to bring about change either by increasing awareness of the people or by providing services in various sectors, but they may show little concern for the processes involved.

Professionals from psychology and other disciplines who act as change agents/interveners are often called upon by GOs and NGOs to help in process management. Sometimes they form their own groups for making interventions. The approach they adopt and the problems they deal with are likely to be dependent on the values of those they represent and their own values.

Interveners adopt one of the three focuses in making interventions:

"BLAMING THE VICTIM" APPROACH The poor state of the individual is attributed by the intervener to certain psychological and social characteristics of the individual. Poverty is often viewed as caused by unfavourable motivational structure; for example, low need for achievement and high need for affiliation, belief in external control, and learned helplessness (D. Sinha, 1975). Similarly, the low educational achievement or the high dropout rate among underprivileged children is due to poor academic self-concept or cultural background not conducive to education, poverty, etc. Such an approach focuses on intervening at the psychological level. For example, it may correct attributional styles or develop proper motivational structures and restructure attitudes and cognitions. The positive gains of this approach are limited. By not addressing the underlying causes of a person's existential condition, one is not able to bring about any enduring changes in the person.

"BLAMING THE SYSTEM" The second focus is on the causes of "underdevelopment", low growth or poor quality of life which are attributed to an unjust social system in which scarce resources have been unequally distributed and have been cornered by a select few. Laws also do not permit a fair allocation of resources. Poor quality of life results from objective conditions as well as making comparisons with people who are better off. If there is little hope of bringing about a change in a particular system one either gives up and becomes alienated or strikes at the system (Crosby, 1982). Intervention strategies using this approach seek to bring about radical change in the way relationships are structured within a system and in the power structure.

Such changes are brought about through restructuring and through techniques of group work which may democratise the system by involving its members at various levels in decisions crucial for them and their lives. Apart from intervening in the existing systems, another approach is to form development partnerships with private voluntary organisations and social scientists and develop "bridging institutions" to provide for greater interorganisational cooperation (Brown 1988). Such institutions are particularly expected to bridge the gaps between the market, the state, and the people.

"BLAMING BOTH SYSTEM AND VICTIM" This seeks a via media and identifies domains of individual behaviour as well as those elements in the system which are not conducive to the organisation's and people's development. The approach attempts to maximise the functioning of individual members and also simultaneously restructure organisations.

Lessons from Studies of Community Interventions in India

The following offers a review of some important studies in which interventions were made in community settings to enhance the overall effectiveness of systems in different sectoral areas. Several reviews of such studies are available (Pareek, 1981; Tripathi, 1988a). The focus here will be on studies which sought to alleviate poverty and bring about a change in the overall quality of life of people. Attention will also be on attempts made to rehabilitate persons with disabilities in community settings.

The maximum number of interventions in the community setting by social scientists in India have been done in rural areas involving farmers. Attempts have been made to bring about changes in the attitudes of farmers towards adoption of agricultural innovations and to inculcate a scientific outlook. These were largely a result of the massive community development (CD) programme launched by the Government of India in the early 1950s. Under this programme, clusters of villages are grouped as blocks within a district. Each block is administered by a Block Development Officer, and each village is provided with village level workers. These functionaries work under the district administration, which receives funds for various development programmes directly from the government. The KAP (Knowledge, Attitude, Practice) model served as the basis of this programme. Block development officers are expected to provide information about modern agricultural implements, improved seeds, and new methods of farming to the villagers. Demonstrations are arranged. Implements and fertilisers are made available to farmers, either free of cost or at subsidised rates. Agricultural extension agencies and research institutes are also involved in these efforts. Radio forums for farmers are organised, where the farmers listen to regular broadcasts of programmes on farming and other related matters and discuss them in groups. The community development programme remains the most ambitious programme undertaken by the Government of India after the independence to change the lives of the rural people. So much so, that a separate Ministry of Community Development was created, headed by a minister of the cabinet rank. Many studies evaluated the success of the community development programme in terms of the social and psychological changes it brought about, besides changes in agroeconomic development. Most studies reported that the community development programme did not make a significant impact on the lives of people and it was not favourably evaluated (Agarwal, 1979; Verma, 1970). Durganand Sinha's (1969; 1974) study, which adopted a longitudinal design, is one of the most extensive studies conducted by a psychologist on understanding the impact of this massive community development programme. On the basis of their degree of economic development, he selected six villages where the CD programme was at various stages, i.e., where it had been in operation for long, and where it had yet to be introduced. He studied the impact of the intervention in terms of fears, aspirations, life goals of villagers, and the extent to which the programme had "modernising" effects on their attitudes towards education, health practices, sanitation, etc. It was observed that even years after the community development programme had been introduced the villagers were not very optimistic about their future. They manifested stagnant aspirations, risk avoidance, and extreme caution. Agroeconomic development was not in any way associated with their motivational structures. Referring to these findings, Sinha (1988a) observed,

> Withdrawal of governmental support after a period of massive developmental activity has often been found to lead to a rapid decline in the areas concerned. The stagnant level of aspirations combined with the absence of striving and risk-taking account for the fact that developmental programmes are not self generating and self-sustaining (p. 37).

Sinha explained the failure of the CD programme in terms of the absence of impact of the programme on psychological structures.

The psychocultural characteristics of Indians have often been cited as lying at the root of low economic development of the country both by Indian and Western social scientists. Max Weber (1958) was the first to find fault with the religions of India and to argue that protestant ethics underlay the spirit of capitalism which flowered in the form of the industrial revolution. Later, McClelland (1961) followed this lead and pointed out that Hinduism did not encourage need for achievement. Hindu parents, according to him, did not insist on their children setting standards of excellence and did not encourage children to achieve those standards. Kapp (1963) isolated the cultural characteristics of Hindus and posited their relationship with economic development; according to him, belief in "cyclical time and cosmological causation belong to those basic categories of Hinduism which stand in the way of the emergence of one basic prerequisite of economic development" (p. 43). Among Indian psychologists, J.B.P. Sinha (1980; 1982) analysed the Indian sociocultural milieu and observed that dependence proneness, emphasis on personal relationships, belief in hierarchy, and soft (*aram*) organisational culture impeded economic development. Pareek's (1970) model of poverty attributes poverty among Indians to low needs for achievement and extension. While analysing factors associated with poverty, D. Sinha (1975) reported that poor people were low on perceptual and linguistic skills, low on achievement and self-esteem, extremely fatalistic, had unrealistic aspirations, and were high on external control. Several authors who have examined the psychocultural characteristics of villagers either directly or obliquely, ascribe the blame to the victims for their existential states.

Some researchers, however, perceived the failure of the CD programme as a failure of the system. Agarwal (1979) and Samanta (1982) ascribed the blame to dissatisfied developmental personnel who feared for their personal safety, lacked power to influence decisions, and had to contend with political interference in their day-to-day working, and found the overall work environment very discouraging. Mehta (1983) noted that the failure of governmental programmes was due to people's poor perception of the role of government, bad demonstration effect, and poor communication between the change agents and targets of change. According to Talib (1981), resistance to change is legitimate on part of Indian peasants because they believe that technological innovations have failed to make basic change in their socioeconomic conditions. Social scientists who attribute failure of governmental programmes to system failure are quick to point out that the strategic organisations entrusted with the responsibility of directing social change and development lack efficiency. They have a poor organisational culture (seen as a result of dysfunctional social values) and have been organised on the basis of the Western bureaucratic model which is alien to the Indian ethos and cultural matrix.

In sharp contrast to the community development programmes of the government, there are two intervention efforts which have been successful and deserve to be mentioned here. This may help us understand what makes such programmes successful. The first one in Tilonia village has continued for a fairly long period of time, in this programme a formal NGO called the Social Work and Research Center (SWRC) located in the village itself was involved (S. Roy, 1988). The second one was more like a field experiment in community intervention and was launched in Singari village, in this social scientists working as external change agents were involved (Chandra & Mehta, 1984).

The main objective of the programme at Tilonia is to bring about integrated rural development by ensuring the minimum needs in the areas of drinking water, education, health, and agriculture. As Roy (1988) explained, the approach adopted at Tilonia makes an attempt to integrate the knowledge and skills of the villagers with urban knowledge, human with financial resources, and the community's needs with services. Members of the SWRC live with the rural people and interact freely with all members of the community. Initially, all villagers were involved but later the organisers came into conflict with the politically and socially powerful section of the village community. They have since focused only on the poor in the community. The programme identifies the skills and knowledge of the members of the rural community and upgrades them so that they can be used for the good of the community. No free service or charity is provided to the members of the community. The programme is highly decentralised. For example, programmes like groundwater location, school education, preventive health schemes, rural industries, animal husbandry, agricultural extension, and women's programmes are managed by the villagers themselves. Initially, they were started by trained urban professionals. Roy identified the various factors contributing to the success of the intervention programme at Tilonia.

1. Support provided by the programme to people in crises.
2. Without an ideological basis, the programme uses multiple methods and approaches.
3. A desire to integrate and learn from the rural people so as to make use of local knowledge.
4 Conscientisation of the poor and training them to become leaders.
5. Giving precedence to skills and knowledge over school degrees. Often a skilled but unschooled villager functions as the supervisor of people with school degrees.

6. Making local organisations accountable to the community.
7. Continuous upgradation of rural technology.

Some of the elements of the approach adopted in the Tilonia project have also been found useful in the context of South Africa. While discussing the use of psychological research in the process of social change, Vlaenderen (1993) observed that two kinds of approaches are possible for understanding and managing social change so far as psychologists are concerned. The first one focuses on helping communities to research problems which they have to contend with. Psychological research is contextualised within a people centred approach. The second approach called the "service approach" not only aids communities in the research process, but also in developing the capacities of their members. To achieve this, it is important to understand and give due credence to local knowledge, i.e., knowledge available in the form of concepts, beliefs and perceptions, and processes through which it is transmitted in the local settings (Chambers, 1985). Empowering rural people by raising their capacities is possible only by resolving the tension that may exist between expert knowledge and local knowledge. Vlaenderen and Gilbert (1990) presented a case study in which rural development involved capacity building of individuals and organisations. This was achieved through participatory research and by utilising local knowledge. The project proposal was written and finalised with the help of external researchers by the members of the community themselves and then ratified by the community. While referring to the outcomes of participatory research, the investigators concluded that besides improving human and organisational capacities for problem solving, this experience enhanced their self-confidence in achieving what they wanted.

The second intervention by Chandra and Mehta (1984) used people's initiative in directing social change and at the same time put emphasis on making the right use of the existing social and political structures. This effort was launched as an experimental project with a view to empowering the poor tribal people to improve their options and life chances. The project started as a night literacy class for the youth of Singari village. Initially, very few youth attended the classes as they did not trust the organisers. An incident involving a policeman, who had extracted a bribe from a villager, was used by the organisers to win the trust of the villagers. First, the youth in the literacy class were informed that the policeman could be made to return the bribe. Of course, they did not believe this but were curious whether it could really be pulled off. The organisers met the concerned officials to inform them about the incident and sought intervention of the top bureaucrats. This helped the organisers. The policeman had to return the bribe he had accepted in the presence of villagers in the village market. This single incident enabled the group organisers to win the confidence of the villagers. Attendance in the literacy class increased and the night school became a kind of a community centre for other activities. The organisers convened a meeting of a group of youth to discuss the problem of rampant drinking in the village and to take some measures to prevent it. The youth organised a large meeting of the villagers in which this problem was discussed. Following this, many villagers decided to give up drinking. A watchdog body in the form of a village council was set up to ensure that those who had given up drinking kept their promise. Voluntary prohibition continued. This boosted the morale of the village council and it decided to take on the village moneylenders who were exploiting them by charging very high interest rates and fudging the accounts against the villagers. The village council discovered that the money which had been paid to them was far more than what was their due. Therefore, the council instructed the villagers not to pay any more money to them. Although death threats were made by the moneylenders, the villagers as a group remained cohesive and no one opposed the decision of the council. Other activities of the council included launching income generating projects with the active help of the district officials. A sense of political efficacy developed among the villagers and they began to actively participate in making decisions vitally related to their lives. It was their active participation in the project which empowered them. The Singari project revealed that external change agents have to be good facilitators of group processes. They can help in the development of democratic values and collective leadership. Another important learning was that external change agents can enable groups to open communication channels with the bureaucrats whose help may be needed in securing loans and support for participation in various governmental programmes. This is important because the poor on their own cannot create any structures although they are eager to improve their quality of life and are ready to learn from others.

The interventions discussed here involved either governmental agencies, voluntary organisations or social service professionals. Recently, a NGO has emerged with active support of the government and some foreign NGOs, it is called "Mahila Samakhya" (MS). Utilising a mixed model, it has taken up the cause of women's empowerment with a great deal of success in six districts in Uttar Pradesh. Mahila Samakhya presents a unique organisational set up and its apex body includes bureaucrats who represent the government and other professionals. Its functioning is completely decentralised and is divided region- and districtwise; it follows a bottom-up approach in programme development and implementation. Large numbers of women from the villages are associated at various levels as *sakhi* (friends), *sahyogini* (associates), and *samanvyak* (coordinator). Mahila Samakhya has organised a women's forum, and has taken up the cause of women in the following areas: (*a*) violence against women, (*b*) fostering a better understanding of the Panchayati Raj (governance through village councils), (*c*) drinking water, and (*d*) labour rates. It has focused on the local needs and helped women to organise around them. They need to be segregated and provided with special facilities as in the case of the blind and deaf and people inflicted with leprosy. In doing so it sets no targets. It focuses primariiy on the process of facilitating empowerment. It has used various cultural devices to increase the awareness of women and the community at large. For example, a traditional way of narrating stories using pictures in Rajasthan is called *Phad*; this method has been successfully utilised to bring to light the way certain village *pradhans* (heads) misused funds allotted for developmental purposes, because of lack of involvement of community members. An interesting project under which women are trained to repair hand pumps has been initiated. This was initially resisted by many male members of the community most concerned about the water problem; since the necessary help from the men was not readily available, they decided to take up this work. They have since successfully looked after the maintenance of water pumps. Mahila Samakhya has fused the formal with the informal, made use of cultural idioms to bring about changes in the attitudes of community members towards women and their place in family and society. Mahila Samakhya's intervention strategy has achieved to a degree the twin criteria of openness and embeddedness.

The discussion so far has focused on interventions which have sought to improve the economic and social conditions of the under-privileged, disadvantaged and poor sections of society. Another section of people, persons with disabilities (PWDs), has attracted the attention of a large number of government organisations and NGOs all over the world. Today, there are at least 1,500 NGOs in India working in this area according to Thomas (1993) but the number could be much higher. The lessons drawn from interventions in the community settings have been used to develop a Community Based Rehabilitation (CBR) approach. For a long time the rehabilitation of physically disabled persons had been the responsibility of charitable organisations. PWDs have been viewed as objects of "sympathy", and at times as "odd balls". They need to be segregated and provided with special facilities as, for instance, the blind and deaf and people suffering from leprosy.

The CBR movement is seen as an offshoot of the current emphasis on social development and the even greater emphasis on involving the local communities in the delivery of health care (Thomas, 1993). In the case of CBR, the main focus is on mainstreaming of disabled persons as they are seen as a human resource rather than a liability. The objectives of the CBR as stated by Lysack and Kaufert (1993) are very similar to those of poverty alleviation programmes (perhaps because there is an intimate relationship between poverty, illiteracy, and disability). These are (*a*) changing attitudes and behaviour towards disability, (*b*) empowerment of persons with disability, (*c*) changing the roles from "boss" to "participants" in health programmes, and (*d*) translating appropriate knowledge to self help skills, etc.

Lysack and Kaufert (1993) recognised the role of cultural factors in intervention when they contrasted the CBR approach with another rehabilitation approach called Independent Living (IL) which emphasises independent control. They opined that the CBR approach is likely to be more successful in Asia than in Northern countries because of cultural factors such as strength of the family unit and strong social norms for providing support from kin and the community. One of the most successful programmes involving CBR which makes use of cultural factors has been launched in Central Java. Here, the existng governmental and nongovernmental organisations have forged links with the village communities through village councils so as to enable them to make greater use of the services which are provided to them. The programme seeks to bring about a change in community behaviour first and only later it addresses issues related to disability. The programme has been successful primarily because of two reasons. It has been able to involve the PKK, a women's voluntary organisation, which is organised at the national and village levels and is already engaged in the delivery of health care and primary prevention. Second, the PKK has successfully utilised certain cultural concepts such as *gotong-royong* (mutual aid/self-help for common benefit) and *kerja-bakti* (community work) for recruiting volunteers from the village communities who devote a great deal of their time to community work. Koentjaraningrat (1982) pointed out that many community projects such as the construction of dams, irrigation works, roads, community buildings, sacred houses, mosques, churches and schools have been made possible because of such community effort. Another set of concepts which Pareek (1988) highlighted, quoting Koentjaraningrat, is of *musyawarah* (consensus) and *mupakat* (unanimous decision). These are used to harmonise the contrasting viewpoints of members by creatively developing a new alternative rather than rejecting any one of them. Since these cultural elements are already in place no additional effort is required by change agents in process facilitation.

Another recent intervention effort involving the CBR approach has also highlighted the role of cultural factors in the success or failure of such programmes. Pande (1994) presented an evaluative report of the CBR programme at Sirathu where it has been in operation for more than a year. It was more of a reflective exercise, since Pande was also one of the initiators of the programme. The programme covered five villages and in tune with the CBR philosophy, sought to empower the PWDs by making them useful members of their communities. This included developing skills so that they were able to avail of institutional and local resources for their upliftment. The programme began with a series of informal meetings called by the initiators of the programme in which the problems of disability and health were raised and the role of the community in primary prevention and in the integration of PWDs highlighted. So far, the programme has only partially achieved its objectives. There are many reasons for this. Pande described how the programme objectives were at variance with the needs of the community, such as the need for safe drinking water. Another problem was related to the role of the initiators who acted more like *data* (donor) rather than as people just like them. Consequently, the initiators received a large number of applications for financial help which they were not able to provide. As a result people may have lost interest in the programme. It was conjectured that as the programme made some headway it disturbed the existing political structure. It was difficult to convey the ideology of the CBR and people were generally not very forthcoming with their efforts and money to help in the integration of the PWDs. They appeared interested only till such time that their selfish ends were met. In India, PWDs remain the responsibility of the family and it is only in the absence of the family members that others may offer help. People's attitudes toward disability also obstruct community interventions (Dalal, personal communication). Indian tradition provides both positive and negative examples of disabled people. Depending on the context, one of these is likely to become more salient. Change agents are likely to succeed to the extent they are able to make use of the cultural idioms.

Utilising Cultural Factors in Community Interventions

The intervention studies which have been reviewed here illustrate where cultural factors enter the intervention process and how they influence outcomes of such interventions. In this section, the discussion will be on some religious movements which have achieved what planned interventions generally purport to, that is, initiate and direct social change, but with a greater degree of success. The purpose here is to understand why such movements succeed, particularly what psychological processes underlie them and are there any lessons to be learnt for making planned interventions. India has seen numerous religious movements which have sought to bring about changes in the existing social system to make it in tune with the times. These movements have sought to "modernise" traditional attitudes, but after retaining the essential features of the Hindu (*Sanatan*) *dharma*. A good twentieth century example of such a movement is that initiated by Swami Vivekanand under the name of Rama Krishna Mission. The Mission has done pioneering work in the fields of education and health, and in many other sectors of community development.

At present there are two movements which have attracted considerable attention of social scientists. These are the Swaminarayan

movement led by Pramukh Swamiji Maharaj and the other is the
Swadhyaya movement led by Shri Pandurang Shastri Athavale.
These movements have attracted attention because of the promise
they hold for bringing about national development (Roy, 1993; Sheth,
1994). The Swaminarayan movement has been in the news recently
in almost all the reputed dailies in the UK because its followers have
built a magnificent new temple in a slum area in Neasden, London.
The British Press has marvelled at how in this modern day and age
it became possible to build such a magnificent temple. One of the
dailies reported:

> There has been an almighty outbreak of Hindu faith and not a
> little Pauline hope and charity.... Its the sort that political parties
> can only dream of harnessing when they talk of community... whole
> families have given months, some years, of their time.... Bankers
> have turned electricians, accountants have laid drains. Some have
> given up their jobs. Solicitors, doctors and architects have sacri-
> ficed annual holidays and been assigned by the saints what might
> be seen as labouring work. Women cook, polish, organize festivi-
> ties... children play their part (quoted in Shourie, 1996a).

Built on a 12 acre plot, the temple is reportedly worth £50 million
and has been constructed entirely through voluntary contributions
not so much in terms of money as in terms of labour. A measure of
this is illustrated by the fact that children went from house to house,
restaurant to restaurant, stadium to stadium to collect some 7 million aluminium cans which they sold to a reprocessing plant and
the earnings were donated for temple construction. Shourie (1996b)
made an important observation regarding the outcomes of this community effort. According to him,

> The blessings such participation spell will be manifest; every
> volunteer worked with his hands and thus learnt the dignity of
> labour: there was no distinction of wealth, caste or any other
> thing else; as every one contributed his mite, everyone sees the
> temple as her and his own; as families have laboured together
> family ties have been strengthened; the community has acquired
> a great symbol (p. 10).

The symbolism observed by Shourie, is making holy what is un-
clean since this breathtakingly beautiful temple actually came up in

a place which was particularly filthy. Just as the lotus remains un-
touched by its surroundings or as the Buddha's shroud was picked
up from a dead man's body, it makes unholy holy. Though the
achievement of the Swaminarayan movement may be belittled by
those who believe that efforts exerted for a religious cause do not
necessarily extend into other areas, they were proved wrong by the
Swadhyaya movement which succeeded in transforming barren
lands into forests and brought about remarkable changes in the
social and personal lives of people. Shastri has imparted a new
meaning to Hindu rituals to bring about this change. Two kinds of
temples have been set up by him: *Vriksha mandirs* (tree temple) and
Amrutalayams (house of nectar). To establish *Vriksha mandirs*, Shastri
tapped the beliefs of the Hindus who venerate certain trees like the
Pipal, the Banyan, the Tulsi, and the Ashok. Using the example of
trees, Shastri explained how one can learn much from them, from
their generosity and compassion: their roots are often used for me-
dicinal purposes, flowers and leaves for worship, and fruits for
satisfying hunger. According to him, God reveals Himself in the
form of trees. What is important here is that this message is not
"constructed". It builds on what people already know and respects
it. Western people may think that such tree worship would only
reinforce irrational beliefs and encourage anti-scientism, but for
Shastri, it signifies giving meaning to life and living. The land for
such tree temples is provided by the villagers all of whom nurture
the tree saplings. Families look after the saplings and trees planted
in the precincts, and keep the temple clean. Similarly, in *Amrutalayams*
there are no idols which are worshipped. The temple is enclosed on
all sides by arches of bamboo on which creepers are trained. Families take turns to serve as "priests" for the period of a week. During
this period they take care of the courtyard and trees, and light the
lamps before other villagers visit the temple. The members of the
family abstain from liquor during this period and follow the path of
truth. Trees, as Shourie (1996a) explained, are used in a symbolic
sense. Trees render service without expecting anything in return.
All the different parts of trees serve one or another purpose. The
followers of Shastri are willing to do *sewa* (service) by offering their
tan (bodily effort), *mun* (emotional investment), and *dhan* (money)
but only in that order. No money is accepted from a person who is
not willing to invest time and effort in the service of the community.
Special skills of the community members are used for generating

economic earnings which are spent on providing succour to the ill and destitute. Any loan from the "temple" is given as *prasada* and, therefore, does not put a person to shame. New traditions have also been developed, on the occasion of festivals members visit each other's houses and eat with them. This weakens the caste distinctions among the villagers. Members of the movement participate in *bhakti-pheries* (devotional tours) for a period of 15 days, the sole objective of this is to reflect on self and knowing others. During these tours, the *pheri-walas* accept nothing from others. Their conduct not only leads to a change in them but also in the people they visit.

Regarding conflict resolution, Shastri's mode of resolving an age-old conflict between two tribal groups is instructive. When approached by the groups, he did not focus on the issue, instead he focused on changing the overall environment. *Swadhyayees* first visited both the communities and when they had won their trust, both groups appealed to Shastri to bring them together. Unlike an OD expert Shastri did not organise any "confrontation" meeting in which issues were raised and mutual give and take agreed upon or a contract drawn up. He simply organised a Satyanarain *puja* involving 1,008 couples belonging to both groups. Couples of the two groups sat alternately using only flowers, water and rice. Lord Satyanarain served as their witness in which community leaders of both groups had resolved to stop their hostilities.

In an attempt to make sense of the two approaches, Shourie (1996a) observed, "These rituals and idols and legends are in the very blood of people, in their breathing itself. Once they are given a new meaning, a meaning suited to the needs of the time, would the task not get done that much sooner and better?" (p. 8).

Some Reflections

What possible lessons can be drawn for developing communities on the basis of studies of community interventions reviewed here, some of which were successful and others not so successful. Srinivas (1995) undertook a metaanalysis of OD efforts in India in terms of organisational development and societal/national development. For national development, he adopted the six criteria suggested by Tripathi (1988b) and Pareek (1988); Tripathi's criteria of openness and embeddedness, and Pareek's extension motivation, proactivity, internality, and creativity. An assessment was done to determine the extent to which the interventions made were based on society's ideology, values, and traditional culture. Of 55 interventions reviewed, only 14 satisfied four out of the six criteria of national development. What was interesting was that these 14 were also among the 17 organisations which were rated successful on organisational criteria. Srinivas compared the rate of success (45 per cent) of such OD efforts with similar efforts in other non-affluent countries (72 per cent) (Golembiewski, 1991) and found it to be much lower. While such comparisons are often not meaningful because of variable socioeconomic and political systems, and interventions in organisations are qualitatively different from community interventions, it is important to improve one's understanding about making interventions. There are certain issues which merit further exploration.

ENTITLEMENT VS AID One of the central issues in community interventions is the removal of blocks in people's quality of life. Both change agents and targets of change (notice the dichotomy) may have differing perceptions of the outcomes that are sought to be achieved and the reasons thereof. While people may perceive themselves as entitled to positive living conditions and feel that they have been unfairly deprived of the facilities others enjoy, change agents and governmental agencies often adopt the stance of "do gooders" and aid providers. These feelings of relative deprivation involving comparisons with others in the community and between communities become a source of distress. Such feelings act as impediments in viewing the community development efforts in a positive light. Governmental programmes often fail to arouse enthusiasm and elicit community members' participation because people perceive government "functionaries" as being paid by them through their taxes. The members of the community feel that they are entitled to their services. The usual perception is: "You are being paid to do your job by us, so why do you ask for our help. We are not being paid". The bureaucratic response to this in many developing countries is: "Be glad and obliged that we are here to provide help to your community, it could have gone to some other community in this scarce resource environment". Such opposing perceptions need to be resolved to enable the change agents and target communities to coordinate their efforts for positive outcomes.

Issues relating to entitlement may also surface, although indirectly, in interventions made by voluntary organisations or other private agencies, particularly when such organisations and agencies do not belong to the community. Feelings of entitlement and accepting aid or help from others are a function of both history as well as sociocultural values of the community. Aid, viewed as *dan* (dole), may not be readily acceptable to people if it is given from an elevated position. *Dan* in the Indian tradition redeems the *data* (aid giver) and not the receiver. A good *data* is expected to be humble while helping others and not obliging. The conflict remains when *dan* is made in non-material terms, such as effort or psychological support.

PEOPLE VS PROGRAMME Another dilemma faced by change agents is the relative emphasis on people versus programme. A change agent who is caught up in the implementation of a particular planned effort may lose the people focus. Therefore, such needs which surface during intervention if they do not fall within the scope of community intervention may often be brushed aside. For example, the intervention made in the CBR programme at Sirathu (Pande, 1994) overlooked the need for drinking water. Those who focus on the programme more are governed by the desire to change and control the behaviour of people and are likely to utilise behaviour modelling techniques and thus adopt a non-holistic approach. However, this does not apply to programmes which focus on people like the Swadhyaya movement, which are more holistic and see the growth of the community in terms of the overall personal and spiritual growth of the community members. Such an approach is likely to be less rational and well planned, more exploratory and eclectic. But such programmes focusing on people are seen as lacking direction, too diffuse, difficult to evaluate and require "charismatic" leaders to guide them. It is important to fuse the two focuses.

LOCAL VS UNIVERSAL KNOWLEDGE At least three successful intervention efforts reviewed here have utilised local knowledge in which the beliefs, traditions, and available knowledge have been adopted to achieve the objectives of the programme. This was obvious in the Tilonia project, the South African project on education, and the Swadhyaya movement. In other projects, in contrast, professional expert help was made available. A conflict may be seen between local and universal knowledge because local knowledge is likely to be based on experience and may lack the required objective validity. The two may not necessarily conflict with each other if beliefs and values do not come into play as in the case of the Tilonia project. However, where traditional beliefs go against the scientific belief (for example, what one should do to attain good health or the curative properties of medicines), problems are likely to arise. Planned efforts need to make room for local knowledge, and if this is done, how would it influence the programme outcomes is a question which remains to be answered.

FORMAL VS VOLUNTARY The dichotomy between formal and voluntary organisations also appears in various intervention efforts reviewed here. Where the change agents have been involved voluntarily, as in the case of the Singari project, or in the two movements, there has been a greater degree of participation of the community as compared to governmental interventions. But the Tilonia project and Mahila Samakhya have adopted a mixed model under which they have regular workers on their staff who are based in the community besides seeking active participation of the community members. Both voluntary organisations and governmental organisations may face the problem of community participation. What may be the right mix of formalisation and volunteerism for community interventions appears to be an issue which calls for further research. A related issue is of the mix between decentralisation and centralisation. Issues like who decides, about what, and in what manner, would be important in this context.

ATTITUDES AND VALUES VS BEHAVIOUR Most intervention programmes seek to change dysfunctional or undesirable behaviours by bringing about a change in attitudes. There is very little evidence of such efforts succeeding. The relationship between attitude and behaviour is tenuous. The reasoned-action theory of attitudes explains why such relationships have not been obtained. Where does one focus? On behaviour, as suggested by J.B.P. Sinha (1990), or on attitudes and values? Or, is there another way? The Swadhyaya movement may provide a clue here. Attitudes have generally been considered cognitive constellations. It is the "affective" component of attitude which has been overlooked. In the Swadhyaya movement, the rituals people are made to observe provide the necessary emotional tone (*bhawana*) to attitudes and values which get stoked and, therefore, become active. In community interventions, ritualistic devices would be needed which would help the change agent to bring about congruence between attitude and the desired behaviours. The model which emerges here is one in which members of the community are helped to reflect on the existing state of their community (or self) in order to recognise the "faults" that may have emerged either in the form of value aberrations or abnegations as a result of coping with the changing environment or for other reasons. To set the system on the right course, one would need to correct these faults by relearning core social values. This will enable the person to rediscover his or her self in the social context which ought to be an important objective of all community intervention programmes.

References

Acharya, S. (1996). Women in the Indian labour force: A temporal and spatial analysis. In S. Horton (Ed.), *Women and industrialisation in Asia* (pp. 43–80). London: Routledge.

Achenbach, T.M. (1991a). *Manual for Youth Self-Report and 1991 Profile.* Burlington, VT: University of Vermont, Department of Psychiatry.

Achenbach, T.M. (1991b). *Manual for the Teacher's Report Form and 1991 Profile.* Burlington, VT: University of Vermont, Department of Psychiatry.

Adair, J.G., & Kagiticibasi, C. (Eds). (1995). National development of psychology. *International Journal of Psychology,* Special issue, *30,* 633–753.

Adair, J.G., Puhan, B.N., & Vohra, N. (1993). Indigenization of psychology. Empirical assessment of progress in Indian research. *International Journal of Psychology, 28,* 149–169.

Agarwal, K.G. (1979). Commitment and effectiveness of change agents. Case of development projects in Ghaziabad district. *National Labour Institute Bulletin, (5, 6),* 14–151.

Agarwal, R., & Misra, G. (1986). A factor analysis of achievement goals and means: An Indian view. *International Journal of Psychology, 21,* 717–731.

Agarwal, R., & Misra, G. (1989). Variations in achievement cognitions: Role of ecology, age and gender. *International Journal of Intercultural Relations, 13,* 93–107.

Aldous, J. (Ed.). (1982). *Two paychecks: Life in dual-earner families.* Beverly Hills, CA: Sage Publications.

Alechina, I. (1982). The contribution of the United Nations system to formulating development concepts. In UNESCO (Ed.), *Different theories and practices of development* (pp. 9–68). Paris: UNESCO.

Andriessen, E.J.H., & Drenth, P.J.D. (1984). Leadership: Theories and models. In P.J.D. Drenth & Thierry et al. (Eds), *Handbook of work and organizational psychology.* New York: Wiley.

Anker, R. (1983). Female labour force participation in developing countries. *International Labour Review, 122* (6).

Anker, R., & Khan, M.E. (1988). *Women's participation in the labour force: A methods test in India.* Geneva: International Labour Organization.

Annamalai, E. (1990). *Linguistic dominance and cultural dominance: A study of tribal bilingualism in India.* Presidential Address, XVII All India Conference of Dravidian Linguistics, Kanyakumari.

Atal, Y. (1981). The call of indigenization. *International Social Science Journal, 33,* 89–97.

Avendaño-Sandoval, R. (1994). *Desarrollo y validacion psicometrica de una escala de abnegacion para adultos. Una aportacion a la etnopsicologia mexicana.* Tesis de Maestria no publicada. Facultad de Psicologia, UNAM, Mexico.

Avendaño-Sandoval, R., & Diaz-Guerrero, R. (1990). El desarrollo de una escala de abnegacion para los mexicanos. In Asociacion Mexicana de Psicologia Social (Coordinadores), *La psicologia social en Mexico, Vol. 3,* (pp. 9–14). Mexico, DF: AMEPSO.

Avendaño-Sandoval, R., & Diaz-Guerrero, R. (1992). Estudio experimental de la abnegacion. *Revista Mexicana de Psicologia, 9* (1), 15–19.

Avolio, B.J., & Bass, B.M. (1988). Transformational leadership, charisma, and beyond. In J.G. Hunt, B.R. Baliga, H.P. Dachler, & C.A. Schriesheim (Eds), *Emerging leadership vistas* (pp. 29–49). Lexington: D.C. Heath and Company.

Baddeley, A. (1986). *Working memory.* Oxford: Clarendon Press.

Baddeley, A., Eldridge, M., & Lewis, V. (1981). The role of subvocalization in reading. *Journal of Experimental Psychology, 33,* 439–454.

Bales, R.F., & Slater, P.E. (1955). Role differentiation in small decision-making groups. In T. Parson, R.F. Bales et al. (Eds), *Family, socialization and interaction process.* Glencoe, Ill: The Free Press.

Balthazar, L. (1995). The dynamics of multi-ethnicity in French-speaking Québec: Towards a new citizenship. *Nationalism and Ethnic Politics, 1,* 82–95.

Bandura, A., Ross, D., & Ross, S.A. (1963). Comparative test of the status envy, social power and the secondary reinforcement theories of identification learning. *Journal of Abnormal and Social Psychology, 67,* 527–534.

Barnes, B., & Shapin, S. (Eds). (1979). *Natural order: Historical studies of scientific culture.* Beverly Hills, CA: Sage Publications.

Baruch, G.K., & Barnett, R. (1983). *Correlates of fathers' participation in family work: A technical report.* Working Paper No. 106. Wellesley, Mass: Wellesley College, Center for Research on Women.

Bass, B.M. (1985). *Leadership performance beyond expectations.* New York: Academic Press.

Bass, B.M. (1990a). *Bass and Stogdill's handbook of leadership* (3rd ed.). New York: The Free Press.

Bass, B.M. (1990b). From transactional to transformational leadership: Learning to share the vision. *Organizational Dynamics,* Winter, 19–32.

Becker, G.S. (1976). *The economic approach to human behavior.* Chicago: The University of Chicago Press.

Beg, M.A.K. (1991). *Psycholinguistics and language acquisition.* New Delhi: Bahri Publications.

Bellah, R.N., Madsen, R., Sullivan, W.M., Swidler, A., & Tipton, S.M. (1985). *Habits of the heart.* Berkeley, CA: University of California Press.

Belshaw, C.S. (1972). Anthropology. *International Social Science Journal, 24,* 80–94.

Bennis, W.G. (1959). Leadership theory and administrative behavior: The problem of authority. *Administrative Science Quarterly, 4*, 259–301.

Bennis, W.G., & Nanus, B. (1985). *Leaders*. New York: Harper & Row.

Berman, J.J. (1990). *Nebraska symposium on motivation 1989. Cross-cultural perspectives* (Vol. 17). Lincoln & London: University of Nebraska Press.

Bernard van Leer Foundation. (1995). *Newsletter*. The Netherlands: Bernard van Leer Foundation.

Bernard, J. (1972). *The future of marriage*. New York: World Publications.

Bernard, J. (1981). The good-provider role: Its rise and fall. *American Psychologist, 36*, 1–12.

Berry, J.W. (1969). On cross-cultural comparability. *International Journal of Psychology, 4*, 119–128.

Berry, J.W. (1974). Canadian psychology: Some social and applied emphases. *Canadian Psychologist, 15*, 132–139.

Berry, J.W. (1980a). Ecological analyses for cross-cultural psychology. In N. Warren (Ed.), *Studies in cross-cultural psychology, Vol. 2* (pp. 157–189). London: Academic Press.

Berry, J.W. (1980b). Introduction. In H.C. Triandis & J.W. Berry (Eds), *Handbook of cross-cultural psychology, methodology, Vol. 2* (pp. 1–28). Boston: Allyn & Bacon.

Berry, J.W. (1980c). Social and cultural change. In H.C. Triandis & R. Brislin (Eds), *Handbook of cross-cultural psychology* (Vol. 5). Boston: Allyn & Bacon.

Berry, J.W. (1983). Textured contexts: Systems and situations in cross-cultural psychology. In S.H. Irvine & J.W. Berry (Eds), *Human assessment and cultural factors* (pp. 117–125). New York: Plenum Press.

Berry, J.W. (1984). Multiculturalism policy in Canada: A social psychological analysis. *Canadian Journal of Behavioural Science, 16*, 353–370.

Berry, J.W. (1986). The comparative study of cognitive abilities. In S.E. Newstead, S.H. Irvine, & P.L. Dann (Eds), *Human assessment: Cognition and motivation*. The Netherlands: Kluwer.

Berry, J.W. (1988). Cognitive values and cognitive competence among the bricoloeus. In J.W. Berry, S.H. Irvine, & E.B. Hunt (Eds), *Indigenous cognition: Functioning in cultural context*. Dordrecht: Nijhoff.

Berry, J.W. (1990). Psychology of acculturation: Understanding individuals moving between cultures. In R.W. Brislin (Ed.), *Applied cross-cultural psychology*. London: Sage Publications.

Berry, J.W., & Kalin, R. (1995). Multicultural and ethnic attitudes in Canada: An overview of the 1991 national survey. *Canadian Journal of Behavioural Science, 27*, 301–320.

Berry, J.W., Kalin, R., & Taylor, D. (1977). *Multiculturalism and ethnic attitudes in Canada*. Ottawa: Supply and Services Canada.

Berry, J.W., & Laponce, J. (Eds). (1994). *Ethnicity and culture in Canada: The research landscape*. Toronto: University of Toronto Press.

Berry, J.W., & Wilde, G.J.S. (Eds). (1972). *Social psychology: The Canadian context*. Toronto: McClelland & Stewart.

Bharat, S. (1992). *The two-pay cheque couples: An analysis of their housework, decision making, sex-role perceptions and attitudes.* Bombay: TISS.

Bharat, S. (1994). Perception of Indian women: A comparison of career and non-career women. *Psychologia, 37* (1), 49–56.

Bharat, S. (1995). Attitude and sex role perceptions among working couples in India. *Journal of Comparative Family Studies, 26,* 371–388.

Bhargava, M., & Aurora, A. (1981). Personality traits as a function of prolonged deprivation. *Indian Journal of Clinical Psychology, 8,* 161–171.

Bharti, A. (1985). The self in Hindu thought and action. In A.J. Marsells, G. DeVos, & F.L.K. Hsu (Eds), *Culture and self: Asian and western perspectives* (pp. 185–230). New York: Tavistock Publications.

Bhattacharyya, K.C. (1931/1954). Swaraj in ideas. *Visvabharati Quarterly, 20,* 103–114.

Birman, B., Orland, M., Jung, R., Anson, R., Garcia, G., Moore, M., Funkhouser, J., Morrison, D., Turnbull, B., & Reisner, E. (1987). *The current operation of the Chapter 1 program.* Washington, DC: Office of Educational Research and Improvement, US Department of Education.

Blake, R.R., & Mouton, J.S. (1964). *The managerial grid.* Houston: Gulf Publishing.

Blau, P.M. (1974). *Exchange and power in social life.* New York: Wiley.

Bowey, J., Cain, M., & Ryan, S. (1992). A reading-level design study of phonological skills underlying fourth-grade children's word reading difficulties. *Child Development, 63,* 999–1011.

Bradley, R.T. (1987). *Charisma and social structure: A study of love and power, wholeness and transformation.* New York: Paragon House.

Breton, R. (1988). From ethnic to civic nationalism: English Canada and Québec. *Ethnic and Racial Studies, 11,* 85–102.

Brislin, R.W. (1983). Cross-cultural research in psychology. *Annual Review of Psychology, 34,* 363–400.

Brophy, J. (1988). Research linking teacher behavior to student achievement: Potential implications for instruction of Chapter 1 students. *Educational Psychologist, 23,* 235–286.

Brown, J. (1973). *A first language: The early stages.* Cambridge, Mass: Harvard University Press.

Brown, L.D. (1988). Private voluntary organizations and development partnerships. In P.N. Khandwalla (Ed.), *Social development: A new role for the organizational sciences.* New Delhi: Sage Publications.

Bruner, J.S. (1986). *Actual minds, possible worlds.* Cambridge, MA: Harvard University Press.

Bruner, J.S. (1990). *Acts of meaning.* Cambridge, MA: Harvard University Press.

Bruner, J.J. (1991). The narrative construction of reality. *Critical Inquiry, 18,* 1–21.

Bryman, A. (1986). *Leadership and organizations.* London: Routledge & Kegan Paul.

Burnet, J. (1975). The policy of multiculturalism within a bilingual framework. In A. Wolfgang (Ed.), *Education of immigrant students.* Toronto: OISE.

Burns, J.M. (1978). *Leadership.* New York: Harper & Row.

Bury, J.B. (1932). *The idea of progress: An inquiry into its origin and growth* (1955 Dover edition). New York: Dover.

Calder, B.J. (1977). An attribution theory of leadership. In B.M. Staw & G.R. Salancik (Eds), *New directions in organizational behavior*. Chicago: St Clair.

Campione, J., & Brown, A. (1987). Blending dynamic assessment with school achievement. In C. Lidz (Ed.), *Dynamic assessment*. New York: Guilford.

Capra, F. (1983). *The Tao of physics*. Boulder: Shambala.

Carlson, J., & Das, J.P. (1992). *The cognitive assessment and remediation of Chapter 1 students*. Riverside, CA: California Educational Research Cooperative.

Carnap, R. (1949). Logical foundations of the Unity of Science. In H. Feigl & W. Sellars (Eds), *Readings in philosophical analysis*. New York: Appleton-Century-Crofts.

Carnap, R. (1932-33/1959). Psychology in physical language (G. Schick, Trans.). In A.J. Ayer (Ed.), *Logical positivism*. Glencoe, Ill: The Free Press.

Carstairs, G.M., & Kapur, R.L. (1976). *The great universe of Kota*. London: Hogarth.

Carter, L. (1982). *The sustaining effects study*. Hearings before the Subcommittee on Elementary, Secondary and Vocational Education of the Committee on Education and Labor, House of Representatives, 97th Congress, second session. Washington, DC: US Government Printing Office.

Carter, L. (1984). The sustaining effects study of compensatory elementary education. *Educational Researcher*, *13*, 4–13.

Cartwright, D. (1965). Leadership, influence and control. In J.G. March (Ed.), *Handbook of organizations*. Chicago: Rand McNally.

Cartwright, D., & Zander, A. (Eds). (1968). *Group dynamics: Research and theory*. New York: Harper & Row.

Chakraborty, K. (1978). *The conflicting worlds of working mothers*. Calcutta: Progressive Publisher.

Chall, J., & Curtis, M. (1990). Diagnostic achievement testing in reading. In C.R. Reynolds & R.W. Kampaus (Eds), *Handbook of psychological and educational assessment of children: Intelligence and achievement*. New York: Guilford.

Chambers, R. (1985). *Rural development: Putting the last first*. London: Longman.

Chandra, N., & Mehta, P. (1984). *People's self-development action: The case of Sinhari*. New Delhi: National Labour Institute.

Chitnis, S. (1988). Feminism: Indian ethos and Indian convictions. In R. Ghadially (Ed.), *Women in Indian society: A reader* (pp. 81–95). New Delhi: Sage Publications.

Chomsky, N. (1957). *Syntactic structures*. The Hague: Mouton.

Chomsky, N. (1965). *Aspects of the theory of syntax*. Cambridge, Mass: The MIT Press.

Chomsky, N. (1986). *Knowledge of language: Its nature, origin and use*. New York: Praeger.

Clifford, J. (1988). *The predicament of culture: Twentieth-century ethnography, literature and art*. Cambridge, MA: Harvard University Press.

Coch, L., & French, J.R.P., Jr (1948). Overcoming resistance to change. *Human Relations*, 1, 512–532.

Cole, M. (1990). Cultural psychology: A once and future discipline? In J.J. Berman (Ed.), *Nebraska symposium on motivation 1989: Cross-cultural perspectives* (Vol. 17, pp. 279–336). Lincoln: University of Nebraska Press.

Collins, A. (1991). From Brahma to a blade of grass: Towards an Indian self psychology. *Journal of Indian Philosophy*, 19, 143–189.

Collins, H.M. (1985). *Changing order: Replication and induction in scientific practice*. London: Sage Publications.

Comer, J.P. (1980). *School power*. New York: The Free Press.

Comer, J.P. (1988). Educating poor minority children. *Scientific American*, 259, 42–48.

Comte, A. (1830/1970). *Introduction to positive philosophy* (F. Ferré, Ed. & Trans.). New York: Bobbs-Merrill.

Conger, J.A. (1985). *Charismatic leadership in business: An exploratory study*. Unpublished doctoral dissertation, School of Business Administration, Harvard University, Mass.

Conger, J.A. (1989). *The charismatic leader* (pp. 12–39). San Francisco, CA: Jossey-Bass.

Conger, J.A. (1990). The dark side of leadership. *Organizational Dynamics*, Winter, 44–55.

Conger, J.A., & Kanungo, R.N. (1987). Towards a behavioral theory of charismatic leadership in organizational settings. *Academy of Management Review*, 13, 471–482.

Conger, J.A., & Kanungo, R.N. (1988a). Behavioral dimensions of charismatic leadership. In J.A. Conger, R.N. Kanungo et al. (Eds), *Charismatic leadership* (pp. 324–336). San Francisco, CA: Jossey-Bass.

Conger, J.A., & Kanungo, R.N. (1988b). Patterns and trends in studying charismatic leadership. In J.A. Conger, R.N. Kanungo et al. (Eds), *Charismatic leadership* (pp. 324–336). San Francisco, CA: Jossey-Bass.

Conger, J.A., & Kanungo, R.N. (1988c). The empowerment process: Integrating theory and practice. *Academy of Management Review*, 13, 471–482.

Conger, J.A., & Kanungo, R.N. (Eds). (1988d). *Charismatic leadership: The elusive factor in organizational effectiveness*. San Francisco, CA: Jossey-Bass.

Coomaraswamy, A.K. (1943). *Hinduism and Buddhism*. Westport, Conn: Greenwood Press.

Coomaraswamy, A.K. (1957). *The dance of Shiva*. New York: Noonday Press.

Cooper, D.G. (1970). *The death of the family*. New York: Pantheon Books.

Coverman, S., & Sheley, J.F. (1986). Change in men's housework and childcare time, 1965–1975. *Journal of Marriage and the Family*, 48, 413–422.

Cowley, W.H. (1928). Three distinctions in the study of leaders. *Journal of Abnormal and Social Psychology*, 23, 144–157.

Crosby, F. (1982). *Relative deprivation and working women*. New York: Oxford University Press.

D'Andrade, R.G. (1990). Culture and personality: A false dichotomy. In D.K. Jordan & M.J. Swartz (Eds), *Personality and the cultural construction of society* (pp. 145–160). Toscaloosa & London: The University of Alabama Press.

Dahl, R.A. (1957). The concept of power. *Behavioral Science, 2,* 210–218.

Dalal, A.K., Singh, A.K., & Misra, G. (1988). Reconceptualization of achievement behaviour: A cognitive approach. In A.K. Dalal (Ed.), *Attribution theory and research* (pp. 82–97). New Delhi: Wiley Eastern.

Daniel, E.V. (1984). *Fluid signs: Being a person the Tamil way.* Berkeley, CA: University of California Press.

Danziger, K. (1990). *Constructing the subject.* Cambridge: Cambridge University Press.

Das, J.P., Kirby, J., & Jarman, R. (1979). *Simultaneous and successive cognitive processes.* New York: Academic Press.

Das, J.P., & Mishra, R. (1991). The relationship between memory span, naming time, speech rate, and reading competence. *Journal of Experimental Education, 59,* 129–139.

Das, J.P., & Naglieri, J. (1989). *The cognitive assessment system: Tryout edition.* San Antonio, TX: The Psychological Corporation.

Das, Veena. (1977). *Structure and cognition: Aspects of Hindu caste and ritual.* New Delhi: Oxford University Press.

Deshpande, M. (1979). History, change and permanence: A classical Indian perspective. In G. Krishna (Ed.), *Contributions to South Asian studies, Vol. 1* (pp. 1–28). New Delhi: Oxford University Press.

Deshpande, S., & Deshpande, L.K. (1992). New economic policy and female employment. *Economic and Political Weekly, 27* (41), 2248–2252.

Devaki, L. (1987). *Learning of morphological rules in children: A comparative study of two cognate languages – Tamil and Kannada.* Unpublished doctoral dissertation, University of Mysore, Mysore.

Devaki, L. (1992). *Development of morphological rules in children.* Mysore: Central Institute of Indian Languages.

Devi, I.M. (1987). *Women, education, employment and family living: A study of emerging Hindu wives in urban India.* Delhi: Gian Publishing House.

Diaz-Guerrero, R. (1959). *Tres contribuciones a la psicoterapia.* Mexico, DF: Facultad de Filosofia Letras, Universidad Nacional Autonoma de Mexico.

Diaz-Guerrero, R. (1967a). Sociocultural premises, attitudes and cross-cultural research. *International Journal of Psychology, 2* (2), 79–87.

Diaz-Guerrero, R. (1967b). The active and the passive syndromes. *Revista Interamericana de Psicologia, 1*(4), 263–272.

Diaz-Guerrero, R. (1979). Origines de la Personnalite Humaine et des Systeme Sociaux. *Revue de Psychologie Appliquee, 29* (2), 139–152.

Diaz-Guerrero, R. (1982). *Psicologia del Mexicano.* Mexico, DF: Trillas.

Diaz-Guerrero, R. (1989a, June 3). Nuestros Primos y Nosotros. La personalidad de Mexicanos y Norteamericanos. Octava parte. Epilogo. *Excelsior,* 4–A, 16–A.

Diaz-Guerrero, R. (1989b). Una etnopsicologia mexicana. *Ciencia y Desarrollo, 15* (86), 69–85.

Diaz-Guerrero, R., & Rodriguez-Velasco, A.M. (1994). El significado subjetivo de la abnegacion y sus sinónimos. *Revista de Psicologia Contemporánea, 1* (1), 16–21.

Diaz-Guerrero, R., & Salas, M. (1975). *El Diferencial Semantico del Idioma Español.* Mexico, DF: Trillas.

Diaz-Loving, R., Andrade-Palos, P., & Nadelsticher, M.S. (1986). Una escala multidimensional de empatia. *Revista de Psicologia Social y Personalidad, 2* (1), 1–11.

Dilthey, W. (1976). *Selected writings* (H.P. Rickman, Ed. & Trans.). Cambridge: Cambridge University Press.

Dove, R. (1993). *British factory-Japanese factory* (pp. 370–384). London: Allen and Unwin.

Downton, J.V., Jr. (1973). *Rebel leadership.* New York: The Free Press.

Drefyus, H.L., & Drefyus, S.E. (1986). *Mind over machine: The power of human intuition and expertise in the era of the computer.* New York: The Free Press.

Dryfoos, J.G. (1994). *Full-service schools: A revolution in health and social services for children, youth, and families.* San Francisco, CA: Jossey-Bass.

Dua, H.R. (1986). Directions of research on multilingualism in India. *Sociolinguistics, XVI* (1), 9–19.

Dube, S.C. (1988). *Modernization and development: The search for alternative paradigms.* Tokyo: The United Nations University.

Eckensberger, L.H. (1979). A metamethodological evaluation of psychological theories from a cross-cultural perspective. In L. Eckensberger, W. Lonner, & Y.H. Poortinga (Eds), *Cross-cultural contributions to psychology* (pp. 255–275). Lisse: Swets & Zeitlinger.

Eichler, A., & Parron, D.L. (1987). *Women's mental health: Agenda for research.* Rockville, MD: National Institute of Mental Health.

Eldering, L., & Leseman, P. (Eds). (1993). *Early intervention and culture.* Paris: UNESCO.

England, J. (1989). *Industrial relations and law in Hong Kong* (2nd ed.). Hong Kong: Oxford University Press.

Enriquez, V.G. (1987). Decolonizing the Filipino psyche: Impetus for the development of psychology in the Philippines. In G.H. Blowers & A.M. Turtle (Eds), *Psychology moving east* (pp. 265–287). Boulder & London: Westview Press.

Epstein, C. (1971). Law partners and marital partners: Strains and solutions in the dual career family enterprise. *Human Relations, 24,* 549–563.

Epstein, S. (1994). Integration of the cognitive and the psychodynamic unconscious. *American Psychologist, 49* (8), 709–724.

Evans, M.G. (1970). The effects of supervisory behavior on the path-goal relationship. *Organizational Behavior and Human Performance, 5,* 277–298.

Fabian, J. (1983). *Time and the other: How anthropology makes its object.* New York: Columbia University Press.

Faucheux, C. (1976). Cross-cultural research in experimental social psychology. *European Journal of Social Psychology, 6,* 269–322.

Feyerabend, P. (1987). *Farewell to reason.* London: Verso.

Feyerabend, P. (1988). *Against method.* London: Verso.

Fiedler, F.E. (1967). *A theory of leadership effectiveness.* New York: McGraw-Hill.

Fiedler, F.E., & Chemers, M.M. (1974). *Leadership and effective management.* Glencoe, Ill: Scott, Foresman.

Fiedler, F.E., & Chemers, M.M. (1984). *Improving leadership effectiveness: The leader-match concept.* New York: Wiley.

Fiske, R.A., & Shweder, R.A. (Eds). (1986). *Metatheory in social science: Pluralisms and subjectivities.* Chicago: The University of Chicago Press.

Fleishman, E.A., Harris, E.F., & Burtt, H.E. (1955). *Leadership and supervision in industry.* Columbus, Ohio: Bureau of Educational Research, Ohio State University.

Fletcher, G.J.O. (1984). Psychology and common sense. *American Psychologist, 39,* 203–213.

Flores-Galaz, M. (1994). *Asertividad: Conceptualizacion, medicion y su relacion con otras variables.* Tesis de Doctorado no publicada. Facultad de Psicologia, UNAM, Mexico.

Flores-Galaz, M., Diaz-Loving, R., & Rivera-Aragon, S. (1987). MERA: Una medida de rasgos asertivos para la cultura mexicana. *Revista Mexicana de Psicologia, 4* (1), 29–35.

Freilich, M.C. (Ed.). (1989). *The relevance of culture.* New York: Bergen and Gravey.

French, J.R.P., & Raven, B.H. (1959). The bases of social power. In D. Cartwright (Ed.), *Studies in social power* (pp. 150–167). Ann Arbor, MI: Institute for Social Research.

Freud, S. (1946). *The ego and the mechanisms of defense.* New York: International Universities Press.

Fyans, L.J., Jr, Salili, F., Maehr, M.L., & Desai, K. (1983). A cross-cultural exploration into the meaning of achievement. *Journal of Personality and Social Psychology, 44,* 1000–1013.

Galanter, M. (1982). Charismatic religious sects and psychiatry: An overview. *American Journal of Psychiatry, 139,* 1539–1548.

Garber, J., & Seligman, M.E.P. (Eds). (1980). *Human helplessness: Theory and applications.* Orlando, FL: Academic Press.

Geertz, C. (1973). *The interpretation of cultures.* New York: Basic Books.

Geertz, C. (1983). *Local knowledge: Further essays in interpretive anthropology.* New York: Basic Books.

Gergen, K.J. (1982). *Toward transformation in social knowledge.* New York: Springer-Verlag.

Gergen, K.J. (1985). The social constructionist movement in modern psychology. *American Psychologist, 40,* 266–275.

Gergen, K.J. (1989). Realities and their relationships. In W.J. Baker, M.E. Hyland, R. Van Hezewizk, & S. Terwee (Eds), *Recent trends in theoretical psychology* (pp. 51–62). New York: Springer-Verlag.

Gergen, K.J. (1990a). Metaphor, metatheory, and the social world. In D.E. Leary (Ed.), *Metaphor in the history of psychology* (pp. 267–299). Cambridge: Cambridge University Press.

Gergen, K.J. (1990b). Social understanding and inscription of self. In J.W. Stigler, R.A. Shweder, & G. Herdt (Eds), *Cultural psychology* (pp. 569–606). Cambridge: Cambridge University Press.

Gergen, K.J. (1991). *The saturated self: Dilemmas of identity in contemporary life.* New York: Basic Books.

Gigerenzer, G. (1991). From tools to theories: A heuristic discovery in cognitive psychology. *Psychological Review, 98,* 254–267.

Gilbert, G.N., & Mulkay, M. (1984). *Opening Pandora's box: A sociological analysis of scientists' discourse.* Cambridge: Cambridge University Press.

Godlier, M. (1986). *The mental and the material.* London: Verso.

Goldscheider, F.K., & Waite, L.J. (1991). *New families, no families: The transformation of the American home.* Berkeley, CA: University of California Press.

Golembiewski, R.T. (1991). Organizational development in the Third World: Values, closeness of fit and culture boundedness. *International Journal of Human Resource Management, 2* (1), 39–53.

Goodenough, W.H. (1989). Culture: Concept and phenomenon. In M.C. Freilich (Ed.), *The relevance of culture* (pp. 93–97). New York: Bergen and Garvey.

Goodnow, J. (1980). Everyday concepts of intelligence and its development. In N. Warren (Ed.), *Studies in cross-cultural psychology* (Vol. 2). London: Academic Press.

Gorden, M. (Ed.). (1972). *The nuclear family in crisis: The search for an alternative.* New York: Harper & Row.

Gore, M.S. (1968). *Urbanization and family change.* Bombay: Popular Prakashan.

Gould, D. (1987). *The lord as guru: Hindi sants in north Indian tradition.* New York: Oxford University Press.

Gudykunst, W., & Bond, M.H. (1997). Intergroup relations across cultures. In J.W. Berry, M.H. Segall, & C. Kagictibasi (Eds), *Handbook of cross-cultural psychology (Vol. 3): Social behavior and applications* (pp. 119–161). Boston: Allyn & Bacon.

Guénon, René. (1945). *Man and his becoming according to the Vedant* (C. Whitby, Trans.). London: Rider & Co.

Gunatilleke, G. (1985). *Changing needs of children: The experience of Sri Lanka.* Colombo: Marga.

Habermas, J. (1971). *Knowledge and human interests* (J.J. Shapiro, Trans.). Boston: Beacon Press. (Original work published 1968.)

Halbfass, W. (1988). *India and Europe: An essay in understanding.* New York: State University of New York Press. (Original German work published 1981.)

Hallowell, A.I. (1953). Culture, personality, and society. In A. Kroeber (Ed.), *Anthropology today: An encyclopedic inventory* (pp. 597–620). Chicago: The University of Chicago Press.

Halpin, A.W., & Winer, B.J. (1952). *The leadership behavior of the airplane commander.* Columbus: Ohio State University Research Foundation.

Hanson, N.R. (1958). *Patterns of discovery*. Cambridge: Cambridge University Press.

Hanushek, (1981). Throwing money at schools. *Journal of Policy Analysis and Management, 1,* 19–41.

Hardesty, C., & Bokemeier, J. (1989). Finding time and making do: Distribution of household labour in non-metropolitan marriages. *Journal of Marriage and the Family, 51,* 253–267.

Harré, R., Clarke, D., & DeCarlo, N. (1985). *Motives and mechanisms*. London: Methuen.

Hartmann, H. (1981). The family as a locus of gender, class and political struggle: The example of housework. *Signs, 6,* 366–394.

Hartnack, C. (1987). British psychoanalysts in colonial India. In M.G. Ash & W.R. Woodward (Eds), *Psychology in twentieth-century thought and society* (pp. 233–253). Cambridge: Cambridge University Press.

Heelas, P., & Lock, A. (1981). *Indigenous psychologies: The anthropology of the self*. New York: Academic Press.

Heesterman, J.C. (1985). *The inner conflict of tradition: Essays in Indian ritual, kinship, and society*. Chicago & London: The University of Chicago Press.

Hegarty, S., & Lucas, D. (1979). *Able to learn: The pursuit of culture-fair assessment*. Slough: NFER.

Heimann, B. (1964). *Facets of Indian thought*. New York: Shirken Books.

Heller, F. (1971). *Managerial decision making: A study of leadership and power sharing among senior managers*. London: Tavistock.

Henriques, J., Hollway, W., Urwin, C., Venn, C., & Walkerdine, V. (1984). *Changing the subject: Psychology social regulation and subjectivity*. London: Methuen.

Hermans, H.J.M., Kempen, H.J.G., & van Loon, Rens, J.P. (1992). The dialogical self: Beyond individualism and rationalism. *American Psychologist, 47,* 23–33.

Herskovits, S.M. (1948). *Man and his works*. New York: Knopf.

Hiriyanna, M. (1932). *The essentials of Indian philosophy*. London: George Allen & Unwin.

Hiriyanna, M. (1952). *Popular essays in Indian philosophy*. Mysore: Kavyalaya Publishers.

Ho, D.Y.F. (1988). Asian psychology: A dialogue on indigenization and beyond. In A.C. Paranjpe, D.Y.F. Ho, & R.W. Rieber (Eds), *Asian contributions to psychology* (pp. 53–77). New York: Praeger.

Hochschild, A. (1989). *The second shift*. New York: Avon Books.

Hofstede, G. (1980). *Culture's consequences: International differences in work-related values*. Beverly Hills, CA: Sage Publications.

Hogan, R., Curphy, G.J., & Hogan, J. (1994). What we know about leadership. *American Psychologist, 49,* 493–504.

Hollander, E.P. (1958). Conformity, status and idiosyncracy credit. *Psychological Review, 65,* 117–127.

Hollander, E.P. (1964). *Leaders, groups and influence*. New York: Oxford University Press.

Hollander, E.P. (1978). *Leadership dynamics.* New York: The Free Press.

Hollander, E.P. (1979). Leadership and social exchange processes. In K. Gergen, M.S. Greenberg, & R.H. Wills (Eds), *Social exchange: Advances in theory and research* (pp. 103–118). New York: Winston-Wiley.

Hollander, E.P. (1986). On the central role of leadership processes. *International Review of Applied Psychology, 35,* 39–52.

Hollander, E.P., & Offermann, L.R. (1990). Power and leadership in organizations. *American Psychologist, 45,* 179–189.

Holtzman, W.H. (1992). Community renewal, family preservation, and child development through the School of the Future. In W.H. Holtzman (Ed.), *School of the Future* (pp. 3–18). Austin, TX: American Psychological Association and Hogg Foundation for Mental Health.

Holtzman, W.H., Evans, R.I., Kennedy, S., & Iscoe, I. (1987). Psychology and health: Contributions of psychology to the improvement of health and health care. *Bulletin of the World Health Organization, 65,* 913–935.

Hong, Ng Sek. (1982). Industrial relations and voluntarism: The Hong Kong dilemma. *International Labour Review, 121* (6), 750.

Hood, J.C. (1983). *Becoming a two-job family.* New York: Praeger.

Hood, J.C. (1986). The provider role: Its meaning and measurement. *Journal of Marriage and the Family, 48,* 349–359.

Hoshino, A., & Umamoto, T. (1987). Japanese psychology: Historical review and recent trends. In G.H. Blowers & A.M. Turtle (Eds), *Psychology moving east* (pp. 183–196). Boulder & London: Westview Press.

House, R.J. (1971). A path-goal theory of leadership effectiveness. *Administrative Science Quarterly,* 321–332.

House, R.J. (1977). A 1976 theory of charismatic leadership. In J.G. Hunt & L.L. Larson (Eds), *Leadership: The cutting edge.* Carbondale: South Illinois University Press.

House, R.J. (1988). Leadership research: Some forgotten, ignored or overlooked findings. In J.G. Hunt, B.R. Baliga, H.P. Dachler, & C.A. Schriesheim (Eds), *Leadership vistas* (pp. 245–260). Lexington: D.C. Heath and Company.

House, R.J., & Dessler, G. (1974). The path-goal theory of leadership: Some post hoc and a priori tests. In J.G. Hunt & L.L. Larson (Eds), *Contingency approaches to leadership* (pp. 29–55). Carbondale: South Illinois University Press.

House, R.J., & Mitchell, T.W. (1974). Path-goal theory of leadership. *Journal of Contemporary Business, 3,* 81–97.

House, R.J., Spangler, W.D., & Woycke, J. (1991). Personality and charisma in US presidency: A psychological theory of leader effectiveness. *Administrative Science Quarterly, 36,* 364–396.

Howarth, C. (1980). The structure of effective psychology. In A.J. Chapman & D.M. Jones (Eds), *Model of man.* Hillsdale, NJ: Lawrence Erlbaum.

Howell, J.M. (1988). The two faces of charisma. In J.A. Conger, R.N. Kanungo et al. (Eds), *Charismatic leadership* (pp. 213–236). San Francisco, CA: Jossey-Bass.

Huber, J., & Spitze, G. (1983). *Sex-stratification: Children, housework and jobs.* Toronto: Academic Press.

Hull, D.L. (1988). *Science as a process: An evolutionary account of the social and conceptual development of science.* Chicago: The University of Chicago Press.

Hunt, J.G. (1984). Organizational leadership: The contingency paradigm and its challenges. In B. Kellerman (Ed.), *Leadership: Multidisciplinary perspectives.* Englewood Cliffs, NJ: Prentice-Hall.

Hunt, J.G., Baliga, B.R., Dachler, H.P., & Schriesheim, C.A. (Eds). (1988). *Emerging leadership vistas.* Lexington, Mass: D.C. Heath & Co.

Hussain, F. (Ed.). (1982). *Indigenous anthropology in non-Western countries.* Durham, North Carolina: Carolina Academic Press.

Husserl, E. (1954/1970). *The crisis of European sciences and transcendental phenomenology.* (D. Carr, Trans.). Evanston, Ill: Northwestern University Press.

Hutnik, N., & Sapru, S. (1996). The salience of ethnicity. *Journal of Social Psychology, 136,* 661–662.

Irvine, S.H., & Berry, J.W. (Eds). (1983). *Human assessment and cultural factors.* New York: Plenum Press.

Irvine, S.H., & Berry, J.W. (Eds). (1988). *Human abilities in cultural context.* New York: Cambridge University Press.

Iscoe, L. (1995a). *A community catalyst: The Austin School of the Future.* Austin, TX: Hogg Foundation for Mental Health.

Iscoe, L. (1995b). *The health clinic: The Houston School of the Future.* Austin, TX: Hogg Foundation for Mental Health.

Iscoe, L. (1995c). *A blue-print for school-based services: The Dallas School of the Future.* Austin, TX: Hogg Foundation for Mental Health.

Iscoe, L. (1995d). *Parent volunteer program: The San Antonio School of the Future.* Austin, TX: Hogg Foundation for Mental Health.

Jago, A. (1982). Leadership: Perspectives in theory and research. *Management Science, 28,* 315–336.

Jahoda, G. (1982). *Psychology and anthropology: A psychological perspective.* London: Academic Press.

Jahoda, G. (1990). Our forgotten ancestors. In J.J. Berman (Ed.), *Nebraska symposium on motivation: Cross-cultural perspectives,* Vol. 17 (pp. 1–40). Lincoln and London: University of Nebraska Press.

Jain, U. (1991). The subjective construction of morality: The Indian experience. *Indian Journal of Social Work, 42,* 379–388.

Jain, U., & Misra, G. (1991). Reflections on psychology's scientific concerns. *Indian Journal of Current Psychological Research, 6,* 83–92.

Kagitcibasi, C., & Berry, J.W. (1989). Cross-cultural psychology: Current research and trends. *Annual Review of Psychology, 40,* 493–531.

Kakar, S. (1978). *The inner world: A psychoanalytic study of childhood and society in India.* New Delhi: Oxford University Press.

Kakar, S. (1979). *Identity and adulthood.* New Delhi: Oxford University Press.

Kalin, R., & Berry, J.W. (1995). Ethnic and civic self-identity in Canada: Analyses of the 1974 and 1991 national surveys. *Canadian Ethnic Studies, 27,* 1–15.

Kalin, R., & Berry, J.W. (1996). Interethnic attitudes in Canada: Ethnocentrism, consensual hierarchy and reciprocity. *Canadian Journal of Behavioural Science, 28,* 253–261.

Kanungo, R.N. (1977). Bases of supervisory power and job satisfaction in bicultural context. In H.C. Jain & R.N. Kanungo (Eds), *Behavioral issues in management: The Canadian context* (pp. 331–344). Toronto: McGraw-Hill Ryerson.

Kanungo, R.N. (1982). *Work alienation.* New York: Praeger.

Kanungo, R.N., & Conger, J.A. (1989). *Charismatic leadership: A behavioral theory and its cross-cultural implications.* Paper presented at the International Association for Cross-Cultural Psychology Conference, Free University, Amsterdam.

Kanungo, R.N., & Conger, J.A. (1993). Promoting altruism as corporate goal. *The Academy of Management Review, 7,* 37–48.

Kanungo, R.N., & Medonca, M. (1994). What leaders cannot do without. In J.A. Conger (Ed.), *Spirit at work* (pp. 162–198). San Francisco, CA: Jossey-Bass.

Kao, H.S.R., & Hong, Ng Sek. (1988). Minimal "self" and Chinese work behaviour: Psychology of the grass-roots. In Durganand Sinha & Henry S.R. Kao (Eds), *Social values and development: Asian perspectives* (pp. 254–272). New Delhi: Sage Publications.

Kao, H.S.R. & Hong, Ng Sek. (1995a). Chinese values in work organization: An alternative approach to change and development. *Journal of Human Values, 1* (2), 183–184.

Kao, H.S.R., & Hong, Ng Sek. (1995b, 27–30 August). *Corporate statesmanship: A cursory note and implications.* Paper presented at the Asian-Pacific Regional Conference of Psychology, Guangzhou, 5–6.

Kao, H.S.R., & Sinha, D. (Eds). (1996). *Effective management and values.* New Delhi: Sage Publications.

Kapp, W.K. (1963). *Hindu culture, economic development and economic planning in India.* Bombay: Asia Publishing House.

Kelman, H.C. (1958). Compliance, identification and internationalization: The process of attitude change. *Journal of Conflict Resolution, 2,* 51–60.

Kennedy, M., Birman, B., & Demaline, R. (1988). *The effectiveness of Chapter 1 services.* Washington, DC: Office of Educational Research and Improvement, US Department of Education.

Kennedy, S., Schierer, J., & Rogers, A. (1984). The price of success: Our monocultural science. *American Psychologist, 39,* 996–997.

Kerr, S., & Jermier, J.M. (1978). Substitutes for leadership: Their meaning and measurement. *Organizational Behaviour and Human Performance, 22,* 375–403.

Kets de Vries, M.F.R. (1988). Origins of charisma: Ties that bind the leader and the led. In J.A. Conger & R.N. Kanungo (Eds), *Charismatic leadership: The elusive factor in organizational effectiveness* (pp. 237–252). San Francisco: Jossey-Bass.

Kets de Vries, M.F.R. (1994). The leadership mystique. *The Academy of Management Executive, 8,* 73–89.

Keyes, C.F., & Daniel, E.V. (1983). *Karma: An anthropological inquiry.* Berkeley, CA: University of California Press.

Khandwalla, P.N. (1988). *Social development: A new role for the organizational sciences.* New Delhi: Sage Publications.

Khanna, G., & Verghese, M.A. (1978). *Indian women today.* Delhi: Vikas Publishing House.

Khubchandani, L.M. (1986). Multilingual societies: Issues of identity and communication. *Sociolinguistics, XVI* (1), 20–34.

Kiggundu, R.H., Jorgensen, J.J., & Hafsi, T. (1983). Administrative theory and practice in developing countries: A synthesis. *Administrative Science Quarterly, 28,* 66–94.

Kim, U. (1995). Psychology, science, and culture: Cross-cultural analysis of national psychologies. *International Journal of Psychology, 30,* 662–679.

Kim, U., & Berry, J.W. (Eds). (1993). *Indigenous psychologies.* Newbury Park, CA: Sage Publications.

Klostermaier, K.K. (1989). *A survey of Hinduism.* Albany: State University of New York Press.

Koch, S. (1985). The nature and limits of psychological knowledge: Lessons of a century qua "science". In S. Koch & D.E. Leary (Eds), *A century of psychology as science* (pp. 75–97). New York: McGraw-Hill.

Koentjaraningrat. (1982). Changing cultural value orientation of Javanese peasants. In G.B. Hansworth (Ed.), *Village-level modernisation in South East Asia.* Vancouver: University of British Columbia Press.

Krishnamurti, B. (1990). The regional language vis-à-vis English as the medium of instruction in higher education: The Indian dilemma. In D.P. Pattanayak (Ed.), *Multilingualism in India.* Clevedon: Multilingual Matters.

Krishnamurthy, J. (1992). *Education and significance of life.* Pondicherry: Krishnamurthy Foundation of India.

Kruglanski, A. (1989). *Lay epistemics and human knowledge.* New York: Plenum Press.

Kuhn, T.S. (1970). *The structure of scientific revolutions.* Chicago: The University of Chicago Press.

Kuhn, T.S. (1977). *The essential tension: Selected studies in scientific tradition and change.* Chicago: The University of Chicago Press.

Kukla, A. (1988). Cross-cultural psychology in a post empiricist era. In M. Bond (Ed.), *The cross-cultural challenge to social psychology* (pp. 141–152). Newbury Park, CA: Sage Publications.

Kumudavalli, S. (1973). *The relationship between articulation and discrimination in Kannada speech sounds in terms of distinctive features.* Unpublished Master's dissertation, Mysore University, Mysore.

La Rosa, J. (1986). *Escalas de Locus de Control y Autoconcepto: Construccion y Validacion.* Tesis de Doctorado no publicada. Facultad de Psicologia, UNAM, Mexico.

La Rosa, J., & Diaz-Loving, R. (1988). Diferencial semantico del autoconcepto en estudiantes. *Revista de Psicologia Social y Personalidad, 4,* 39–58.

La Rosa, J., & Diaz-Loving, R. (1991). Evaluacion del autoconcepto. Una escala multidimensional. *Revista Latinoamericana de Psicologia, 23* (1), 15–33.

Lakshmi Bai, B. (1983/1984). Case relations and case forms in child language. *Osmania Papers in Linguistics, 9&10,* 73–101.

Lakshmi Bai, B. (1984). Dative in Dravidian: A perspective from child language. *Psycho-Lingua, XVI* (2), 135–144.

Lakshmi Bai, B. (1986). Development of negation in Tamil-Telugu bilingual children. In J.A. Fishman (Ed.), *The Fergusonian impact, Vol. 1: From phonology to society.* New York: Mouton de Gruyter.

Lamb, M.E. (1982). *Non-traditional families: Parenting and child development.* Hillsdale, NJ: Lawrence Erlbaum.

Langner, E.J. (1983). *The psychology of control.* Beverly Hills, CA: Sage Publications.

Larson, G.J. (1990). India through Hindu categories: A Samkhya response. *Contributions to Indian Sociology, 24,* 237–249.

Lasch, C. (1991). *The true and only heaven: Progress and its critics.* New York: W.W. Norton.

Latour, B. (1987). *Science in action.* Cambridge, Mass: Harvard University Press.

Latour, B., & Woolgar, S. (1986). *Laboratory life: The construction of scientific facts.* Princeton, NJ: Princeton University Press.

Leahey, T.H. (1987). *A history of psychology: Main currents in psychological writings* (2nd ed.). Englewood Cliffs, NJ: Prentice-Hall.

Leary, D.E. (1987). Telling likely stories: The rhetoric of the new psychology, 1880–1920. *Journal of the History of the Behavioral Sciences, 13,* 315–331.

Lein, L., Radle, P., & Radle, R. (1992). San Antonio family support program: Reflections on the School of Future in the center of a public housing project. In W.H. Holtzman (Ed.), *School of the Future.* Austin, TX: American Psychological Association and Hogg Foundation for Mental Health.

Lett, J. (1987). *The human enterprise: A critical introduction to anthropological theory.* Boulder & London: Westview Press.

Lewin, K., Lippitt, R., & White, R.K. (1939). Patterns of aggressive behavior in experimentally created social climates. *Journal of Social Psychology, 10,* 271–299.

Likert, R. (1961). *New patterns of management.* New York: McGraw-Hill.

Lippitt, R., & White, R.K. (1947). An experimental study of leadership and group life. In E.E. Maccoby, T.M. Newcomb, & E.C. Hartley (Eds), *Readings in social psychology* (pp. 496–511). New York: Holt, Rinehart, & Winston.

Little, T., Das, J.P., Carlson, J., & Yachimowicz, D. (1994). The role of hierarchical skills in cognitive ability as moderators of deficits in academic performance. *Learning and Individual Differences, 5,* 219–240.

Lodahl, A. (1982). *Crises in values and the success of the unification church.* Unpublished Bachelor's dissertation, Cornell University, Ithaca.

Longino, H.E. (1990). *Science as social knowledge.* Princeton, NJ: Princeton University Press.

Lovett, M., Ransby, M., Hardwick, N., Johns, & Donaldson, S. (1989). Can dyslexia be treated? Treatment specific and generalized treatment effects in dyslexic children's response to remediation. *Brain and Language, 37,* 90–121.

Luthans, F., & Kreitner, R. (1975). *Organizational behavior modification.* Glenview, Ill: Scott, Foresman.

Lysack, C., & Kaufert, J. (1993, 29–30 October). *Conflicting ideologies: Independent living models versus conjoint development in community based rehabilitation.* Paper presented at the Conference on Asia in the 1990's Meeting and Making a New World, Queen's University, Ontario.

Macaulay, T.B. (1835/1972). Minute on Indian education. In T.B. Macaulay, *Selected writings* (J. Clive & T. Pinney, Eds) (pp. 237–251). Chicago: The University of Chicago Press.

Macklin, E.D. (1987). Non traditional family norms. In M.B. Sussman & S.K. Steinmetz (Eds), *Handbook of marriage and the family.* New York: Plenum Press.

Madan, T.N. (1987). *Non-renunciation: Themes and interpretations of Hindu culture.* New Delhi: Oxford University Press.

Malpass, R.S., & Poortinga, Y.H. (1986). Strategies for design and analysis. In W.J. Lonner & J.W. Berry (Eds), *Field methods in cross-cultural research* (pp. 47–84). Beverly Hills, CA: Sage Publications.

Manganaro, M. (1990). Textual play, power, cultural critique: An orientation to modernist anthropology. In M. Manganaro (Ed.), *Modernist anthropology: From fieldwork to text* (pp. 3–50). Princeton, NJ: Princeton University Press.

Markus, H.R., & Kitayama, S. (1991). Culture and self: Implications for cognition, emotion, and motivation. *Psychological Review, 98,* 224–253.

Marriot, M. (1976). Hindu transactions: Diversity with dualism. In B. Kapferer (Ed.), *Transaction and meaning: Directions in the anthropology of exchange and symbolic behavior* (pp. 109–142). Philadelphia: Institute for the Study of Human Issues.

Marriot, M. (Ed.). (1990). *India through Hindu categories.* New Delhi: Sage Publications.

Martinko, M.J., & Gardner, W.L. (1982). Learned helplessness: An alternative explanation for performance deficits. *Academy of Management Review, 7,* 195–204.

McClelland, D.C. (1961). *The achieving society.* New York: John Wiley & Sons.

McClelland, D.C. (1975). *Power: The inner experience.* New York: Irvington.

McClelland, D.C., & Winter, D.G. (1969). *Motivating economic achievement.* New York: The Free Press.

McGregor, D. (1960). *The human side of enterprise.* New York: McGraw-Hill.

Mead, M. (1931). *Growing up in New Guinea.* London: Routledge.

Mehta, S.R. (1983). Acceptance of change. *Social Change, 13,* 31–55.

Meindl, J.R., Ehrlich, S.B., & Dukerich, J.M. (1985). The romance of leadership. *Administrative Science Quarterly, 30,* 78–102.

Melgoza-Enriquez, E. (1990). *Evaluacion de Algunas Facetas de la Personaliddad en Docentes Mexicanos, Partiendo de la Etnopsicologia Mexicana.* Tesis de Licenciatura no publicada. Facultad de Psicologia, UNAM, Mexico.

Melgoza-Enriquez, E., & Diaz-Guerrero, R. (1990). El desarrollo de una escala de flexibilidad en sujtos mexicanos. In Asociacion Mexicana de Psicologia Social (Coordinadores), *La Psicologia Social en Mexico*, Vol. 3 (pp. 20–24). Mexico, DF: AMEPSO.

Meyer, M. (1922). *Psychology of the other-one* (2nd ed.). Columbia, NO: Missouri Book Company.

Michael, J.M. (1982). The second revolution in health: Health promotion and its environmental base. *American Psychologist, 37,* 936–941.

Millea, S., & Coleman, M.T. (1992). Creating a sense of community: The Austin School of the Future. In W.H. Holtzman (Ed.), *School of the Future.* Austin, TX: American Psychological Association and Hogg Foundation for Mental Health.

Mintzberg, H. (1982). If you are not serving Bill and Barbara, then you are not serving leadership. In J.G. Hunt, U. Sekaran, & C.A. Schriesheim (Eds), *Leadership: Beyond establishment views.* Carbondale: Southern Illinois University Press.

Mishra, B. (1994). *Word order in expression of bitransitive verbs in Hindi: Impact of deprivation.* Paper presented at the international conference on Early Childhood Communication, Utkal University, Bhubaneswar.

Mishra, B., & Dubey, J. (1987). Pragmatic strategy in word order of children's expression of locative preposition *on* in Hindi. *Indian Journal of Current Psychological Research, 2* (2), 93–97.

Mishra, K. (1997). *Maitri bhavana: Implications for the development of self as well as others.* Paper presented at the seminar on Challenges of Multiculturalism: India and Canada, Banaras Hindu University, Varanasi.

Mishra, R.C. (1988). Field dependence-independence as related to face recognition and eye contact among tribal adolescents. *Indian Psychologist, 5,* 21–26.

Mishra, R.C. (1990). Cognitive stimulation, training, and perceptual-cognitive task performance by socially deprived children. *Indian Journal of Current Psychological Research, 5,* 1–9.

Mishra, R.C. (1996). Perceptual differentiation in relation to children's daily life activities. *Social Science International, 12,* 1–11.

Mishra, R.C., & Sinha, D. (1985). *Acculturation, cognitive changes and interpersonal adjustment: A study of some changing tribes of Bihar.* A preliminary report presented to the ICSSR, New Delhi.

Mishra, R.C., Sinha, D., & Berry, J.W. (1990). *Some aspects of cognitive functioning of Birhor and Oraon children.* Proceedings of the X Congress of the IACCP, Nara.

Mishra, R.C., Sinha, D., & Berry, J.W. (1996). *Ecology acculturation and psychological adaptation: A study of adivasis in Bihar.* New Delhi: Sage Publications.

Misra, G. (1983, January). Deprivation and development: A review of Indian studies. *Indian Educational Review,* 1–21.

Misra, G. (1988). Relevance of Indian thought to contemporary psychology. In F.M. Sahoo (Ed.), *Psychology in Indian context* (pp. 16–21). Agra: National Psychological Corporation.

Misra, G. (1989). Intrinsic motivation, extrinsic reward and performance. *Indian Educational Review, 24,* 17–35.

Misra, G. (1990). *Applied social psychology in India.* New Delhi: Sage Publications.

Misra, G. (1991a). Socio-cultural influences on moral behaviour. *Indian Journal of Social Work, 42,* 179–194.

Misra, G. (1991b). *Forms and foundations of psychological knowledge. Study on progress.* Swarthmore, Penn: Swarthmore College.

Misra, G., & Agarwal, R. (1985). The meaning of achievement: Implications for a cross-cultural theory of achievement motivation. In I.R. Lagunes & Ype H. Poortinga (Eds), *From a different perspective: Studies of behavior across cultures* (pp. 250–266). Lisse: Swets & Zeitlinger.

Misra, G., & Gergen, K.J. (1993). On the place of culture in psychological science. *International Journal of Psychology, 28,* 225–243.

Misra, G., & Tripathi, L.B. (1980). *Psychological consequences of prolonged deprivation.* Agra: National Psychological Corporation.

Misra, V.N. (1971). Relevance of the Indian concept of civilization in the modern context. *Journal of Ganganatha Jha Kendriya Sanskrit Vidyapeeth, 27,* 363–373.

Misumi, J. (1988). *The meaning of work (MOW) for the Japanese and action research on small group activities in Japanese industrial organizations.* Paper presented at the international symposium on Social Values and Effective Organizations, Taipei.

Moghaddam, F.M. (1987). Psychology in the three worlds: As reflected by the crisis in social psychology and the move toward indigenous third-world psychology. *American Psychologist, 42,* 912–920.

Mohanty, A.K. (1988). Beyond the horizon of Indian psychology: The Yankee doodler. In F.M. Sahoo (Ed.), *Psychology in Indian context.* Agra: National Psychological Corporation.

Mohanty, A.K. (1990). Psychological consequences of mother tongue maintenance and language literacy for linguistic minorities in India. *Psychology and Developing Societies, 2* (1), 31–51.

Mohanty, A.K. (1991). Social psychological aspects of languages in contact in multilingual societies. In G. Misra (Ed.), *Applied social psychology in India.* New Delhi: Sage Publications.

Mohanty, A.K. (1992/1993). Classification and assessment of bilinguals: An overview of issues and implications. *JEFL (Journal of the Central Institute of English and Foreign Languages), 10–11,* 139–148.

Mohanty, A.K. (1994a). *Bilingualism in a multilingual society.* Mysore: Central Institute of Indian Languages.

Mohanty, A.K. (1994b). *Socialization for multilingual communication.* Paper presented at the international conference on Early Childhood Communication, Utkal University, Bhubaneswar.

Mohanty, A.K. (2000). Language behaviour and processes. In J. Pandey (Ed.), *Psychology in India revisited – Developments in the discipline. Vol. 1: Physiological foundation and human cognition*. New Delhi: Sage Publications.

Mohanty, A.K., & Mishra, B. (1982). Effect of context on word order of children's expression of locative propositions. *Psychological Reports, 50*, 1163–1166.

Mohanty, A.K., & Mishra, M. (1985). Expression and comprehension of Oriya bitransitive sentences: Effect of word order. *Psycho-Lingua, XV* (1), 7–18.

Mohanty, A.K., & Mohanty, N. (1981). Effect of word order and reversibility on comprehension of Oriya locative sentences. *Indian Journal of Psychology, 56*, 59–66.

Mohanty, A.K., Panda, S., & Mishra, B. (1999). Language socialization in a multilingual society. In T.S. Saraswathi (Ed.), *Culture, socialization and human development: Theory, research and applications in India*. New Delhi: Sage Publications.

Mohanty, A.K., & Perregaux, C. (1997). Language acquisition and bilingualism. In J.W. Berry, P.R. Dasen, & T.S. Saraswathi (Eds), *Handbook of cross-cultural psychology, Vol. 2: Basic processes and human development* (2nd ed.). Boston: Allyn & Bacon.

Mohite, P. (1983). Development of language curriculum for preschool children. *Child Psychiatry Quarterly, 16* (4), 168–184.

Morawski, J.G. (Ed.). (1988). *The rise of experimentation in American psychology*. New Haven, CT: Yale University Press.

Moscovici, S. (1972). Society and theory in social psychology. In J. Israel & H. Tajfel (Eds), *The content of social psychology* (pp. 17–68). London: Academic Press.

Much, W. (1995). Cultural psychology. In J.A. Smith, R. Harré, & L.K. Langenhove (Eds), *Rethinking psychology*. Thousand Oaks, CA: Sage Publications.

Murphy, G., & Murphy, L.B. (Eds). (1968). *Asian psychology*. New York: Harper.

Murti, T.V.S. (1955). *The central philosophy of Buddhism*. London: Allen & Unwin.

Nadler, D.A., & Tushman, M.L. (1990). Beyond the charismatic leader: Leadership and organizational change. *California Management Review*, Winter, 77–97.

Nagaraja, J. (1983). Mental health limits, priorities and psychoethics. *Indian Journal of Psychiatry, 25*, 3–6.

Naglieri, J. (1992). Two roads diverged in a wood: Choosing g or PASS cognitive processes. In J. Carlson (Ed.), *Advances in cognition and educational practice* (Vol. 1, part A). Greenwich, CT: JAI Press.

Nakajima, H. (1994). Health, population and development. *World Health, 47*, 3.

Nakamura, H. (1964). *Ways of thinking of eastern people: India, Tibet and Japan*. Honolulu: The University Press of Hawaii.

Nandy, A. (1983). *The intimate enemy: Loss and recovery of self under colonialism*. New Delhi: Oxford University Press.

Narsimha Reddy, D. (1979). Female work participation in India: Facts, problems and policies. *Indian Journal of Industrial Relations, 15* (2), 197–212.

Neki, J.S. (1973). Guru–chela relationship: The possibility of a therapeutic paradigm. *American Journal of Orthopsychiatry, 43,* 755–766.

Neki, J.S. (1976). An examination of the cultural relation of dependence as a dynamic of social and therapeutic relationships in social development. *British Journal of Medical Psychology, 49,* 1–10.

Nerlove, S.B., & Snipper, S. (1981). Cognitive consequences of cultural opportunity. In R.H. Munroe, R.L. Munroe, & B.B. Whiting (Eds), *Handbook of cross-cultural human development.* New York: Garland.

Neufeldt, R.W. (1986). *Karma and rebirth: Post classical developments.* Albany: State University of New York Press.

Newland, T.F. (1980). Psychological assessment of exceptional children and youth. In W. Cruickshank (Ed.), *Psychology of exceptional children and youth.* Englewood Cliffs, NJ: Prentice-Hall.

Nickols, S.Y., & Metzen, E.J. (1978). Housework time of husband and wife. *Home Economics Research Journal, 7,* 142–156.

Nirmala, C. (1981a). *First language (Telugu) development: A short descriptive study.* Unpublished doctoral dissertation, Osmania University, Hyderabad.

Nirmala, C. (1981b). Medial consonant cluster acquisition by Telugu children. *Journal of Child Language, 8,* 63–73.

Nirmala, C. (1983/1984). Development of plural in Telugu children. *Osmania Papers in Linguistics, 9 & 10,* 1–20.

Nisbet, R.A. (1966). *The sociological tradition.* New York: Basic Books.

O'Flaherty, W.D. (1980). *Karma and rebirth in classical Indian traditions.* Berkeley, CA: University of California Press.

Ochs, E. (1986). Introduction. In B.B. Schieffelin & E. Ochs (Eds), *Language socialization across cultures.* Cambridge, Mass: Cambridge University Press.

Oldham, G.R. (1976). The motivation strategies used by supervisors. *Organizational Behavior and Human Performance, 15,* 66–86.

Organ, T.W.C. (1990). *The Hindu quest for the perfection of man.* Athens, Ohio: Ohio University Press.

Orley, J.K.M. (1994). *Quality of life assessment: International perspective.* Berlin: Springer.

Osgood, C.E., May, W.H., & Miron, M.S. (1975). *Cross-cultural universals of affective meaning.* Urbana, Ill: University of Illinois Press.

Osgood, C.E., Suci, G.J., & Tannenbaum, P.H. (1957). *The measurement of meaning.* Urbana, Ill: University of Illinois Press.

Ostor, A. (1980). *The play of the gods: Locality, ideology and time in the festivals of a Bengali town.* Chicago: The University of Chicago Press.

Overman, E.S. (1989). *Methodology and epistemology for social science: Selected papers by Donald T. Campbell.* Chicago: The University of Chicago Press.

Packer, M.J. (1985). Hermeneutic inquiry in the study of human conduct. *American Psychologist, 40,* 1081–1093.

Pande, N. (1994). *Evaluation in report of the CBR demonstration project at Sirathu: Reflections over the achievements and failures.* Unpublished manuscript, Department of Psychology, University of Allahabad, Allahabad.

Pandey, G.C. (1972). *The meaning and process of culture*. Agra: S.L. Agarwala & Company.

Pandey, G.C. (1984). *Foundations of Indian culture: Spiritual vision and symbolic forms in ancient India*. New Delhi: Books & Books.

Pandey, J. (Ed.). (1981). *Perspectives on experimental social psychology in India*. New Delhi: Sage Publications.

Pandey, J. (Ed.). (1988a). *Psychology in India: The state-of-the-art* (3 vols). New Delhi: Sage Publications.

Pandey, J. (Ed.). (1988b). *Social reality: Perspectives and understanding*. New Delhi: Concept.

Pandey, N., & Naidu, R.K. (1986). Effort and outcome orientations as moderators of stress-strain relationship. *Psychological Studies*, 32, 207–214.

Pandian, J. (1985). *Anthropology and the western tradition: Toward an authentic anthropology*. Illinois: Wareland.

Paranjpe, A.C. (1984). *Theoretical psychology: The meeting of East and West*. New York: Plenum Press.

Paranjpe, A.C. (1988). A personality theory according to Vedanta. In A.C. Paranjpe, D.Y.F. Ho, & R.W. Ribber (Eds), *Asian contributions to psychology* (pp. 185–213). New York: Praeger.

Paranjpe, A.C., Ho, D.Y.F., & Rieber, R.W. (Eds). (1988). *Asian contributions to psychology*. New York: Praeger.

Pareek, U. (1970). Poverty and motivation: Figure and ground. In V. Allen (Ed.), *Psychological factors in poverty*. Chicago: Markham Publishing House.

Pareek, U. (1981). Dynamics of social change. In U. Pareek (Ed.), *A survey of research in psychology, 1971–76* (Part II). Bombay: Popular Prakashan.

Pareek, U. (1988). Culture and development: The case of Indonesia. In D. Sinha & H.S.R. Kao (Eds), *Social values and development: Asian perspectives* (pp. 175–196). New Delhi: Sage Publications.

Passmore, J. (1967). Logical positivism. In *Encyclopaedia of philosophy* (Vol. 5, pp. 52–57). New York: The Free Press.

Patnaik, N., & Rath, R. (1982). Effect of cognitive training on the achievement of socially disadvantaged lone achievers. In R. Rath, H.S. Asthana, D. Sinha, & J.B.P. Sinha (Eds), *Diversity and unity in cross-cultural psychology*. Lisse: Swets & Zeitlinger.

Pattanayak, D.P. (1981). *Multilingualism and mother tongue education*. New Delhi: Oxford University Press.

Pattanayak, D.P. (Ed.). (1990). *Multilingualism in India*. Clevedon: Multilingual Matters.

Pederson, P. (1979). Non-western psychology: The search for alternatives. In A.J. Marsella, R.G. Tharp, & T.J. Ciborowski (Eds), *Perspectives on cross-cultural psychology*. New York: Academic Press.

Pepitone, A. (1989). Toward a cultural social psychology. *Psychology and Developing Societies*, 1 (1), 5–19.

Pfeffer, J. (1977). The ambiguity of leadership. *Academy of Management Review*, 2, 104–112.

Pleck, J.H. (1985). *Working wives/working husbands*. Beverly Hills, CA: Sage Publications.

Podsakoff, P.M., Todor, W.D., & Skov, R. (1982). Effect of leader contingent and non-contingent reward and punishment behaviors on subordinate performance and satisfaction. *Academy of Management Journal, 25*, 810–821.

Poloma, M.M. (1972). Role conflict and the married professional woman. In C. Safilios-Rothschild (Ed.), *Toward a sociology of women*. Lexington, Mass: Xerox Press.

Poortinga, Y.H., & Van der Flier (1988). The meaning of item bias in ability tests. In S.H. Irvine & J.W. Berry (Eds), *Human abilities in cultural context*. New York: Cambridge University Press.

Potter, J., & Wetherell, M. (1987). *Discourse and social psychology: Beyond attitudes and behaviors*. London: Sage Publications.

Powell, R., Bhatt, G., Grady, B., Tonks, R., & Carpendale, J. (1991). *United we stand? Our disciplinary commitment as psychologists*. Paper presented at the annual convention of the Canadian Psychological Association, Calgary.

Price-Williams, D.R. (1985). Cultural psychology. In G. Lindzey & E. Aronson (Eds), *Handbook of social psychology, Vol. II, Special fields and application* (pp. 993–1042). New York: Random House.

Puhan, B.N., & Sahoo, F.M. (1991). Indigenization of psychological studies: Research agenda. *Indian Journal of Current Psychological Research, 6*, 101–107.

Rabinow, P., & Sullivan, W.M. (Eds). (1979). *Interpretive social science: A reader*. Berkeley, CA: University of California Press.

Radhakrishnan, S. (1927). *The Hindu view of life*. London: George Allen & Unwin.

Raju, P.T. (1985). *Structural depths of Indian thought*. Albany: State University of New York Press.

Ramanujan, A.K. (1990). Is there an Indian way of thinking? An informal essay. In M. Marriot (Ed.), *India through Hindu categories*. New Delhi: Sage Publications.

Ramu, G.N. (1989). *Women, work and marriage in urban India: A study of dual and single earner couples*. New Delhi: Sage Publications.

Rani, K. (1976). *Role conflict and working women*. New Delhi: Chetna Publishers.

Rao, V.V.P., & Rao, V.N. (1988). Sex role attitudes of college students in India. In R. Ghadially (Ed.), *Women in Indian society: A reader*. New Delhi: Sage Publications.

Rapoport, R., & Rapoport, R. (1980). Three generations of dual career family research. In F. Pepitone-Rockwell (Ed.), *Dual career couples*. Beverly Hills, CA: Sage Publications.

Rath, R., & Patnaik, N. (1979). Effect of training on some cognitive abilities. *Journal of Psychological Researches, 23*, 81–92.

Ravetz, J.R. (1990). *The merger of knowledge with power: Essays in critical science*. London: Mansell Publishing House.

Rawlinson, A. (1981). Yoga psychology. In P. Heelas & A. Lock (Eds), *Indigenous psychologies: The anthropology of the self* (pp. 247–264). London: Academic Press.

Reddy, P. (1984). Impact of culture on organization design. *Vikalpa, 9*, 145–158.

Reichenbach, B.R. (1990). *The law of karma: A philosophical inquiry*. Honolulu: University of Hawaii Press.

Richler, M. (1992). *Oh Canada! Oh Québec!* Toronto: Penguin.

Roberts, N. (1985). Transforming leadership: A process of collective action. *Human Relations, 38*, 1023–1046.

Rodman, H. (1972). Marital power and the theory of resources in cultural context. *Journal of Comparative Family Studies, 3*, 50–67.

Rogoff, B. (1981). Schooling and the development of cognitive skills. In H.C. Triandis & A. Heron (Eds), *Handbook of cross-cultural psychology, Vol. 4*. Boston: Allyn & Bacon.

Rohner, R. (1984). Toward a conception of culture for cross-cultural psychology. *Journal of Cross-Cultural Psychology, 15*, 111–138.

Roland, A. (1988). *In search of self in India and Japan: Toward a cross-cultural psychology*. Princeton, NJ: Princeton University Press.

Rorty, R. (1979). *Philosophy and the mirror of nature*. Princeton, NJ: Princeton University Press.

Rosaldo, M. (1980). *Knowledge and passion: Ilongot notions of self and social life*. Cambridge and New York: Cambridge University Press.

Rose, N. (1985). *The psychological complex: Psychology, politics and society in England, 1869–1939*. London: Allen & Unwin.

Rosenberg, M. (1965). *Society and the adolescent self-image*. Princeton, NJ: Princeton University Press.

Ross, A.D. (1961). *The Hindu family and its urban setting*. New Delhi: Oxford University Press.

Rouse, J. (1987). *Knowledge and power: Toward a political philosophy of science*. Ithaca & London: Cornell University Press.

Rowan, B., & Guthrie, L. (1988). *The quality of Chapter 1 instruction: Results from a study of 24 schools*. San Francisco, CA: Far West Laboratory for Educational Research and Development.

Roy, R. (1993). Swadhyaya: Values and message. In P. Wignaraja (Ed.), *New social movements in the south: Empowering the people*. London: Zed Books Ltd.

Roy, R., & Srivastava, R.K. (1986). *Dialogues on development*. New Delhi: Sage Publications.

Roy, S. (1988). The Tilonia model as a new approach. In P.N. Khandwalla (Ed.), *Social development* (pp. 203–205). New Delhi: Sage Publications.

Russell, R.W. (1984). Psychology in its world context. *American Psychologist, 39*, 1017–1025.

Russo, N.F. (1985). *Developing a national agenda to address women's mental health needs*. Washington, DC: American Psychological Association.

Safilios-Rothschild, C. (1982). Female power, autonomy and demographic change in the third world. In R. Anker, M. Buvinic, & Youssef (Eds), *Women's roles and population trends in the third world*. London: International Labour Organization.

Safilios-Rothschild, C. (1990). Socio-economic determinants of the outcomes of women's income-generation in developing countries. In S. Stichter & J.L. Parpart (Eds), *Women, employment and the family in the international division of labour*. London: The Macmillan Press.

Sahu, S., & Swain, J.B. (1985). Effect of language training programme on low language achievers. *Perspectives on Psychological Researches, 8* (2), 1–8.

Sailaja, V. (1989). *Role of word order in the acquisition of Telugu*. Paper presented at the national seminar on Language Processes and Language Disorders, Department of Linguistics, Osmania University, Hyderabad.

Samanta, R.K. (1982). Work environment of ULWs in Meghalaya. *Social Change, 12,* 34–38.

Sampson, E.E. (1977). Psychology and the American ideal. *Journal of Personality and Social Psychology, 35,* 767–782.

Sampson, E.E. (1988). The debate on individualism: Indigenous psychologies of the individual and their role in personal and societal functioning. *American Psychologist, 43,* 15–22.

Sanchez, E. (1995). Community participation from the perspective of social psychology. *InterAmerican Journal of Psychology, 29,* 227–242.

Sashkin, M. (1988). The visionary leader. In J.A. Conger, R.N. Kanungo et al., (Eds), *Charismatic leadership*. San Francisco, CA: Jossey-Bass.

Savara, M. (1986). *Changing trends in women's employment: A case study of textile industry in Bombay*. Bombay: Himalaya Publishing House.

Scanzoni, J., & Polonka, K. (1980). A conceptual approach to explicit marital negotiation. *Journal of Marriage and the Family, 42,* 31–44.

Scheler, M. (1970). On the positivistic philosophy of the history of knowledge and its Law of Three Stages. In J.E. Curtis & J.W. Petras (Eds), *The sociology of knowledge*. New York: Praeger. (Date of original work unknown.)

Schwartz, B. (1986). *The battle for human nature: Science, morality and modern life*. New York & London: W.W. Norton.

Schwindler, W. (1984). UNESCO's project on the exchange of knowledge for endogenous development. *International Journal of Psychology, 19,* 3–15.

Segall, M.H. (1983). On the search for the independent variable in cross-cultural psychology. In S.H. Irvine & J.W. Berry (Eds), *Human assessment and cultural factors* (pp. 127–138). New York: Plenum Press.

Segall, M.H. (1984). More than we need to know about culture but are afraid not to ask. *Journal of Cross-Cultural Psychology, 15,* 153–162.

Segall, M.H. (1986). *Culture and behavior in global perspective: An introduction to cross-cultural psychology*. New York: Pergamon Press.

Segall, M.H., Dasen, P.R., Berry, J.W., & Poortinga, Ype H. (1990). *Human behavior in global perspective*. New York: Pergamon Press.

Semin, G.R., & Gergen, K.J. (1990). *Everyday understanding: Social and scientific implications*. London: Sage Publications.

Sengupta, S. (1965). *Tree symbol worship in India: A new survey of a pattern of folk religion*. Calcutta: Indian Publications.

Serpell, R. (1982). *Planning and delivery of community-based services for mentally handicapped children in Africa.* Paper presented at the Eighth World Congress of ILSMH, Nairobi.

Serpell, R. (1988). Childhood disability in the socio-cultural context: Assessment and information needs for effective services. In P.R. Dasen, J.W. Berry, & N. Sartorius (Eds), *Health and cross-cultural psychology: Towards applications.* Newbury Park, CA: Sage Publications.

Sexton, V.S., & Misiak, A. (1984). American psychologist and psychology abroad. *American Psychologist, 39,* 1026–1031.

Shah, A.V. (1982). Integration of mental health. *Indian Journal of Psychiatry, 24,* 3–7.

Shamgar-Handelman, L., & Palomba, R. (1987). *Alternative patterns of family life in modern societies.* Rome: Collana Monografie.

Shamir, B., House, R.J., & Arthur, M.B. (1989). *The transformational effects of charismatic leadership: A motivational theory.* Working Paper, Reginald Jones Center for Strategic Management, Wharton School of Management, Philadelphia.

Share, D., & Stanovich, K. (1995). Cognitive processes in early reading development: Accommodating individual differences into a model of acquisition. *Issues in Education: Contributions from Educational Psychology, 1,* 1–57.

Sharma, S. (1978). Research on anxiety in India: A review. *Indian Journal of Psychology, 53,* 29–43.

Sharma, S. (1988). Stress and anxiety. In J. Pandey (Ed.), *Psychology in India: The state-of-the-art.* New Delhi: Sage Publications.

Sharma, U. (1990). Public employment and private relations: Women and work in India. In S. Stichter & J.L. Parpart (Eds), *Women, employment and the family in the international division of labour.* London: The Macmillan Press.

Sharma, V. (1969). *A linguistic study of speech development in early childhood.* Unpublished doctoral dissertation, Agra University, Agra.

Sheth, N.R. (1994). *Children of the same God: A spiritual approach to social transformation.* Working Paper 59. Ahmedabad: Gujarat Institute of Development Research.

Shotter, J. (1990). *Knowing of the third kind.* Utrecht: ISROR.

Shourie, A. (1996a, 14 January). Rituals, idols, have great significance. *Pioneer, 8.*

Shourie, A. (1996b, 21 January). The Buddha's garment. *Pioneer, 10.*

Shukla, A. (1987). Decision making in single- and dual-career families in India. *Journal of Marriage and the Family, 49,* 621–629.

Shweder, R.A. (1990). Cultural psychology—What is it? In J.W. Stigler, R.A. Shweder, & G. Herdt (Eds), *Cultural psychology: Essays on comparative development* (pp. 1–42). Cambridge: Cambridge University Press.

Shweder, R.A. (1991). *Thinking through cultures: Expeditions in indigenous psychologies.* Cambridge, Mass: Harvard University Press.

Shweder, R.A., & LeVine, R.A. (Eds). (1984). *Culture theory: Essays on mind, self and emotion.* Cambridge: Cambridge University Press.

Shweder, R.A., Mohapatra, M., & Miller, J.G. (1987). Culture and moral development. In J. Kagan & S. Lamb (Eds), *The emergence of morality in young children*. Chicago & London: The University of Chicago Press.

Siegel, L. (1989). IQ is irrelevant to the defintion of learning disabilities. *Journal of Learning Disabilities, 22*, 469–479.

Sims, H.P. (1977). The leader as manager in reinforcement contingencies: An empirical example and a model. In J.G. Hunt & L.L. Larson (Eds), *Leadership: The cutting edge* (pp. 121–137). Carbondale, Ill: Southern Illinois University Press.

Sinari, R. (1965). The method of phenomenological reduction in Yoga. *Philosophy of East and West, 15*, 217–228.

Singh, A. (1987). *Certain deprivational factors in language development in children*. Unpublished doctoral dissertation, University of Allahabad, Allahabad.

Singh, A.K. (1981). *Poverty and prejudice in India: Psychological studies in dehumanization*. Unpublished manuscript, Ranchi University, Ranchi.

Singh, A.K. (1988). Intergroup relations and social tensions. In J. Pandey (Ed.), *Psychology in India: The state-of-the-art* (Vol. 2, pp. 159–223). New Delhi: Sage Publications.

Sinha, D. (1965). The integration of modern psychology with Indian thought. *Journal of Humanistic Psychology, 5*, 6–17.

Sinha, D. (1969). *Indian villages in transition: A motivational analysis*. New Delhi: Associated Publishing House.

Sinha, D. (1974). *Motivation and rural development*. Calcutta: Minerva.

Sinha, D. (1975, 29–31 December). *Study of psychological dimensions of poverty: A challenge and necessity*. Presidential address, 13th annual conference of the Indian Academy of Applied Psychology, Karnataka University, Dharwar.

Sinha, D. (1977a). Orientation and attitude of the social psychologist in a developing country: The Indian case. *International Review of Applied Psychology, 26*, 1–10.

Sinha, D. (1977b). Some social disadvantages and development of certain perceptual skills. *Indian Journal of Psychology, 52*, 115–132.

Sinha, D. (1978). Story-Pictorial E.F.T.: A culturally appropriate test for perceptual disembedding. *Indian Journal of Psychology, 52*, 160–171.

Sinha, D. (1979). Perceptual style among nomadic and transitional agriculturist Birhors. In L.H. Eckensberger, W.J. Lonner, & Y.H. Poortinga (Eds), *Cross-cultural contributions to psychology*. Lisse: Swets & Zeitlinger.

Sinha, D. (1980, 5–12 July). *Towards out-growing the alien framework. A review of some recent trends in psychological researches in India*. Paper presented at the XXII International Congress of Psychology, Leipzig.

Sinha, D. (1981a). Non-western perspectives in psychology: Why, what and whither? *Journal of Indian Psychology, 3*, 1–9.

Sinha, D. (1981b). Social psychology in India: A historical perspective. In J. Pandey (Ed.), *Perspectives on experimental social psychology in India* (pp. 3–17). New Delhi: Concept.

Sinha, D. (1982). Socio-cultural factors and the development of perceptual and cognitive skills. In W.W. Hartup (Ed.), *Review of child development research* (Vol. 6). Chicago: The University of Chicago Press.

Sinha, D. (1983). Human assessment in the Indian context. In S.H. Irvine & J.W. Berry (Eds), *Human assessment and cultural factors*. New York: Plenum Press.

Sinha, D. (1984a). *Manual for Story-Pictorial EFT and Indo-African EFT*. Varanasi: Rupa Psychological Centre.

Sinha, D. (1984b). Psychology in the context of third world development. *International Journal of Psychology, 19*, 17–29.

Sinha, D. (1984c). Some recent changes in the Indian family and their implications for socialization. *The Indian Journal of Social Work, XLV* (3), 271–286.

Sinha, D. (1986). *Psychology in a third world country: The Indian experience*. New Delhi: Sage Publications.

Sinha, D. (1988a). Basic Indian values and behaviour dispositions in the context of national development. An appraisal. In D. Sinha & H.S.R. Kao (Eds), *Social values and development: Asian perspectives* (pp. 31–55). New Delhi: Sage Publications.

Sinha, D. (1988b). The family scenario in a developing country and its implications for mental health. The case in India. In P.R. Dasen, J.W. Berry, & N. Sartorius (Eds), *Health and cross-cultural psychology toward applications*. (pp. 48–70) Newbury Park, CA: Sage Publications.

Sinha, D. (1989). Cross-cultural psychology and the process of indigenization: A second view from the third world. In D.M. Keats, D. Munroe, & L. Mann (Eds), *Heterogeneity in cross-cultural psychology*. Lisse: Swets & Zeitlinger.

Sinha, D. (1990). Concept of psycho-social well-being: Western and Indian perspectives. *National Institute of Mental Health and Neurosciences Journal, 8*, 1–11.

Sinha, D. (1993). Indigenization of psychology in India and its relevance. In U. Kim & J.W. Berry (Eds), *Indigenous psychologies: Research and experience in cultural contexts* (pp. 30–43). Newbury Park, CA: Sage Publications.

Sinha, D. (1997). Indigenizing psychology. In J.W. Berry, Y.H. Poortinga, & J. Pandey (Eds), *Handbook of cross-cultural psychology, Vol. 1* (pp. 129–169). Boston: Allyn & Bacon.

Sinha, D., & Bharat, S. (1985). Three types of family structure and psychological differentiation: A study among the Jaunsar-Bawar society. *International Journal of Psychology, 20*, 693–700.

Sinha, D., & Kao, H.S.R. (Eds). (1988). *Social values and development: Asian perspectives*. New Delhi: Sage Publications.

Sinha, D., & Mishra, R.C. (1993). Some methodological issues related to research in developmental psychology in the context of policy and intervention programmes. In T.S. Saraswathi & B. Kaur (Eds), *Human development and family studies in India: An agenda for research and policy*. New Delhi: Sage Publications.

Sinha, D., & Shrestha, A.B. (1992). Ecocultural factors in cognitive style among children from hills and plains of Nepal. *International Journal of Psychology, 20*, 693–708.

288 🎋 Psychology in Human and Social Development

Sinha, D., Tripathi, R.C., & Misra, G. (Eds). (1982). *Deprivation: Its social roots and psychological consequences.* New Delhi: Concept.

Sinha, G. (1988). Exposure to industrial and urban environments, and formal schooling as factors in psychological differentiation. *International Journal of Psychology, 23,* 707–719.

Sinha, J.B.P. (1980). *The nurturant task leader.* New Delhi: Concept Publishing Company.

Sinha, J.B.P. (1982). The Hindu (Indian) identity. *Dynamic Psychiatry, 15* (74/75), 148–160.

Sinha, J.B.P. (1988). Reorganizing values for development. In D. Sinha & H.S.R. Kao (Eds), *Social values and development: Asian perspectives* (pp. 275–284). New Delhi: Sage Publications.

Sinha, J.B.P. (1990, 22–27 July). *Developing psychology as a policy science: Prospects and problems.* Invited address at the International Congress of Applied Psychology, Kyoto.

Sinha, J.B.P. (1995). Factors facilitating and impeding the growth of psychology in South Asia with special reference in India. *International Journal of Psychology, 30,* 741–753.

Sinha, R., & Prabhu, S. (1988). Status equilibrium of working women. In T.M. Dak (Ed.), *Women and work in Indian society.* Delhi: Discovery Publishing House.

Slobin, D.I. (1982). Universal and particular in the acquisition of language. In E. Wanner & L.R. Gleitman (Eds), *Language acquisition: The state of the art.* Cambridge, Mass: Cambridge University Press.

Slocum, W.L., & Nye, I.F. (1976). Provider and housekeeper roles. In I.F. Nye (Ed.), *Role structure and analysis of the family.* Beverly Hills, CA: Sage Publications.

Smedslund, J. (1995). Psychologic: Common sense and the pseudo empirical. In J.A. Smith, R. Harré, & L.K. Langenhove (Eds), *Rethinking psychology.* Thousand Oaks, CA: Sage Publications.

Smith, J.A., Harré, R., & Langenhove, L.K. (Eds). (1995). *Rethinking psychology.* Thousand Oaks, CA: Sage Publications.

Sniderman, P., et al. (1993). Psychological and cultural foundations of prejudice: The case of anti-Semitism in Québec. *Canadian Review of Sociology and Anthropology, 30,* 242–270.

Snow, C.P. (1956/1963). The two cultures. In S. Weintraub (Ed.), *C.P. Snow: A spectrum.* New York: Charles Scribner's.

Southworth, F.C. (1980). Functional aspects of bilingualism. *International Journal of Dravidian Linguistics, IX* (1), 74–108.

Spiro, M. (1972). An overview and a suggested reorientation. In F.L.K. Hsu (Ed.), *Psychological anthropology* (pp. 573–607). Cambridge, Mass: Schenkman.

Sridevi, S.V. (1976). *The aspects of acquisition of Kannada by 2+ year old children.* Unpublished Master's dissertation, All India Institute of Speech and Hearing, Mysore.

Srinivas, K.M. (1995). Achieving excellence in Indian organizations: New opportunities for psychologists. *Psychology and Developing Societies*, 7 (2), 185–216.

Srinivas, M.N. (1952). *Religion and society among the Coorgs of south India*. London: Oxford University Press.

Sripat, K. (1989). Changing perception of women: Implications for change and development. In A.K. Dalal & A.K. Singh (Eds), *Human resources development: Psychological perspectives*. Gurgaon: Academic Press.

Srivastava, A.K. (1990). Multilingualism and school education in India: Special features, problems and prospects. In D.P. Pattanayak (Ed.), *Multilingualism in India*. Clevedon: Multilingual Matters.

Srivastava, A.K., & Khatoon, P. (1980). Effect of difference between mother tongue and another language as medium of instruction on mental ability, achievement and creativity of VII standard children. In E. Annamalai (Ed.), *Bilingualism and achievement in schools*. Mysore: Central Institute of Indian Languages.

Srivastava, A.K., & Ramaswamy, K. (1987). Bilingualism, SES, sex and personality development in school going children. *Scholar Critic*, 5 (9), 75–90.

Srivastava, R.N. (1977). Indian bilingualism: Myth and reality. In P.G. Sharma & S. Kumar (Eds), *Indian bilingualism*. Agra: Kendriya Hindi Sansthan.

Srivastava, R.N., & Gupta, R.S. (1990). Literacy in a multilingual context. In D.P. Pattanayak (Ed.), *Multilingualism in India*. Clevedon: Multilingual Matters.

Standing, R. (1991). *Dependence and autonomy: Women's employment and the family in Calcutta*. London: Routledge.

Stanovich, K. (1988). Explaining the differences between the dyslexic and garden-variety poor reader: The phonological-core variable difference model. *Journal of Learning Disabilities*, 21, 590–604.

Stephan, C., Passer, N.R., Kennedy, J.C., & Aronson, E. (1978). Attributions to success and failure in cooperative, competitive and independent interactions. *European Journal of Social Psychology*, 8, 269–274.

Stewart, S., Hong, Ng Sek, & Ting, C.F. (1993). *Wages, incentives and productivity linkages in Hong Kong*. Unpublished monograph.

Stichter, S., & Parpart, J.L. (1990). *Women, employment and the family in the international division of labour*. London: The Macmillan Press.

Stogdill, R.M. (1974). *Handbook of leadership*. New York: The Free Press.

Student, K.R. (1968). Supervisory influence and work-group performance. *Journal of Applied Psychology*, 52, 188–194.

Super, C.M., & Harkness, S. (1986). The developmental niche: A conceptualization at the interface of child and culture. *International Journal of Behavioral Development*, 9, 545–569.

Super, C.M., & Harkness, S. (1997). The cultural structuring of child development. In J.W. Berry, P.R. Dasen, & T.S. Saraswathi (Eds), *Handbook of cross-cultural psychology*, Vol. 2 (pp. 1–39). Boston: Allyn & Bacon.

Tajfel, H. (1978). *Differentiation between social groups: Studies in the social psychology of intergroup relations*. London: Academic Press.

Talib, M. (1981). Resistances to development—A view from below. *Man and Development, 3,* 136–145.

Tannenbaum, R., & Schmidt, W.H. (1958, March–April). How to choose a leadership pattern. *Harvard Business Review.*

Taylor, S.E. (1990). Health psychology. *American Psychologist, 45,* 40–50.

The WHO QOL Group. (1996). What is quality of life? *World Health Forum, 17,* 354–356.

Thirumalai, M.S. (1972). Some aspects of 4 year plus old stage in the acquisition of Tamil phonology. *Journal of AIISH, 3,* 7–12.

Thomas, A.B. (1988). Does leadership make a difference to organizational performance. *Administrative Science Quarterly, 33,* 388–400.

Thomas, K.W., & Velthouse, B.A. (1990). Cognitive elements in empowerment: An interpretive model of intrinsic task motivation. *Academy of Management Review, 15,* 666–681.

Thomas, M. (1993, 29–31 October). *Disability and rehabilitation: The emergence of community based rehabilitation approach in India.* Paper presented at the conference on Asia in the 1990's Meeting and Making a New World, Queens University, Ontario.

Torgesen, J. (1995). Instruction for reading disabled children: Questions about knowledge and practice. *Issues in Education: Contributions from Educational Psychology, 1,* 91–96.

Torgesen, J., & Houck, G. (1980). Processing deficiencies in learning disabled children who perform poorly on the digit span task. *Journal of Educational Psychology, 72,* 141–160.

Torgesen, J., Kistner, J., & Morgan, S. (1987). Component processes in working memory. In J. Borkowski & J. Day (Eds), *Memory and cognition in special children: Perspectives on retardation, learning disabilities and giftedness.* Norwood, NJ: Ablex.

Torgesen, J., Wagner, R., Simmons, K., & Laughon, R. (1990). Identifying phonological coding problems in disabled readers: Naming, counting, or span measures? *Learning Disability Quarterly, 13,* 236–243.

Triandis, H.C. (1972). *The analysis of subjective culture.* New York: John Wiley.

Triandis, H.C. (1980). Introduction. In H.C. Triandis & W.W. Lambert (Eds), *Handbook of cross-cultural psychology perspectives* (Vol. 1, pp. 15–30). Boston: Allyn & Bacon.

Triandis, H.C. (1988). Collectivism vs. individualism: A reconceptualization of a basic concept in cross-cultural psychology. In C. Bagley & G.K. Verma (Eds), *Personality, cognition and values: Cross-cultural perspectives of childhood and adolescence* (pp. 60–95). London: McMillan.

Triandis, H.C. (1989). The self and social behavior in differing cultural contexts. *Psychological Review, 996,* 506–520.

Triandis, H.C. (1990). Cross-cultural studies of individualism and collectivism. In J.J. Berman (Ed.), *Nebraska symposium on motivation 1989: Cross-cultural perspectives* (pp. 41–134). Lincoln & London: University of Nebraska Press.

Tripathi, R.C. (1988a). Applied social psychology. In J. Pandey (Ed.), *Psychology in India: The state-of-the-art* (Vol. 2, pp. 95–158). New Delhi: Sage Publications.

Tripathi, R.C. (1988b). Aligning development to values in India. In D. Sinha & H.S.R. Kao (Eds), *Social values and development: Asian perspectives* (pp. 314–332). New Delhi: Sage Publications.

Usha Devi, A. (1990). *Acquisition of syntax: A case study of Telugu*. New Delhi: Bahri.

Vaidyanathan, R. (1984). *Verbal environment and early language acquisition: A pragmatic approach*. Unpublished doctoral dissertation, Bombay.

Vaidyanathan, R. (1988). Development of form and functions of interrogatives in children: A longitudinal study in Tamil. *Journal of Child Language, 15,* 533–551.

Valdez-Medina, J.L. (1994). *El Autoconcepto del Mexicano. Estudios de Validacion*. Tesis de Doctorado no publicada. Facultad de Psicologia, UNAM, Mexico.

Van de Vijver, F.J.R., & Poortinga, Y.H. (1982). Cross-cultural generalization and universality. *Journal of Cross-Cultural Psychology, 13,* 387–408.

Varma, T. (1979). Stage I speech of a Hindi speaking child. *Journal of Child Language, 6,* 167–173.

Vasanta, D. (1992). Phonological development and phonological disorders: A review article. In T. Balasubramaniam & V. Prakasam (Eds), *Sound patterns for the phonetician: Studies in phonetics and phonology in honour of J.C. Catford*. Madras: T.R. Publications.

Vasanta, D., & Sailaja, V. (1993). *Psycholinguistic evidence for word order variation within dative constructions in Telugu*. Paper presented at the national seminar on Word Order in Indian Languages, Osmania University, Hyderabad.

Vasanta, D., Sastry, J.V., & Ravi Maruth, P. (1994). *Grammaticality judgement of Telugu speaking elementary school children*. Paper presented at the national seminar on Language Development and Language Disorders, Osmania University, Hyderabad.

Verma, A.S. (1970). *A sociological analysis of rural reconstruction and community development programs in Uttar Pradesh with special reference to Gorakhpur division*. Unpublished doctoral dissertation, Lucknow University, Lucknow.

Vlaenderen, H.V. (1993). Psychological research in the process of social change: A contribution to community development. *Psychology and Developing Societies, 5* (1), 95–109.

Vlaenderen, H.J., & Gilbert, A.J. (1990, 3-5 September). *Participatory research for human capacity building in rural development*. Paper presented at the Congress of the Psychological Association of South Africa, University of Port Elizabeth.

Vroom, V.H., & Yetton, E.W. (1973). *Leadership and decision making*. Pittsburgh: University of Pittsburgh Press.

Vygotsky, L. (1962). *Thought and language*. Cambridge, MA: The MIT Press.

Vygotsky, L. (1978). *Mind in society*. Cambridge, Mass: Harvard University Press.

Wadhera, K. (1976). *The new bread winners*. New Delhi: Vishwa Yuvak Kendra.

Wadley, S. (1988). Women and the Hindu tradition. In R. Ghadially (Ed.), *Women in Indian society: A reader* (pp. 23–43). New Delhi: Sage Publications.

Wagner, P., & Wittrock, B. (1990). States, institutions, discourses: A comparative perspective on the structuration of the social sciences. *Discourses on Society, 15,* 331–357.

Walberg, J. (1984). *Federal (Chapter 1) educational spending and effects on poor children.* Washington, DC: Learn, Inc.

Weber, M. (1958). *The religions of India: The sociology of Hinduism and Buddhism.* Glencoe, CT: The Free Press.

Weiner, B. (1991). Metaphors in motivation and attribution. *American Psychologist, 46,* 921–930.

Westley, F., & Mintzberg, H. (1988). Profiles of strategic vision: Levesque and Iacocca. In J.A. Conger, R.N. Kanungo et al. (Eds), *Charismatic leadership.* San Francisco, CA: Jossey-Bass.

White, G.M., & Kirkpatrick, M. (1985). *Person, self, and experience: Exploring Pacific ethnopsychologies.* Berkeley, CA: University of California Press.

Wig, N.N. (1979). Mental health and population growth. *Indian Journal of Psychology, 21,* 12–33.

Wilkinson, A., & Diamond, P. (in press). Achenbach's Youth Self-Report refined: A four-factor model for use with non-clinical populations of predominantly Mexican-origin youth. *Journal of Youth and Adolescence.*

Wilner, A.R. (1984). *The spellbinders: Charismatic political leadership.* New Haven: Yale University Press.

Wing Lung Bank Limited. (1993). *Sixty years of banking services: Annual report 1992* (p. 29). Hong Kong: Wing Lung Bank.

Witkin, H.A., & Goodenough, D.R. (1981). *Cognitive style: Essence and origins.* New York: International University Press.

Wolf, E. (1982). *Europe and the people without history.* Berkeley, CA: University of California Press.

Woolgar, S. (1988). *Science: The very idea.* Chichester: Ellis Horwood.

World Bank (1993). *World development report: Investing in health.* Washington, DC: Oxford University Press.

World Health Organization. (1988). *Charter for action to achieve health for all.* Geneva: WHO.

World Neighbors. (1995). *World neighbors in action: Learning with the community through participatory rural appraisal.* Oklahoma City, OK: World Neighbors.

Wright, R.M. (1988). Anthropological presupposition of indigenous advocacy. *Annual Review of Anthropology, 17,* 365–390.

Wundt, W. (1900–1920). *Völkerpsychologie* (Psychology of societies). Leipzig: Englemann.

Yee, C.W., Hong, C.S., & Chung, L. (1995). *Headship, motivation and corporate culture: Using Kowloon dairy for analysis.* A student research project, Department of Psychology, University of Hong Kong, Hong Kong.

Yogev, S. (1981). Do professional women have egalitarian marital relationship? *Journal of Marriage and the Family, 43*, 865–871.

Yukl, C.A. (1989). *Leadership in organizations*. Englewood Cliffs, NJ: Prentice-Hall.

Zaleznik, A. (1977, May–June). Managers and leaders: Are they different? *Harvard Business Review*, 67–78.

Zaleznik, A. (1990). The leadership gap. *The Academy of Management, 4*, 7–22.

Zigler, E.F. (1989). Addressing the nation's child care crises: The school of the 21st century. *American Journal of Orthopsychiatry, 59*, 485–491.

Notes on Contributors

John W. Berry is Professor Emeritus of Psychology at Queen's University, Kingston, Canada. He received his BA from Sir George Williams University, Montreal and his doctorate from the University of Edinburgh. He has been a Lecturer at the University of Sydney, a Fellow of the Netherlands Institute for Advanced Study, and a Visiting Professor at the Universities of Nice, Geneva and Oxford. Prof. Berry has served as Secretary-General and President of the International Association for Cross-Cultural Psychology, where he is currently an Honorary Fellow. He has authored and edited over 20 books in the areas of cross-cultural, social and cognitive psychology, and is particularly interested in the application of cross-cultural psychology to public policy and programmes in the areas of acculturation, multiculturalism, immigration, health, and education. He was Associate Editor of the *Journal of Cross-Cultural Psychology*, and co-editor of the three-volume *Handbook of Cross-Cultural Psychology*.

Shalini Bharat is Reader at the Tata Institute of Social Sciences, Mumbai. A doctorate in psychology from the University of Allahabad, she is involved in applied and interdisciplinary research on diverse aspects of the family. Her recent work focuses on adoptive families; women, work and family; and familial and social dimensions of HIV/AIDS. Her publications include *Family Measurement in India*, *Child Adoption: Trends and Emerging Issues*, and *Research on Families with Problems in India*. She is a member of the Editorial Board of the *Indian Psychological Abstracts and Reviews*.

Jerry S. Carlson was formerly Professor at the University of California, Riverside. Following his early retirement, he has taught at the University of Washington, Seattle. Prof. Carlson has made significant contributions to research on intelligence, especially dynamic assessment and learning disabilities. He has published extensively in the areas of educational psychology and science education, and is the Editor of the journal *Issues in Education*. Prof. Carlson founded the International Association of Cognitive Education and has also served as its President.

J.A. Conger is Chairman and Executive Director of The Leadership Institute at the University of Southern California. He has done extensive work in the areas of executive leadership, corporate boards, the management of organisational change, and the training and development of leaders and managers. An outstanding teacher, he was selected by *Business Week* to teach leadership to executives. In recognition of his work on leadership education, he assisted the Harvard Business School to redesign the school's organisational behaviour course around leadership issues. He has authored over 60 articles and seven books.

J.P. Das is Emeritus Professor of Educational Psychology, and Research Professor at the Developmental Disabilities Centre, University of Alberta, Canada. He has previously taught at Utkal University, the UCLA, and Vanderbilt University. Professor Das has done extensive work in the areas of intelligence and cognitive dysfunctions including learning disabilities and mental retardation. He is a Fellow of the Royal Society, Canada.

Rogelio Diaz-Guerrero is Research Professor at the National University of Mexico (UNAM). His main areas of research are culture and personality and cross-cultural psychology. He has authored, co-authored or edited many books and has published over 250 journal articles and chapters in specialised books. He has received awards from the Interamerican, the Spanish and the Mexican Societies of Psychology, and honorary memberships from the International Association for Cross-Cultural Psychology and the International Union of Psychological Science. The National University of Mexico conferred upon him an award for research in the behavioural sciences, and the National Systems of Research in Mexico named him the Distinguished Emeritus Research Scientist. His book *Psicologia del Mexicano* is in its sixth edition.

Wayne H. Holtzman is Hogg Professor of Psychology and Education at the University of Texas at Austin. He holds a doctoral degree from Stanford University and was Fellow at the Centre for Advanced Study in the Behavioural Sciences. Professor Holtzman has been President of the Hogg Foundation for Mental Health; and Secretary-

General and President of the International Union of Psychological Science. The American Psychological Association conferred upon him the Award for Distinguished International Contributions to Psychology, and the Southwestern University conferred upon him an honorary doctorate. He has contributed extensively to scientific journals and has authored a number of books.

Ng Sek Hong is Senior Lecturer in the Department of Management Studies, University of Hong Kong. He obtained his Master's degree from the London School of Economics and Political Science, University of London. His research interests include work and work organisations.

R.N. Kanungo is Professor of Organizational Behavior and holds the Faculty of Management Chair at McGill University, Canada. He has published over 100 papers in both basic and applied areas of psychology and management, and has authored/edited many books on a wide range of topics related to motivation and leadership. In recognition of his contributions to psychology and management, he was elected Fellow of the Canadian Psychological Association and was conferred the Commonwealth Seagram Senior Faculty Fellowship and Best Paper awards.

Henry S.R. Kao is Professor of Psychology at the University of Hong Kong. He has previously taught at Purdue University, and was Visiting Professor at the East China Normal University, Shanghai; Shaanxi Teachers' University, Xian; and South China Normal University, Guangzhou. Professor Kao has published extensively and his books include *Psychology of Chinese Calligraphy and Organizational Behaviour* (co-authored), *Social Values and Development* (co-edited), *Asian Perspectives on Psychology* (co-edited), *Chinese and the Chinese Mind* (co-edited), and *Effective Organizations and Social Values* (co-edited).

R.C. Mishra is Professor of Psychology at Banaras Hindu University since 1992. He joined the University as a Lecturer and became a Reader in 1984. A doctorate from the University of Allahabad, he has been a Post-doctoral Research Fellow, a Shastri Research Fellow, and a Visiting Fellow at Queen's University, Canada. He has also been a Visiting Professor at the University of Geneva. Professor Mishra is primarily interested in cultural influence on human development. He has contributed extensively to professional journals and edited volumes in the fields of cognition, acculturation, school-ing and cross-cultural studies.

Girishwar Misra is Professor of Psychology at the University of Delhi. He has earlier taught at the Universities of Gorakhpur, Allahabad and Bhopal, and was a Fulbright Fellow at Swarthmore College and the University of Michigan. Professor Misra has pub-lished extensively in the areas of cultural psychology, applied so-cial psychology and human development and has authored/edited *Psychological Consequences of Prolonged Deprivation, Deprivation: Its Social Roots and Psychological Consequences, Foundations of Social Psychol-ogy, General Psychology, Applied Social Psychology in India, Psychol-ogy of Poverty and Disadvantage, Perspectives on Indigenous Psychology,* and *Psychological Perspectives on Stress and Health.* In recognition of his contributions to social science teaching and research, the Gov-ernment of Madhya Pradesh conferred upon him the Radhakrishnan Award (1991) and Dr Hari Singh Gaur Award (1992).

Ajit K. Mohanty is Coordinator at the Centre of Advanced Study in Psychology, Utkal University, Bhubaneswar, where he has been Pro-fessor since 1983. He was Killam Doctoral Scholar at the University of Alberta, Fulbright Post-doctoral Scholar at the University of Wis-consin, Visiting Scholar at the University of Geneva, and Senior Fellow at the Central Institute of Indian Languages. A psycholinguist specialising in multilingualism, reading and language acquisition, Professor Mohanty has published extensively and is the author of *Bilingualism in a Multilingual Society* and editor of *Psychology of Pov-erty and Disadvantage.*

A.C. Paranjpe is Professor of Psychology at Simon Fraser Univer-sity, Canada, where he has been teaching since 1967. After completing his doctorate from the University of Poona, he was awarded a Smith-Mundt scholarship and a Fulbright travel grant for post-doctoral research with Professor Erik H. Erikson at Harvard University. His early works are *Caste, Prejudice, and the Individual* and *In Search of Identity.* His research interests focus on the examination of psycho-logical theories in their historical and cultural contexts, especially with reference to the intellectual traditions of Europe and India. His other publications in this field include *Theoretical Psychology: The Meeting of East and West, Asian Contributions to Psychology,* and *Self and Identity in Modern Psychology and Indian Thought.*

T.S. Saraswathi is Professor at the Department of Human Development and Family Studies at the Maharaja Sayajirao University of Baroda. She has received numerous professional awards and international fellowships for her contributions to the field of developmental psychology. Prof. Saraswathi has contributed articles to reputed journals and edited books. Her publications include *Trends and Issues in Child Development, Invisible Boundaries: Grooming for Adult Roles, Developmental Psychology in India: An Annotated Bibliography, Culture, Socialization and Human Development: Theory Research and Applications in India, Human Development and Family Studies in India: An Agenda for Research and Policy* (co-edited), *Capturing Complexities: A Methodological Study of Women, Households and Development* (co-edited), and the three-volume *Handbook of Cross-Cultural Psychology* (co-edited).

R.C. Tripathi is currently Professor and Head of the Department of Psychology and the Centre of Advanced Studies in Psychology at the University of Allahabad. He joined the University as a Lecturer in 1963 and became a Reader in 1972. He has been a Fulbright Fellow at the University of Michigan and Visiting Professor at both Tilburg and Wake Forest Universities. Prof. Tripathi is particularly interested in the application of psychology to human resource development. Apart from numerous articles in national and international journals of repute, he has authored/edited *Environment and Structure of Organizations, Deprivation: Its Social Roots and Psychological Consequences,* and *Norm Violation and Intergroup Relations.*

Index

Heart of Worcestershire College, Redditch, Bromsgrove and Osprey House.

Books should be returned or renewed on or before the last date below.

You can renew: in person at any Learning Centre
by phone: (01905) 725661
by e-mail: renewals @ howcollege.ac.uk
Online: http://circa.howcollege.ac.uk/Heritage
FINES ARE CHARGED FOR LATE RETURN

14 OCT 2016

1 7 NOV 2017

2 7 JAN 2020

0 6 DEC 2021

Please note by borrowing this item
you are agreeing to abide by College rules,
including the payment of fines for late return.
NB: loss or damage to any item will be charged.